Ecclesiological Investigations

Series Editor

Gerard Mannion

Volume 14

Church, Liberation and World Religions:
Towards a Christian-Buddhist Dialogue

Other titles in the series:

Receiving 'The Nature and Mission of the Church'
Christian Community Now
Comparative Ecclesiology: Critical Investigations
Church and Religious 'Other'
Ecumenical Ecclesiology
Globalization and the Mission of the Church
Friendship Exploring its Implications for the Church in Postmodernity
Agreeable Agreement
Being Faithful
Communion, Diversity and Salvation
Dumitru Staniloae: An Ecumenical Ecclesiology
Doctrine, Dynamic and Difference

Church, Liberation and World Religions: Towards a Christian-Buddhist Dialogue

Mario I. Aguilar

BLOOMSBURY
LONDON · NEW DELHI · NEW YORK · SYDNEY

Bloomsbury T&T Clark
An imprint of Bloomsbury Publishing Plc

50 Bedford Square	1385 Broadway
London	New York
WC1B 3DP	NY 10018
UK	USA

www.bloomsbury.com

Bloomsbury is a registered trade mark of Bloomsbury Publishing Plc

First published 2012
Paperback edition first published 2014

© Mario I. Aguilar, 2012

All rights reserved. No part of this publication may be reproduced or transmitted in any form or by any means, electronic or mechanical, including photocopying, recording, or any information storage or retrieval system, without prior permission in writing from the publishers.

Mario I. Aguilar has asserted his right under the Copyright, Designs and Patents Act, 1988, to be identified as Author of this work.

No responsibility for loss caused to any individual or organization acting on or refraining from action as a result of the material in this publication can be accepted by Bloomsbury or the author.

British Library Cataloguing-in-Publication Data
A catalogue record for this book is available from the British Library.

ISBN: HB: 978-0-567-27324-6
PB: 978-0-567-25575-4

Library of Congress Cataloging-in-Publication Data
A catalog record for this book is available from the Library of Congress.

Typeset by Newgen Imaging Systems Pvt Ltd, Chennai, India

This book is dedicated to Glenda Tello
Fortiter in re, suaviter in modo [memento] coelum
non animum mutant qui trans mare currunt

Contents

Acknowledgments · viii

INTRODUCTION: TOWARDS A CHRISTIAN BUDDHIST DIALOGUE · 1

Chapter 1	DIALOGUE IN VATICAN II	16
Chapter 2	LATIN AMERICAN PRAXIS	36
Chapter 3	CONTEMPORARY DIALOGUES: THE TRAPPISTS OF ALGERIA	55
Chapter 4	BUDDHISM AND A SECULARIZED DIALOGUE	74
Chapter 5	THOMAS MERTON AND THE DALAI LAMA	87
Chapter 6	MEDELLIN AND THE SERVICE TO THE POOR	106
Chapter 7	BASIC TENETS	126
Chapter 8	A FRESH CHRISTIAN ECCLESIOLOGY AND BUDDHIST CHALLENGES	143

Index · 161

Acknowledgments

Every book is like an empty canvas, a tapestry on which choices of subject, colour, style and aesthetic narrative are the choice of the artist. However, during the time in which the artist works and recreates the canvas or the page he is influenced by the people, beauty, suffering and life that surrounds him. Thus, my acknowledgements are to those who have made this process of filling this particular canvas with fruitful, painful, controversial and even personal depictions.

I realize that this theological exploration was inspired through my younger years by Catholic missionaries who had gone to India and with whom I shared life in London and Nairobi. They were the kind of missionaries of dialogue who had not been happy to 'bring the gospel' to Asia but had recognized that ancient civilizations and ancient religions were also a manifestation of God's grace. Among many others I would like to acknowledge the witness to dialogue and mission in the Catholic Church of Walter Boyle, Brendan O'Reilly and Tom Lynch. Tom Lynch, an Irish Catholic priest, died in 2010 in India where he had lived in an ashram as a contemplative for many years. He had decided that his best contribution to dialogue was to die in India rather than in his native Ireland.

I am grateful to colleagues at St Mary's College, University of St Andrews, and especially to Dr Eric Stoddart for encouraging this kind of research and for their friendship. I have discussed parts of this book with some of my doctoral students, that is Dr Alejandro Chávez, Clair Linzey, Gordon Barclay, Denis Dragovic, Estifanos Zewde, Milton Nunez-Coba and Ross Wissmann. I thank all of them for their ideas and challenges. Part of this book was delivered in a series of seminars at the Centre for the Study of Religion and Politics (CSRP) of the University of St Andrews at a time when Burcu Sunar, a Turkish scholar, was staying at the centre. I am grateful to her, a Muslim, for some conversations on dialogue and her convictions about the role of the world religions in the world.

Acknowledgments

There is no doubt that my personal life as a Camaldolese Benedictine Oblate has made me ask many questions about the church's life and dialogue with the world religions and I acknowledge the influence of three great contemplatives: Thomas Merton, the fourteenth Dalai Lama and Swami Abhishiktananda (Henri Le Saux).

Mario I. Aguilar
St Andrews, February 2012

Introduction: Towards a Christian Buddhist Dialogue

The visit of the fourteenth Dalai Lama to the Cistercian Abbey of Gethsemani in Kentucky (United States of America) in July 1996 triggered the imagination of a Christian world that seems to be forever challenged by the developments of modernity, postmodernity and globalization.[1] The visit of the Dalai Lama to the tomb of Thomas Merton, monk and scholar, continued their own previous encounter in India in 1968 and it was a sign of a dialogue that had already started 28 years earlier in Dharamsala, India.[2] On that occasion, the fourteenth Dalai Lama arrived in a helicopter amid tight security to take part in an event of East–West monastic dialogue organized by the organization Monastic Interreligious Dialogue.[3] While visiting Merton's grave and after a period of meditation sitting on the ground, accompanied by Abbott Timothy Kelly OCSO, the Dalai Lama said 'I am now in touch with his spirit'.[4]

These experiences and any interest in Christian–Buddhist dialogue seem to be at first an isolated event; however, at least a Roman Catholic experience of this kind of dialogue has been growing since the openings provided by the Second Vatican Council (see Chapter 1). In fact, while less publicized by the media, Christian or otherwise, the experiences of Christian–Buddhist dialogue and indeed the experiences of Christian dialogue with other world religions seems to be more common than suspected and it has not been confined to the Roman Catholic Church only. Thus, it is a fact that while the Roman Catholic Church implemented instances of dialogue after the end of Vatican II, the World Council of Churches (WCC) also explored avenues of dialogue with other world religions.

The WCC fostered a consultation on inter-faith dialogue in Ajaltoun, Lebanon, in 1970 (16–25 March). Those participating were three Hindus, four Buddhists, twenty-eight Christians (including five members of staff of the WCC) and three Muslims; in all representing seventeen countries. Margrethe Brown of the Commission on Ecumenical Mission and Relations of the United Presbyterian Church (United States of America) who reported on this meeting finished her report with a challenging comment: 'It is evident that we have by no means exhausted our understanding of the nature of the Church.' Shortly after, the WCC started a programme entitled 'Dialogue with People of Living Faiths'. Following such a programme delegates meeting at the Nairobi Assembly in 1975 commented on a section of the programme's document entitled 'Seeking Community' which in turn called for new ways to relate to other religions by building a community across barriers of a religious nature. It is important to note that European delegates present at the meeting rejected the idea while delegates from the southern hemisphere were quite positive about these new developments.[5] Real efforts did not prosper and other ecclesial concerns became part of the antics for the WCC's reshaping of the 1980s.

The Experience of Dialogue

As in the case of Christian and Buddhist monks meeting at the Abbey of Gethsemani interreligious dialogue seems a challenging and rewarding activity in which Christians and Buddhist practitioners share some commonality, conviviality and a sense of joy in their spiritual practices. However, this is certainly not the ordinary experience of most Christians despite the fact that dialogue with the world religions has become a more common experience among the Christian monastic orders. The sociopolitical bases for further religious dialogue are there but social conflict and mistrust sometimes bring the same attitudes to Christians who in fact should be at the centre of fostering dialogue within sectors of society even in the most difficult circumstances. The Church follows the same contradictions in that while she is at the centre of the task of bringing Good News, hope and love of a neighbour, she has also erred at times in keeping to herself and ministering only to those who are following the 'truth' as an exclusive and isolating discourse.

Nevertheless, the experience of globalization as a common search for understanding has been theologically nurtured by the contributions to a more inclusive world by well-known figures such as the fourteenth Dalai Lama (Tibet), Archbishop Desmond Tutu (South Africa), Bishop Oscar Romero (El Salvador) and Mother Teresa (Calcutta).[6] These religious figures have been assumed as making a positive contribution to a world in which war, international tensions and the abuse of human rights have been significant since the hopeful moments of hope marked by the end of apartheid in South Africa, the fall of the Berlin Wall and the end of the military regimes in Latin America. I have expanded on the impact of these and other comparable religious and public figures in previous works arguing that there is a clear connection between contemplation as a personal spiritual dialogue and the effects of contemplation and prayer within human communities.[7] Thus, I have suggested that Christians in their own lives and in their own spaces change structures of death into structures of life by nourishing with an ongoing process of contemplation their daily contributions to the politics of human life and death.[8] By contemplating God in the awareness of a political and human world every Christian and every follower of Christ acquires attitudes and sentiments of peace with God that in turn allow for a gentler and compassionate attitude towards others in daily life. Those 'others' include marginalized members of our own social communities, be they religious or political, and those who are very different in life and belief. After all, all human beings are equals in their dignity as the children of God, be they Christians or non-Christians alike.[9] Thus, this re-creation of God's peace in dialogue and diversity becomes a common experience not only for contemplatives but also for Christian activists and political activists in general.[10]

In this work I explore some of the possible theological avenues for the churches' dialogue with the world religions and particularly with Buddhism. I argue for an ecclesiology of service and dialogue instead of one of magisterium and theological separation. I argue that dialogue is a work in progress, a daily movement towards an ongoing movement of service that includes a Christian dialogue with Buddhism as an active dialogue between Christians and Buddhists. I suggest that dialogue is an ongoing part of the self-reflection of a church open to the Spirit in the twenty-first century, a church that within the twentieth century confronted the possibility of a dialogue that had previously been negated by Vatican I with its emphasis on the primacy and centrality of the papacy during the nineteenth century.[11]

The seminal documents on dialogue with other religions and a secularized world arose out of the deliberations of the Second Vatican Council (1962–5). At Vatican II the fathers of the council and their advisors asked hard questions about the world, other religions and the possibilities of salvation, dialogue and the action of God in the world as a whole rather than the world as contained within the Catholic Church. In fact, the Declaration on the Relations of the Church to Non-Christian Religions (*Nostra Aetate*, 28 October 1965) cannot be understood without looking closely at the church's relocation of herself within the world through the Pastoral Constitution on the Church in the Modern World (*Gaudium et Spes*, 7 December 1965) and the reaffirmation of the centrality of human dignity (*Humanae Personae Dignitatem*, 28 August 1968).[12]

John Hick has correctly argued that the occasions for dialogue between people of one faith and another increased within the late twentieth century; however, he also poignantly argued that there is a following step in all dialogue: 'dialogue between people who accept the genuine religious equality of the other, so that they can then benefit freely from one another's distinctive spiritual insights and be free to join together in facing the massive social and economic and political problems of the world'.[13]

Theological Suggestions

This work outlines some of the possibilities for dialogue, that is theological, prophetic and social, particularly the possibilities of a Christian dialogue with Buddhism. Historical aspects of dialogue (or the absence of it) with Islam and Judaism are also explored; such dialogue should be easier because of the common tenet that a Creator God exists. This has not always been an easy dialogue despite the fact that it is a truism to affirm that any dialogue centred on the goodness of God is good and necessary as a central tenet for any religious dialogue. To suggest the tenets of a religious or non-religious dialogue with Buddhism is another matter because Buddhism as a philosophical and religious system does not adhere to a belief in God.[14] Thus, Buddhism does not uphold a belief in a God that creates the world or human life or a God that judges a person at the end of a life or biological span. In theological terms Buddhism does not have doctrines that relate creation or eschatology to human life or death. Further, Buddhists believe in reincarnation and a cycle of life that continues through several human biological cycles based on principles of human suffering, the possibility of human enlightenment and the power of the mind to control the senses in order to perceive human and animal life as common and closely related. In these tenets of philosophical understanding Hinduism and Buddhism continue to be closely related.[15]

These reflections and theological investigations are marked by my personal experience as a Roman Catholic, as a theologian and a contemplative hermit living a call to prayer and inter-religious dialogue within the Benedictine tradition of the Camaldolese Benedictines.[16] The Camaldolese Constitution expresses this desire for communion and dialogue with other world religions as follows:

> The whole world is aware of a new ecumenical climate which is creating, or enhancing the condition for dialogue among believers of the great living faiths. Catholics, Christians of other confessions, Jews, Muslims, Hindus, Buddhists, and all persons of good will are seeking new ways of growing in the truth and in communion.[17]

Such *koinonia* between the different faiths and religions is only a reflection of the communion between Father, Son and Holy Spirit and the fact that God is Love (1 Jn 4.8, 17).[18] Thus, this work presupposes an experience of Church and it is aimed at an experience of dialogue that arises out of a Christian experience within the Church fostered by the aggiornamento of the Catholic Church at the Second Vatican Council. It argues for a return to the spirit of Vatican II: a spirit of openness to the possible surprises of God's action in the world. It is a theological exploration that discusses critically the attempts by Pope Benedict XVI's to problematize the nature of churches to the detriment of years of inter-faith dialogue by the Catholic Church. I refer here to the publication of *Dominus Jesus* in the year 2000 by Cardinal Ratzinger, later to become Pope Benedict XVI. *Dominus Jesus* deals with the relation of the Catholic Church with other churches and other religions and strongly suggests that other faiths and other churches are imperfect and incomplete in relation to the Catholic Church. In the words of Leonardo Boff there exists in this document a 'Roman Catholic fundamentalism' as the document puts forward the view that 'the Roman Catholic Church is the only Church of Christ'.[19]

This work argues that dialogue with the world religions presupposes that, as outlined by Erik Borgman, 'theology has always had to deal with the fact that its object – for classical theology that is God – is beyond comprehension in our limited attempts to rationalize reality'.[20] It is with this somehow limited understanding of a supra-reality that the experience of dialogue does not become normative or authoritative but an expression of a wider conversation about divine dialogues and human manifestations. This sense of a wider protocol of religious significance challenges any exclusion or exclusivity in the religious imagination and adheres to an ever-increasing exploration of the world religions assuming the Church as not being the religious norm but as a partner of human and divine realities. This work argues that dialogue does not come from seeking mutual understandings; instead it assumes mutual differences in answering questions, or better in asking questions, about the beginning and the end of one's life. These questions remain human questions that aided with a theological refection point to a God who loves all human beings equally and offers grace, freely given, to all, within and without the Church.

Human Dialogue and Ecclesial Experience

In his assessment of the dialogue with other religions forwarded by Vatican II Donald Nicholl has argued that 'the fact is that inter-faith experience for most human beings is something strange and almost entirely unprecedented'.[21] All human beings as human beings are nurtured and nourished by a particular family, group, society and state with customs, ideas and common understandings that become assumed as 'truths' – be they sociocultural, historical or religious. The family becomes the unit of divine manifestation and the 'truths' passed unto the children a way of life for them throughout their lives.[22] Thus, social and cultural truths become personal truths to be reaffirmed against other beliefs, other cultural truths and other mores. This passing on of truths is a classical Christian theological vision that creates a notion of a Church that teaches, leads the way and is the recipient of divine and human truths.

This vision of a church at the centre of the world evolved over centuries and was not there within the early Church. For at the start, under the Roman persecution and the Greek influences on the churches founded by the apostle Paul, the followers of Christ were part of a movement labelled the Way within the Acts of the Apostles. The movement was small and the followers had to navigate the tensions with a Jewish cultural tradition, the possibilities of knowing and gnosis in a Greek world and the challenges of a Roman imperial religion based on the emperor and not on the Christ. Within this period of encounter by Christ's followers Christian churches showed certain diversity and were not able to exercise any religious or political power over others. Thus, Leonardo Boff has clearly argued that the beginnings of the church, what he calls the 'ecclesio-genesis', carried with it a diversified ecclesial tension between the local churches and their cultural milieu that was rather different than the growing centralized political and social influence exercised by Christianity later on. From the fourth century onwards Christianity became the official religion of the empire of Constantine and later of Europe as well as the religion of the colonies of European colonial powers in Latin America, Africa and Asia.

This situation of Christian establishment was to prevail until the 1960s when a changing and evermore secularized Europe started to challenge the primacy of a Church centred in her, be the church reformed or non-reformed in doctrine and practice. As a result, the Roman Catholic Church which for centuries had proclaimed the dictum *extra ecclesiam nulla salus* (there is no salvation outside the Church) found herself challenged by John XXIII's call for an ecumenical council and for the establishment of a church of the poor in 1959. As a result, the advent of the Second Vatican Council opened the Catholic Church to the world not for the first time but certainly at a level of doctrinal hermeneutics in which the world outside the church was seen as positive and creative. Thus, the Catholic Church expressed a very concrete desire of being associated with all human beings and their lives. After all and within this fresh reflection on the world, the Catholic Church recognized that God is associated with all human beings through the very act of creation.

Within this refreshed conciliar reflection religious values and customs remain as signs of a person's human dignity, a person created by God and affirmed by natural rights so that according to *Dignitatis Humanae* 'this right of the human person to religious freedom must be given such recognition in the constitutional order of society as will make it a civil right'.[23] The language of Vatican II opened a reflection towards equality and human dignity within and without the church with clear consequences for intra-religious dialogue and the dialogue with those who profess other faiths and no faith at all. For Vatican II religious, civil and natural rights become interconnected and theological premises inform a Christian community immersed with a diversity and variety of beliefs united under the umbrella of 'the people of God'.[24]

The results of this pastoral shift undertaken by the fathers of the council did not change the 'Catholic truths' about God and human beings but allowed for a God-centric emphasis within the Catholic Church. Within this ecclesiologically refreshed option God's plan of salvation could be inclusive of other faiths while the Christian option remained Christ-centred in the Church with a Christ in dialogue with all and who embraces different human and spiritual realities. God did not change but the social position of a church evolved from the monarchic institution of Pious XII to the 'church of the poor' of John XXIII and the servant church of Vatican II and Paul VI. While Vatican II took place before the 1968 student riots in Paris, the escalation of the Vietnam War and the secularization of Europe, Vatican II prepared the Catholic Church to be open to the 'signs of the times' and open to a servant dialogue with other faiths and non-faiths searching for the humbleness of a servant church rather than the centrality of a monarchical church.

I have, somewhere else, expanded ideas on the humbleness of a theologian who instead of upholding sacred truths that cannot be further understood examines changes and human realities of understanding and allows for a reflection that encourages inter-religious dialogue rather than exclusion.[25] Within this renewed theological work, sets of theological premises uphold within the centrality of dialogue creating the possibility of a common conversation with other faiths and those who profess no faith at all. Within this framework of a Christian–Buddhist dialogue the possibility of a pastoral kindness towards other religions exists. Nevertheless, theological dialogue does not take place when examining creation and eschatology.

Fifty years after Vatican II I would argue that there is now a need to conceptualize those attempts at a theological dialogue. Theology, understood as 'faith seeking understanding', has many tasks and one of them is to foster dialogue between those created in the image of God. If for some theologians the study and reflection on doctrine and tradition is their main theological task, I am more minded to argue with John McDade that the task of theology 'is not to update a previously constituted body of truth – interpretative hermeneutics is insufficient – but to articulate present experiences so that they stand in a creative and critical relationship to the tradition'.[26]

The articulation of present experiences gives the possibility of a theological reflection on the relation between the Church as instrument of liberation from sin and oppression, from injustice and poverty and from personal greed, and the other world religions as sources of eschatological thinking and ethical acting in return. Jesus Christ liberates from sin, sickness and darkness sharing with the Lord Buddha the possibility of the centrality of a metaphysic reflection on life that eventually leads to a close common relation to the spiritual and metaphysical world rather than any clinging to material goods, materiality and self-centeredness.

Dialogue as Presence

Most of the contemporary examples of 'canonical' dialogue have been meetings by invitation only in which practitioners of different faiths have talked to each other. However, within the ongoing dialogue between Christians and Buddhists there has been a sustained effort by Buddhist and Roman Catholic monks to gather together to pray and meditate. This expression of a bodily presence has had a profound sensorial effect on others as photographs of the fourteenth Dalai Lama meditating beside the tomb of Thomas Merton in 1995 caught the inter-faith imagination and the longings of a secularized world that still searches for a spirituality separated from established religion.[27]

The physical presence and bodily stillness between practitioners of Christianity and Buddhism speak loudly as an accomplishment of a presence of the human and the divine. It is a fact that intellectual discussions do not have the same impact and that journeys of inter-faith dialogue require experience and action rather than an agreement on the unity of creeds. The central dialogic point of encounter is actually the *koinonia* of those who treasure the journey, the sign of those who in communion with others search on the one hand for God's presence (Christians) and on the other for God's absence (Buddhists). Human dialogue then becomes an ecclesial experience in which members of the Body of Christ find partners on their journey. Those partners in dialogue have a deep respect for all human beings, for all sentient beings and for contemplation, meditation and liberation from the primacy of the material, expressed in contemporary choices such as consumerism, greed and selfishness.

Dialogue as Absence

It is in the silence and the stillness that Christians can encounter the wisdom of the absence of an absolute material truth and dialogue can commence. In the middle of the night with its silence one encounters the voice of the Absolute; however, slowly the voice disappears and it becomes a presence of stillness that quickly turns into absence. I am thinking here of the possible understanding of a Christian and a Buddhist who in the silence of the night liberate themselves of the noise and the distractions of the presence of thousands of preoccupations and the noise (expressed as intercessory prayer) that supposedly is required in order to communicate with God. The Jesuit Dan Berrigan has expressed this particular experience in his self-reflection on a period of reading and contemplation that he undertook in Paris in the early 1970s. During that time he dialogued with the Zen Master Thich Nhat Hanh.[28] Berrigan had been in prison for burning US government files related to the drafting of young Americans into the US Army for the purpose of fighting in Vietnam.[29] While 'eager for personal healing and time for reflection', Berrigan had welcomed an invitation to spend time with Buddhists in Paris.[30] That fruitful dialogue, inscribed later in the form of a book, was paced by the stillness of prayer as Berrigan recalls 25 years later: 'Every evening we prayed together in silence, "for the space of a candle," at Nhat Hahn's gentle leading'.[31] The transcripts of those conversations, as interpreted by Robert Elsberg, witnessed to the fact that the conversations had long pauses for prayer and meditation.[32] In my own interpretation the conversations provided room for the silence of the stillness, for the listening and the liberating sound of the silenced emptying (see Chapter 4).

Dialogue as Knowledge

It is also in the knowledge of other religions that one can find the seeds for an ecclesiology of mutual understanding.[33] Discrimination and strife arise out of ignorance while distrust of others comes out of an ongoing narrative of misinformation that leads to false argumentations, false understandings and even violence. For knowledge does not bring harmony by itself but provides the possibility of peace among the world religions. Hans Küng, being one of the main proponents of a doctrine of peace that can affect and effect peace among nations, helped us not only with a reflection on dialogue that took place after the events in the United States on 9/11 but also triggered further questions from those involved in the creation of an inter-faith knowledge.[34] Following that spirit of a search for knowledge, John Hick, Perry Schmidt-Leukel, Leonard Swidler and Paul Knitter organized a conference whose participants were those who felt comfortable with a 'pluralist model'. The invitation to such gathering included 35 religious scholars from Europe, Asia and the United States who gathered in Birmingham, UK (6–9 September 2003).[35] This group of scholars was united by a common faith stand: they all believed in a pluralistic model related to the common assumption that 'they no longer have to insist that they had the only, or the final, or the superior path to God and absolute Truth'.[36] The meeting of religious scholars with knowledge of Christianity and other traditions secured an important step in what Paul Knitter has summarized as a goal of this dialogue in pluralism: that 'Christianity would remain important and distinctive, but so would other religions'.[37]

The common agreements within those religious scholars remain an important portfolio for any advancement or critical reflection on the knowledge of other religious traditions and a foundation and *modus vivendi* for any interfaith dialogue:

(1) All the religions possess the resources within their own traditions to adopt the pluralist model.
(2) Differences matter.
(3) All religious traditions, in varying ways, recognize that the ultimate reality or truth that is the object of their quest or discoveries is beyond the scope of a complete human understanding.
(4) Pluralism does not imply relativism.
(5) The most urgent (though not the only) form of an interreligious encounter today is an ethical dialogue among the religions.
(6) In all their encounters and dialogues, the religions must respect the freedom of conscience.[38]

The reflections of this group of scholars opened the way for further cooperation and dialogue in 'pluralism' at a high level of engagement and reflection. However, it is my argument in this work that a grass root argument for experience is also needed in order to be consequent to the change of metaphors and language that are being expressed. After all, the divine reality does not change; we pretend it changes. In connection with a possible diversity, John Hick has reminded us that 'all the world religions speak in their different ways of a limitlessly important reality that both transcends the material universe and is also present within it'.[39]

Dialogue and a Common Humanity

Many inter-faith commissions and study groups have advanced the possibilities of dialogue and in turn have fostered dialogue; however, the reality of dialogue is that fear and distrust also coexist. In many ways, the certainty wanted by all religious practitioners blocks the possibilities of advancing the knowledge and commitment to dialogue. For it would be a truism to suggest that honest religious practitioners have found a clear religious path in which they believe and they are less interested in other people's paths. In fact, the difficulties of accepting a common humanity have their roots in theologies that locate the whole world under Christ and perceive the Church as the only custodian of this central tenet. Paul Knitter has called this understanding 'religious superiority', a sentiment that arose out of an absolute certainty that Christianity is the only path to God and that Christ willed everybody to be saved in his name. Theologically this sentiment should not affect non-Christians; however, the dictum implemented through colonial expeditions and European missionaries' preaching to non-Christians expressed clearly the accepted dictum *extra ecclesiam nulla salus* (outside the church there is no salvation). This theological understanding created a church that was not able to accept anything other than a European Christianity and this sentiment remains engraved in many traditional quarters of the Catholic Church and the Reformed Churches. In turn, it became a dictum of the reformed churches that were influenced by Karl Barth's theology. For Barth has no time for other faiths and as a result he ignores any possible dialogue with other religions completely.

In this work and through eight chapters I explore the history of dialogue in the twentieth century and I offer some theological reflections on a central part of the reality of the Kingdom of God: the values of the Kingdom of God foster a Church that serves, that enters into dialogue and that praises God through the activity of serving all in the spirit of a common humanity.

Chapter 1 outlines the impact of Vatican II on dialogue within the Catholic Church. Vatican II not only sanctioned in its documents the respect and dignity of other world religions but also stressed the dignity of the human and the central role of conscience within the freedom of religion in society. The notion of 'the people of God' expanded the church's understanding of God's work in the world and in the religions of the world while triggering a fresh awakening to a positive outlook towards the contemporary world. This chapter examines some of the documents on inter-religious dialogue that followed Vatican II and some figures within the Catholic Church who had already lived a dialogue with the world religions in their own lives well before the calling of the council.

Chapter 2 connects the end of Vatican II with a pastoral aggiornamento in Latin America where the majority of Christians of the world lived at that time. A wave of pastoral and theological reflection triggered by Vatican II made possible a fresh look at Christian life in Latin America where a 'preferential option for the poor' and the rise of the lay Christian communities reflected the call of the council to the 'people of God' to make a better world. Latin American theology reflected on processes of social and personal 'liberation' using the same word that Buddhists use and therefore creating a bridge between the centrality of human rights and the respect for a common humanity. This chapter argues that this kind of reflection about commonality in respect for all human beings is a central part of an ongoing theological reflection on dialogue.

Chapter 3 examines a particular example of a very fruitful dialogue between a Catholic Trappist monastic community in Algeria and the Muslim community living in the area where the monastery was. In this case the ties of service and common respect created a strong socioreligious bond between Christian monks and Muslim people so that when the Algerian civil war started the monks decided not to leave the area. In 1996 they were kidnapped by a group of fanatic Muslim fighters and were decapitated. The monks' reflections, life and written narratives provide an important example of experiential inter-religious dialogue based on the service to God and to others.

Chapter 4 examines two different examples of Christian dialogue with Buddhism. In the first example, it outlines the arrival of the Jesuits in Tibet in the eighteenth century and the dialogue that followed. This was an experience in which languages and customs were studied by the Jesuits inside Tibet but where dialogue was of an apologetic nature and did not conduce to a better understanding of Christianity and Buddhism. The Jesuits were removed from Tibet by Propaganda Fidei and their mission did not succeed but their presence in Tibet became an important marker of an encounter between Christianity and Tibetan Buddhism. In the second example this chapter examines the dialogue between another Jesuit, Dan Berrigan SJ and the Vietnamese Buddhist monk Thich Nhat Hanh. This was a positive set of conversations aimed at a Buddhist–Christian 'awareness' in which both participants not only spent time talking about common grounds but also meditating together.

Chapter 5 examines the encounter of the Trappist monk Thomas Merton with the fourteenth Dalai Lama in Dharamsala, India, in 1968. Through three separate meetings Merton and the Dalai Lama shared their common monastic understanding and discussed important points of meditation, philosophy and human values.

Chapter 6 examines the Latin American 'preferential option for the poor' that arose out of the Christian experience in the 1970s Latin America. The service to the poor and the option for a simpler lifestyle with the poor in mind, the chapter suggests, can also be a point of encounter between a more radical Christianity and Buddhism. For, both Christianity and Buddhism profess a personal and experiential way of approaching the spiritual incorporating changes in one's lifestyle with simplicity and meditation as part of an ongoing process of personal liberation and of help to the needy, to the poor and the marginalized of this world.

Chapter 7 explores some of the basic tenets of Christianity as expressed in gospel texts such as Lk. 4.16–30 and Mt. 25.31–46 where the mission of the Church and the basis of dialogue appear because of a commitment to action and to embracing those who suffer. Buddhism recognizes the awareness of suffering as central to Buddhist life and Christianity sees the awareness of God's presence through the service to those who suffer. This chapter outlines some of the contemporary reflections of a Christian philosopher and politician, the Italian Gianni Vattimo, who has strongly argued for an 'after Christianity' paradigm in which humanism and a common humanity remain ethical values attached to all societies. This chapter examines the implications of some of these basic tenets for our relation with a world of the market and of personal enrichment, a world that is challenged by the common values of humanity at the centre as proclaimed by Christianity and Buddhism.

Chapter 8 proposes some challenges for an ongoing Christian–Buddhist dialogue based on a fresh ecclesiology of service and contemplation that actualizes dialogue as love, liberation, personal reshaping, religious contradiction and as a 'second step'. These characteristics for dialogue reshape the Church into a servant Church as witness to dialogue rather than a teaching body of exclusive commands and unique norms and regulations for human life.

It is my general conclusion throughout this work that the experience of a common humanity is the common experience of those who follow a particular path towards an ultimate spiritual reality. They are united in explanations about life and death that convey metaphysical understandings and that impact on their ethical life and their relations with others. It is possible and desirable for all in general and for the Church in particular to dialogue with others maintaining metaphysical realities at the centre of life, be it a Christian or Buddhist life or both.[40]

Notes

1 For details of the visit see 'The Dalai Lama visits Gethsemani', *St. Anthony's Messenger*, January 1997.
2 For an account of Merton's visit to Dharamsala in 1968 see Thomas Merton, *November Circular Letter to Friends*, New Delhi: India, 9 November 1968, published as 'Appendix VI' in *The Asian Journal of Thomas Merton*, New York: New Directions, 1975, pp. 320–5; Merton's visit is also mentioned in Michael Harris Goodman, *The Last Dalai Lama: A Biography*, London: Sidgwick & Jackson, 1986, p. 325. For an annotated account of Merton's visit see Mario I. Aguilar, *Thomas Merton: Contemplation and Political Action*, London: SPCK, 2011.
3 Dialogue Interreligieux Monastique / Monastic Interreligious Dialogue (DIMMID) is an international monastic organization that promotes and supports dialogue, especially dialogue at the level of religious experience and practice, between Christian monastic men and women and followers of other religions. DIMMID is a commission of the Benedictine Confederation with formal links to both branches of the Cistercian order. It acts in liaison with the Holy See's Pontifical Council for Interreligious Dialogue and welcomes collaboration with other organizations that foster interreligious dialogue. DIMMID is civilly incorporated in the state of Minnesota (United States of America) as a non-profit, tax-exempt institution operating exclusively for charitable, educational, and religious purposes, see www.dimmid.org/
4 William H. Shannon, 'Dalai Lama (Tenzin Gyatso)', in William H. Shannon, Christine M. Bochen and Patrick F. O'Connell, eds. *The Thomas Merton Encyclopedia*, Maryknoll, NY: Orbis, 2002, pp. 98–9 at p. 99.

5 Weley S. Ariarajah, 'Power, Politics and Plurality: The Struggles of the World Council of Churches to Deal with Religious Plurality', in Paul F. Knitter, ed. *The Myth of Religious Superiority: Multifaith Explorations of Religious Pluralism*, Maryknoll, NY: Orbis, 2005, pp. 176–93 at p. 184.

6 I recognize here that there is a certain negativity about globalization expressed by many Christians, negativity that has also been explored and challenged by great Christians such as Thomas Merton, Dan Berrigan or Bede Griffiths.

7 For a summary of important contributions to dialogue and peace by religious figures of the twentieth century see Mario I. Aguilar, *Contemplating God, Changing the World*, London: SPCK, 2008.

8 Aguilar, *Contemplating God*, pp. xxi–xxii.

9 See for example the conversation between the Jesuit Daniel Berrigan and the Vietnamese monk and Zen master Thich Nhat Hanh, where the Buddhist monk suggests that 'once drawn into politics you are caught. A monk is much listened to by the people [. . .] As a monk he speaks out of his wisdom, his spirituality'; see Thich Nhat Hanh and Daniel Berrigan, *The Raft is not the Shore: Conversations Toward a Buddhist-Christian Awareness*, Maryknoll, NY: Orbis, 2001, p. 93.

10 See the reflections on Christian political activism and the peace movement by John Dear, *The God of Peace: Toward a Theology of Nonviolence*, Maryknoll, NY: Orbis, 1994 and *Peace Behind Bars: A Peacemaking Priest's Journal from Jail*, Franklin, WI: Sheed & Ward, 1995.

11 See Adrian Hastings, 'Catholic History from Vatican I to John Paul II', in Adrian Hastings, ed. *Modern Catholicism: Vatican II and After*, London: SPCK and New York: Oxford University Press, 1991, pp. 1–13.

12 See Austin Flanney OP, *Vatican Council II: The Conciliar and Post-conciliar Documents*, New York: Costello Publishing Company and Dublin: Dominican Publications, 1975; Austin Flannery OP, *Vatican Council II: More Post-conciliar Documents*, New York: Costello Publishing Company and Dublin: Dominican Publications 1983 and Walter M. Abbott SJ, *The Documents of Vatican II*, London: Geoffrey Chapman, 1966.

13 John Hick, 'The Next Step beyond Dialogue', in Paul Knitter, ed. *The Myth of Religious Superiority: Multifaith Explorations of Religious Pluralism*, Maryknoll, NY: Orbis, 2005, pp. 3–12 at p. 3.

14 Perry Schmidt-Leukel, *Understanding Buddhism*, Edinburgh: Dunedin Academic Press, 2006 and (ed.) *Buddhism and Religious Diversity*, London: Routledge, 2012.

15 Ananda Coomaraswamy, *Hinduism and Buddhism*, Mountain View, CA: Golden Elixir Press, 2011.

16 For an overview of the history and spirituality of the Camaldolese see Peter-Damian Belisle, 'Overview of Camaldolese History and Spirituality', in Peter-Damian Belisle, ed. *The Privilege of Love: Camaldolese Benedictine Spirituality*, Collegeville, MI: Liturgical Press, 2002.

17 Camaldolese Congregation of the Order of Saint Benedict, *Constitutions and Declarations*, Camaldoli, 1985, see Constitution § 125.

18 Robert Hale, 'Koinonia: The Privilege of Love', in Peter-Damian Belisle, ed. *The Privilege of Love: Camaldolese Benedictine Spirituality*. Collegeville, MI: Liturgical Press, 2002, pp. 99–114 at p. 99.

19 Leonardo Boff, *Fundamentalism, Terrorism and the Future of Humanity*. London: SPCK, 2006, p. 9.

20 Erik Borgman, 'Theology: Discipline at the Limits', in Erik Borgman and Felix Wilfred, eds. 'Theology in a World of Specialization', *Concilium*, 2006, 2, pp. 141–51 at p. 148.
21 Donald Nicholl, 'Other Religions (Nostra Aetate)', in Adrian Hastings, ed. *Modern Catholicism: Vatican II and After*, London: SPCK and New York: Oxford University Press, 1991, pp. 126–34 at p. 132.
22 This centrality of the family as the nurturing unit of Christians was already re-emphasized by Pope Leo XIII, *Arcanum* ('On Christian Marriage'), 10 February 1880.
23 Vatican II, *Dignitatis Humanae* § 2.
24 *Lumen Gentium* § 9–17.
25 Mario I. Aguilar, 'Public Theology from the Periphery: Victims and Theologians', *International Journal of Public Theology*, 2007, 1, pp. 321–37.
26 John McDade SJ, 'Catholic Theology in the Post-Conciliar Period', in Adrian Hastings, ed. *Modern Catholicism: Vatican II and After*, London: SPCK and New York: Oxford University Press, 1991, pp. 422–43 at p. 430.
27 Photograph available in William H. Shannon, Christine M. Bochen and Patrick F. O'Connell, eds. *The Thomas Merton Encyclopedia*, Maryknoll, NY: Orbis, 2002, p. 99.
28 Daniel Berrigan, 'Afterward', in Thich Nhat Hanh and Daniel Berrigan, *The Raft is not the Shore: Conversations Toward a Buddhist-Christian Awareness*, Maryknoll, NY: Orbis, 2001, pp. 151–3.
29 Murray Polner and Jim O'Grady, *Disarmed and Dangerous: The Radical Lives and Times of Daniel and Philip Berrigan*, New York: Basic Books, 1997, pp. 195–217.
30 Robert Elsberg, 'Introduction', in Thich Nhat Hanh and Daniel Berrigan, *The Raft is not the Shore: Conversations Toward a Buddhist-Christian Awareness*, Maryknoll, NY: Orbis, 2001, pp. xi–xii.
31 Berrigan, 'Afterward', p. 152.
32 Elsberg, 'Introduction', p. xii.
33 Roger Corless, 'The Christian Exploration of Non-Christian Religions: Merton's Example of Where it Might Lead Us', in Victor A. Kramer, ed. *The Merton Annual: Studies in Culture, Spirituality and Social Concerns*, 2007, 20, pp. 206–24.
34 Hans Küng, *Global Responsibility: In Search of a New World Ethic*, New York: Crossroad, 1991.
35 John Hick, 'Pluralism Conference', *Buddhist-Christian Studies*, 2004, 24, p. 253.
36 Paul F. Knitter, 'Introduction', in Paul F. Knitter, ed. *The Myth of Religious Superiority: Multifaith Explorations of Religious Pluralism*, Maryknoll, NY: Orbis, 2005, pp. vii–xi at p. vii.
37 Ibid.
38 Ibid., pp. vii–xi at pp. x–xi.
39 Hick, 'The Next Step beyond Dialogue', pp. 3–12 at p. 5.
40 Rose Drew, *Buddhist and Christian? An Exploration of Dual Belonging*, London: Routledge, 2011 and Paul F. Knitter, *Without Buddha I Could Not Be a Christian*, London: Oneworld, 2009.

Chapter 1

DIALOGUE IN VATICAN II

More than 50 years have passed since John XXIII called a council on 25 January 1959 in order to reflect on the role of the Church within the contemporary world.[1] Previous councils had been called to deal with a crisis in the mere existence of the Catholic Church: the Council of Trent (1545) dealt with the rising Protestant Reformation in Europe and Vatican I (1869) reasserted the church's position against liberalism and the results of the Enlightenment.[2] John XXIII paved the way to his public announcement by privately telling of his wish for a council to 17 Roman cardinals present at the chapter house of the abbey of St Paul's-without-the-walls – who did not react with enthusiasm but with silence.[3] In his own later personal reflections he mentioned that 'it was completely unexpected, like a flash of heavenly light, shedding sweetness in eyes and hearts. And at the same time it gave rise to a great fervour throughout the world in expectation of the holding of the Council'.[4]

John XXIII clarified that the council should emphasize the positive aspects of the modern world seeking always the justice of the Kingdom of God first and implement a magisterium that is pastoral in nature. In the words of Robert Schreiter: 'the church should contribute to the unity of humankind and present its teachings in ways understandable to people who live in the modern world.'[5] John XXIII could be deemed a radical in that he spoke in his public discourse about the church of the poor and his own wish for a church that could be less monarchic and more understood by the contemporary world of Europe. However, it is a fact that new developments on dialogue and a very strong process of secularization in Europe have made some of the fresh and inclusive insights of Vatican II less relevant to most people. It is possible to argue that there has been an effort to forget the council during the pontificates of John Paul II and Benedict XVI. Clearly these two popes forwarded a model of communion between the local churches and Rome that became more centralized and more traditional in the way of appointing bishops and the actual role of the Church. This role changed from being that of a servant church at the Council to a teaching church with Benedict XVI. As a result, bishops canonically in charge of teaching within the Catholic Church became more central to the structure of the Catholic Church leaving less room for a collegial cooperation between local churches and assigning less power of decision to the local Episcopal Conferences.[6]

This model affected modes and ways of fostering dialogue between Christians and those of other faiths and no-faiths. It is a fact that John Paul II and Benedict XVI became a sign of dialogue by their appearances in world events of inter-faith prayer such as encounters in Assisi and by visiting synagogues and mosques thereby showing enormous respect for other faiths, particularly those of the Abrahamic faiths, that is Muslims and Jews.[7] However, their teaching concerning dialogue with other religions reinforced the primacy of the Catholic Church as the church of Christ and little encouragement was given to Christian communities already engaged in dialogue. In the case of Christian–Buddhist relations there was nevertheless an increase in the appreciation of Buddhist philosophy and meditation by sectors of Christians everywhere but particularly among the youth of Europe. In fact, a number of Christians started asserting a dual belonging: to Christianity as well as to Buddhism.[8]

It is crucial in order to critically discuss dialogue, I would argue, to first re-examine the teachings of Vatican II regarding inter-faith dialogue and to revisit the spirit of the council regarding dialogue with other human beings, particular with those such as Buddhists who do not adhere to a belief in a creator God.

The Issue of Conscience and Human Dignity

Two issues for discussion became central within Vatican II: conscience and human dignity. Without the two agreements on the freedom of conscience given by God to all human beings and therefore the assertion of the dignity of each human being made in the image of God further discussions on an inclusive church would have been extremely difficult. Thus, it is difficult to separate the document on other religions, the *Nostra Aetate*, from the *Constitution on the Church* (*Lumen Gentium*), the *Pastoral Constitution on the Church in the Modern World* (*Gaudium et Spes*) and the *Declaration on Religious Liberty* (*Dignitatis Humanae*).

Dignitatis Humanae (7 December 1965), a document that was embryonically prepared by the American theologian John Courtney Murray SJ, made the religious freedom of the individual part of official church teaching.[9] This was a complete turn of affairs since Pious IX who in his *Syllabus of Errors* had not included any religious or political pluralism.[10] It was indeed a change that was particularly needed by Catholics living in mostly Protestant societies such as the United States. *Dignitatis Humanae* argued that there is no recognition of a church's authority by a believing state; the church's authority adheres to freedom rather than to the establishment.[11] The ground for this change in doctrine breaking with Constantine, Justinian and Charlemagne is an examination of the dignity of the human individual.[12] This right to individual freedom extends to groups of believers and it includes freedom of enquiry, association, communication, finance, public testimony, worship and common moral endeavour.[13] The document puts a newly strong emphasis on individual conscience stating that 'it is through this conscience that man sees and recognizes the demands of the divine law'.[14]

For a contemporary generation that has enjoyed the fruits of Vatican II it is difficult to grasp the enormous and central change that this emphasis on the freedom of the individual meant to Catholics as well as non-Catholics. It must be remembered that at the time of the council Catholics were restricted in their freedom of belief, public testimony, communication, worship and moral guidance.[15] Thus, by the publication of works in the *Index* of forbidden books Catholics were banned from reading works by non-Catholics and they needed an episcopal *imprimatur* – a permission to publish on issues of religion and morality – while all clerics needed an imprimatur for anything they were intending to publish. Catholics could not attend other churches' worship thus being controlled by a clearly hierarchical system that was accountable to the Holy Office.

Nostra Aetate

The Declaration on the Relations of the Church to Non-Christian Religions (*Nostra Aetate*, October 1965) was truly the work of the council because nobody could have predicted before the council that the Fathers of the Council would engage with other religions apart from Judaism.[16] It was a process of reflection that was clearly aided by John XXIII and was prepared through the appointment of Cardinal Bea as the president of the secretariat for promoting Christian unity in June 1960. Bea was also asked to work on a schema on the Jews, a particular preoccupation of the council.

The schema on the Jews was abandoned at a meeting of the Central Commission for preparing the Council in June 1962 because of considerations on the ongoing political animosity between Arabs and Jews. This was providential in that the schema was diversified and even when *Nostra Aetate* deals mainly with Judaism without the events that took place in Palestine in June 1962 it would have most probably evolved into a declaration on inter-faith dialogue solely with the Jews. Despite the death of John XXIII in June 1963 a new schema was introduced in November 1963 containing three chapters on the Christian churches, one on the Jews and a fifth one dealing with religious freedom. Discussions were influenced heavily by the possibility that words about the Jews could endanger the existence of Christians within Israel and Palestine as well as by fear of a reaction by Muslims if they were to be mentioned within paragraphs on ecumenism or paired with the Jews. Thus, even when there was no clear discussion on religious freedom it was clear that the council document had to evolve as to include other religions without pairing them with the Jews and a whole discussion on anti-Semitism within the church.

In May 1964 Paul VI solved this previous impasse by giving more importance to the relations with other religions expressed through the founding of a special Secretariat for the development of relations with other religions under the leadership of Cardinal Marella. Three months later Paul VI issued the encyclical *Ecclesiam Suam*, the most comprehensive church document related to the spirituality of dialogue.

On 25 September 1964 Cardinal Bea reported, to great applause, to the eighty-eighth congregation on his report titled *Declaratio de Judaeis et de non-Christianis*.[17] Before the session the German Bishops had produced a document agreeing with the approval of Bea's document and remembering that serious injustices had been committed against the Jewish people in the name of the German people. The genesis of the document had been of particular concern to Cardinal Bea triggered by the personal concern on this matter expressed by John XXIII. On 28 September 1964 the text on dialogue presented to the council was broadened as to include the mention of Muslims and other religions as well as Jews. As a result of this extended preparation the declaration *Nostra Aetate* was approved at the first vote in November 1964. The document was finally promulgated on 28 October 1965 with the title *Declaration on the Relation of the Church to Non-Christian Religions*.

Already at the start of the document the fathers of the council outlined the common human need for asking questions about life and death, judgement, sinfulness and indeed human life as a whole.[18] Further, the document recognized the existence of religions belonging to advanced civilizations that have systematized some of the answers to the questions about life and death.[19] It mentions Hinduism and Buddhism suggesting that 'Buddhism in its various forms testifies to the essential inadequacy of this changing world. It proposes a way of life by which men can, with confidence and trust, attain a state of perfect liberation and reach supreme illumination either through their own efforts or by the aid of divine help'.[20]

The sentence that follows was a bomb shell, outlining a newness of the acceptance of diversity that marked an end to the enmity of many centuries between the Catholic Church and other religions. For the fathers of the council state plainly that,

> The Catholic Church rejects nothing of what is true and holy in these religions. She has a high regard for the manner of life and conduct, the precepts and doctrines which, although differing in many ways from her own teaching, nevertheless often reflect a ray of that truth which enlightens all men.[21]

However, the document also stressed the fact that for Christians, thus, their name, the way to 'the fullness' of religious life is found in Christ.[22] Christians are to engage 'with prudence and charity into discussions and collaboration with members of other religions' preserving and encouraging other faiths while bearing witness to their own.

Regarding Islam the document makes a clear connection between the roots of faith in Abraham and the daily life of prayer, alms-deed and fasting that connect Christians and Muslims.[23] There is a plea to forget a past with 'many quarrels and dissensions' between Christian and Muslims and a fresh call is made to promote 'peace, liberty, social justice and moral values'.[24]

The document, initially concerned with Christian Jewish relations continues to stress the roots of both faith in Abraham, Moses and the Prophets recalling the fact that the Jews did not recognize Jesus as the Messiah but they remain 'very dear to God'.[25] Thus, there is a common spiritual heritage that should be encouraged by biblical and theological studies and through what the council calls 'friendly discussions'.[26] It is at this point that the document dealt with the most difficult historical stumbling block of Christian–Jewish relations: the death of Christ. The passage of Jn 19.6 where the Jewish authorities and the people themselves press for the death of Christ was used through centuries to accuse the Jews of the death of Christ, an account that created a growing anti-Semitism within the church. *Nostra Aetate* was absolutely clear in stating that 'neither all Jews indiscriminately at that time, nor Jews today, can be charged with the crimes committed during his passion'.[27]

A warning follows for those who distort the truth of the Gospel and the affirmation that the church 'reproves every form of persecution against whomsoever it may be directed'.[28] Finally, the document condemns any discrimination or harassment against people because of race, colour and condition in life or religion.[29]

It is clear from reading this document that the Catholic Church went a long way to establish a principle of respect and cooperation with other religions that would have been unthinkable at the start of the twentieth century.

Ecclesiam Suam

The council established a magisterial principle of inclusion for the world religions that was based not on an exceptional state of affairs but on a return to an inclusivist understanding of church and a refreshed sense of a spirit of dialogue. Both understandings were set up by Paul VI in the encyclical letter 'On the Church' (*Ecclesiam Suam*), promulgated on 6 August 1964.[30] The encyclical manifested an openness that had been denied previously; however, this openness was a significant necessity in order to enhance the work of the church. According to Cardinal F. König, President of the Secretariat for Nonbelievers, in an interview given to Vatican Radio 'the Church was called to dialogue, but only in order to carry out its proper task, namely the saving proclamation of Christ'.[31]

The first of Paul VI's encyclicals, *Ecclesiam Suam* is divided into three parts – self-awareness, renewal and dialogue – and it describes the church in relation to society with the church entrusted with one task, 'to serve society'.[32] Within this service the church must reflect 'on its own nature, the better to appreciate the divine plan which it is the Church's task to implement'.[33] For the Church, according to Paul VI, belongs to the world 'even though distinguished from it by its own altogether unique characteristics'.[34] Further, 'the Church is deeply rooted in the world'; 'it exists in the world and draws its members from the world'.[35] However, because it exists in the world it is bound to feel the tensions and the pressures of an ever-changing world.[36] Thus, it is necessary, according to Paul VI, to revisit the church's own existence in the scriptures and the apostolic tradition.[37]

Paul VI returns to two previous documents that shed important light on the activities and the task of the church: the encyclical *Satis cognitum* (Leo XIII, 1896) and the encyclical *Mystici corporis* (Pious XII, 1943).[38] The strengthening of understanding of the Mystical Body of Christ, according to Paul VI, could create the conditions in which a spiritual uplifting should come from a deep reflection on the nature of the union between Christ and his church.[39] Further, this self-reflection could create a 'renewed discovery of its vital bond of union with Christ'.[40] However, for Paul VI the nature of the church is not a matter for speculative theology but it has to be lived 'so that the faithful may have a kind of intuitive experience of it, even before they come to understand it clearly'.[41] Thus, the importance of baptism whereby the baptized rejoices in a new life and sees baptism as a new 'illumination' that 'draws down upon his soul the life-giving radiance of divine truth'.[42]

Once and again Paul VI stressed the importance of the conciliar deliberations on the church and lay the foundational principle for a church immersed in the world defined as 'in the world, but not of it'.[43] He reminded readers of

John XXIII's word for the council, 'aggiornamento', and his own adherence to it as a significant marker of the need for the church to be immersed in the contemporary world and to look for the 'signs of the time'.[44] One of the important points for the renewal of the church in general and the renewal of ecclesiastical life in particular mentioned by Paul VI was 'the spirit of poverty, or rather, the zeal for preserving this spirit'.[45] Such is the centrality that Paul VI gives to the spirit of poverty that he asserts that 'it is a fundamental element of that divine plan by which we are destined to win the Kingdom of God, and yet it is greatly jeopardized by the modern trend to set so much store by wealth'.[46] The Pope recognizes the difficulties that everyone has on keeping a spirit of poverty and announces particular canonical regulations and directives regarding poverty as to highlight clearly that 'spiritual goods far outweigh economic goods, the possession and use of which should be regulated and subordinated to the conduct and advantage of our apostolic mission'.[47] Regarding wealth the Pope encourages the understanding of economics and the actual use of wealth not as a source of tension but to help those who are in need; thus wealth should be used 'justly and equitable for the good of all' and ultimately redistributed.[48] Together with the spirit of poverty charity emerges as 'the very heart and centre of the plan of God's providence as revealed in both the Old and the New Testament'.[49] Paul VI uses the word 'charity' instead of 'love' and argues strongly following Paul's hymn of love (1 Corinthians 13) that 'charity is the key to everything. It sets all to rights. There is nothing which charity cannot achieve and renew'.[50]

The third part of *Ecclesiam Suam* deals with the issue of dialogue and particularly with dialogue with the world.[51] The world for Paul VI is defined as:

> Either those human beings who are opposed to the light of faith and the gift of grace, those whose naive optimism betrays them into thinking that their own energies suffice to win them complete, lasting, and gainful prosperity, or, finally, those who take refuge in an aggressively pessimistic outlook on life and maintain that their vices, weaknesses and moral ailments are inevitable, incurable, or perhaps even desirable as sure manifestations of personal freedom and sincerity.[52]

Paul VI reminds Catholics that Christians are different than people in 'the world' by the fact that they have been justified which in Catholic terms alludes to the theological understanding that they are participants in the Paschal Mystery through Baptism, 'which is truly a rebirth'.[53] Christians differentiate themselves from the world without indifference, fear or contempt for the world; on the contrary the church distinguishes her from humanity in order to become closer to humanity, showing more concern and more love for all.[54] Thus, the church must enter into dialogue with the world because it has something to say, a message to give and a communication to make.[55]

Even when the aim of this dialogue is 'to win souls' Paul VI acknowledges that issues of dialogue with the world have a previous foundation given by Leo XIII, Pious XI, Pious XII and John XXIII.[56] Those popes have shown that if the church is to bring people to Christ and to the church she must engage herself in dialogue, in a conversation with the world.[57] Thus, dialogue arises out of the experience of God in prayer and in discernment because dialogue has God Himself as 'the noble origin of this dialogue'.[58] It is in the dialogue between Christ and human beings that He reveals how He wishes to be known: as pure love.[59] Thus, Paul VI stresses the dialogue established by the Father who sent his Son and who is in dialogue with us through the church, a paradigm of dialogue that should be established with the whole of humanity.[60] In his reflection, Paul VI stressed the fact that God initiated this dialogue first in love and this is an important characteristic of the church's dialogue with others: it should be initiated by the church without waiting for others and in the spirit of love.[61] In fact, God's dialogue was not initiated on merit or with particular objectives but it was conducted freely, without coercion in a spirit of conversational openness. The same process of dialogue with others in 'human friendliness, interior persuasion, and ordinary conversation' is expected of the church.[62]

Within Paul VI's teachings dialogue is catholic (universal), perseverant with the church taking the initiative; thus, dialogue becomes the method for the relations between the church and the world.[63] In order to respect a human being's freedom and dignity Paul VI suggests that dialogue has the following characteristics: (i) dialogue should be intelligible, (ii) it should be humble, truthful and peaceful, (iii) it should carry confidence on the power of words as well as on the good will of the other party and (iv) it should be conducted with the prudence of a teacher.[64]

In the final part of *Ecclessiam Suam* Paul VI provided a positive view to developments and changes in the world stating that,

> All things human are our concern. We share with the whole of the human race a common nature, a common life, with all its gifts and all its problems. We are ready to play our part in this primary, universal society, to acknowledge the insistent demands of its fundamental needs, and to applaud the new and often sublime expressions of its genius.[65]

Among the most difficult sectors of society with whom the church could dialogue Paul VI mentioned those who followed atheism and communism.[66] Among the very positive partners in dialogue Paul VI mentioned those who seek and work for peace, those who share a faith in One God (Jewish and Moslem) and those who follow Afro-Asiatic religions.[67] Thus, regarding those who follow non-Christian religions Paul VI asserted,

> We desire to join with them in promoting and defending common ideals in the spheres of religious liberty, human brotherhood, education, culture, social welfare, and civic order. Dialogue is possible in all these great projects, which are our concern as much as theirs, and we will not fail to offer opportunities for discussion in the event of such an offer being favourably received in genuine, mutual respect.[68]

Finally Paul VI referred to those who share a belief in Christ stressing the commonalities between the Christian churches rather than the differences.[69] The fact that representatives of all the Christian churches were present at the Second Vatican Council (properly labelled 'ecumenical') was already a sign of the things to come.

As a result of all those reflections dialogue was to be central to the life of the church in a post-conciliar climate and in the case of Jewish–Christian relations many groups started conversations and lives in dialogue. As Donald Nicholl has argued 'the depth of that change is probably hard for anyone to measure who was not personally acquainted with the situation before the Second Vatican Council'.[70]

Despite appearances and before Vatican II, there had been pioneers of interfaith dialogue who had been very active in pursuing the possibilities of bringing the Gospel to Muslims and Hindus. In the process of trying to do so they became immersed in a dualistic world of two religions and in the subsequent tensions and joys of a practising inter-faith dialogue through their own lives.

Dialogue before the Council

The contact between Europe and Asia, with their diverse cultures and religions, had been indirectly fostered by the expansion of European colonialism from the nineteenth century onwards. The encounter between Christianity and Hinduism in India was an example of respect within the perils of colonialism while African religions were the recipients of a colonial Christianity that over imposed religious categories on a continent with hundreds of religious traditions that for the most part were non-literal. Colonial functionaries, military and Christian missionaries posted to all corners of European empires encountered millions of religious practitioners of other religions and the impact was clear. Particularly in India the British colonial administration had encountered a region where millions of people practiced religious festivals and rites publicly and fervently. As a result, the first dialogue with Muslims, Hindus and Buddhists came through the daily life of European civil servants and their families who in some cases became fascinated by the extent of religious fervour, the colourful temples and the respect offered to holy men and women in India and Africa.

Therefore it is a fact of history and the history of missions that some of those exchanges had already influenced the life of dialogue between the different religions, a fact of life that helped to create a positive preparation for dialogue in the documents of Vatican II. Missionary congregations such as the Jesuits, the Missionaries of Africa (White Fathers) or the Society of the Divine Word played an important part in the positive preparation on the council's reflections on mission individuals who were not Christians and in the positive outlook shown by John XXIII and Paul VI towards non-Christian religions.

Christianity and Judaism

Relations between Christians and Jews throughout the centuries had been quite strained. They became more strained during and after World War II because of the passivity on the part of the German Bishops. They did not risk their close relations with Catholic members of the Nazi Party and the ambivalent reaction of the Vatican blamed later on the inability of Pious XII to challenge the Nazi regime in a public way. Thus, in the years before the council there were fresh attempts to foster Jewish–Christian relations from the roots by those Christian and Jewish theologians who had condemned the silence of the Church or were reflecting on the absence of God during the Shoah.

Among the few that were actively in dialogue with the church one could mention here the influence exercised by Rabbi Abraham Heschel (1907–72), who was consulted by John XXIII and Paul VI, consultation that certainly influenced the final texts on dialogue produced by the council. Rabbi Heschel, a liberal rabbi born in Poland, studied in Berlin and was living in Frankfurt in 1938 when he was arrested by the Gestapo and deported to Poland. He lectured on Jewish philosophy and Torah at the Warsaw's Institute for Jewish Studies. Six weeks before the German invasion of Poland he left for London aided by the Hebrew Union College that had been working to secure visas for Jewish scholars in Europe. Rabbi Heschel's sister Esther was killed in a bombing, his mother was killed by the Nazis and two of his sisters, Gittel and Devorah, died in Nazi concentration camps. Heschel arrived in New York in 1940 and taught at the Hebrew Union College in Cincinnati for 5 years. In 1946 he moved to the Jewish Theological Seminary of America, the main seminary for Conservative Judaism, where he taught Jewish Ethics and Mysticism until 1972. He saw the books of the prophets as a call for social action in the United States and as a result he supported black civil rights and protested against the Vietnam War.[71] At Vatican II he represented American Jews, particularly with a vision that religious experience, including Judaism, could be understood as a human impulse and that no faith could claim the absolute truth.

Christianity and Islam

In the case of Islam there were close contacts between the Vatican and the French Arabist Louis Massignon (1883–1962).[72] In 1926 Massignon was appointed to the Chair of Muslim Sociology and Sociography at the Collège de France in Paris and in 1933 he became director of studies for Islam at the École Pratique des Hautes Études within the religious studies section. In the same year he was elected a member of the Academy of the Arabic Language in Cairo, a place where he spent every winter during his academic career. He died at the beginning of the council but had been quite influential in the perception of Islam by Pius XII and John XXIII by the fact that he was a Catholic who tried to study and understand Islam from within.[73]

Louis Massignon grew up in Paris where he pursued different disciplines within the humanities division at the university, including Arabic. Between 1906 and 1910 he resided in Cairo where he studied Arabic and conducted research in Iraq and Istanbul. Between 1912 and 1913 he returned to Cairo as visiting professor at the Egyptian University (later renamed University of Cairo). In 1922 Massignon submitted the required two doctoral theses to the University of Paris. The theses concerned two different themes: al-Ḥallāj and early Islamic mysticism and his works were published that year in two volumes under the title *La passion d'al-Hosayn-ibn-Mansour al'Hallâj, martyr mystique de l'Islam exécuté à Bagdad le 26 mars 922*.[74]

Massignon had various mystical and spiritual experiences in his travels as a postgraduate student through Algeria and Morocco. However, a central experience that marked him for life took place in 1908 in Mesopotamia. A year before he arrived in Baghdad as a member of an archaeological team and as a guest of the Alusi family, a prominent Muslim family. However, while in the desert he was taken prisoner by Turkish forces involved in the Turkish revolution and accused of being a spy. He was freed due to negotiations conducted by the Alusi who showed him the values of Arab hospitality and helped him to gather sources for his work on al-Ḥallāj. During his captivity he experienced a numbness and illness due to what he would interpret as the presence of God as 'a visitation of a stranger'. He had a second episode of this inability to function corporeally and underwent a moment of conversion towards Christianity. He travelled to Beirut accompanied by the Iraqi Carmelite priest Père Anastase-Marie de Saint Elie who heard his confession in Beirut.

Massignon described his conversion as a moment that was brought about by friends of his who had experienced God in a Muslim context and mentioned specifically Charles de Foucault.[75] He later became the executor of Charles de Foucault spiritual legacy, namely the 'directoire' – a rule for the foundation of the congregation of the Little Brothers of Jesus. This took him some time because of the reluctance by the Vatican to grant the imprimatur to publish the rule, publication that finally took place in 1928. Massignon had been invited by Charles de Foucault to join him as a hermit among the Tuareg at Tamanrasset but he declined such invitation.

After his marriage and during the 1930s Massignon became a member of the third order of Franciscans, a lay organization inspired by the figure of St Francis of Assisi, and he took the name of Ibrahim. As part of this spiritual development Massignon, together with a friend Mary Kahil, visited the abandoned Franciscan Church in Damietta, Egypt, where Francis had met Sultan al-Malik al-Kamil in 1219. Both of them took a vow of *Badaliya* (Arabic = substitution), offering their lives for the Muslims. The vow did not ask for their conversion but that God's purpose is realized in them, a prayer that led to the formation of the Badaliya prayer association in 1947.

On 5 February 1949 Massignon became, with the permission of Pious XII, a Melkite Greek Catholic, thus no longer a Roman Catholic but an Arab Catholic who took part in the Byzantine Rite celebrated in Arabic. On 28 January 1958 he became a priest in the Greek Catholic Rite having being ordained by Bishop Kamel Medawar and with the permission of Patriarch Maximos IV. There was some opposition from the Vatican to this ordination but he fulfilled his wish of becoming an offering for Muslims. He died on 30 October 1962 having made a clear bridge between France and the Arab world and between Catholicism and Islam. His two main contributions to a Christian–Muslim dialogue were expressed in his life through sacred hospitality and mystical substitution, theological concepts and practical actions present in Christianity and Islam.

Christianity and Hinduism

The ongoing life-dialogue between Christian monks and the world of Hinduism before Vatican II outlines similar and significant parameters of understanding within Christian–Buddhist relations after Vatican II. Hinduism and Buddhism are interconnected in their understanding of creation from energy rather than from the wish of a superior being and not only in both being religious traditions; both also stand as world religious faiths outside the Abrahamic family.

Further, Hinduism and Buddhism function without the concept of an afterlife represented by a final judgement and an eternal life related to a creator God.

I shall return to some of these textual theoretical differences later in the book; however, at this stage it is important to outline three important Christian contributions for Christian–Hindu dialogue that started before Vatican II and continued after the council. These three pioneers had an influence on the breadth of dialogue and recognition of the sacredness of Hinduism within the Catholic Church.[76] The three of them belonged to the Benedictine monastic family and lived in India as Christians inspired by Hinduism. They were Abbé Jules Monchanin (1895–1957), Dom Henri Le Saux (1910–73) and Dom Bede Griffiths (1906–93).

There were others who also became engaged in a religious life informed by Hindu practices, among them Father Francis Mahieu, a Belgian Trapppist who stayed in Bombay after arrival from Europe and later moved to Kerala, and who considered becoming a postulant at Shantivanam, the ashram started by Monchanin and Le Saux.[77] Mahieu stayed for a few months at Shantivanam; however he decided to move away looking for his own place, having a very distant personal relationship with Le Saux.[78] On moving away from Shantivanam he started another ashram, named as Kurisumala in Kerala, together with Bede Griffin.[79] In 1969 Mahieu almost took over Le Saux's ashram, a place eventually taken by Griffiths.[80] Mahieu remained in Kerala most of his life, thus geographically apart from Monchanin, Le Saux and Griffiths, exercising a less compelling influence on the attempts to link Christianity and Hinduism in India and within the Catholic Church.[81]

The first pioneer of a Christian–Hindu dialogue was Abbé Jules Monchanin (1895–1957; Hindu name = Swāmi Paramārūbyānanda).[82] Born near Lyons in 1895 Monchanin was ordained as a Catholic priest in 1922 and proceeded to work in a miner's parish in a poor suburb of Lyons.[83] After serving in three parishes he developed ill health and was moved as a chaplain first to an orphanage and later to a boy's boarding school. He pursued his interest in India studying Sanskrit and Indian subjects in general and at the same time longing for a Christian monastic life in India. In 1939 Monchanin received permission from the Bishop of Tiruchirapalli to work with the few Christians who lived in the diocese and in May of that year he left for India. For the next decade Monchanin worked in the diocese of Tiruchirapalli feeling physical hardship and an acute loneliness. However, he immersed himself in the study of the Tamil language learning about all things Indian, specially the *Gita*.[84] In 1950 he started a monastic hermitage on the banks of the Kavery River.[85]

The year 1950 coincided with the arrival of Le Saux in India and on the feast of St Benedict on 21 March 1950 the ashram was opened with various names: Eremus Sanctissimae Trinitatis (Hermitage of the Most Holy Trinity), Shantivanam (Grove of Peace) and Saccidananda (after the Vedantic ternary Being-Awareness-Bliss).[86] The foundation of the ashram pioneered Christian–Hindu dialogue and the foundation document stated its goal as 'to form the first nucleus of a monastery (or rather a *laura*, a grouping of neighbouring anchorites like the ancient laura of St. Sabas in Palestine) which buttresses the Rule of St. Benedict – a primitive, sober, discrete rule. Only one purpose: to seek God. And the monastery will be Indian style'.[87]

Monchanin's companion was to be another pioneer of Christian–Hindu dialogue, the Benedictine Dom Henri Le Saux (Hindu name Swami Abhishiktananda), a French Benedictine who went to India in 1948 in order to devote his life as a living bridge between Christianity and Hinduism.[88] Born in Saint Briac, Brittany, France in August 1910 Le Saux entered the diocesan seminary but by age 19 he felt called to the contemplative life and entered the Benedictine Abbey of Saint Anne of Kergonan. There he developed a desire to bring Christianity to India and to enter into dialogue with Hinduism so that once and for all Indians would understand the nature of Christianity.

The life of dialogue, as lived by Dom Henri, outlined the possibility of an ever-changing stage of dialogue. Dialogue becomes a process, a journey that keeps changing, and in the case of dialogue with Hinduism (and Buddhism) it requires a self-emptying and inward journey that prevails over documents or social encounters. Thus, in the first part of his dialogue Dom Henri saw his call as to bring Christianity to India and Christianity as the fulfilment of Hinduism.[89] In a second phase this kind of dialogue (or missionary work) changed as he went deeper and deeper into his *advatain* experiences, the search for an emptiness of non-duality.[90] Those experiences were deepened by his meeting with Sri Ramana Maharshi and by his solitary meditations during his long retreats to the mountain of Arunachala.[91] This phase created a clear tension and spiritual struggle that only solved itself in a third phase of his life. During those final years of his life he had a disciple, the French theological student Marc Chaduc, and finally the struggle resolved itself in favour of *advaita*. For *advaita*, understood as a non-duality, both as doctrine and as experience brought a personal crisis on Abhishiktananda. For Dom Henri, according to Henry Olmeadow, *advaita* is 'an "inner" awareness of the Real (Self/Atman-Brahman/God/Divine Presence) in which all dualities disappear, including that of "experience" and "experiencer," of subject and object'.[92] Abhishiktanada went all the way risking the possibility that his previous Christian knowledge could not help him to attain *advaita* and that a sensorial search for understanding and experience of Hinduism could not bring him to the emptiness of non-duality, the presence of the One in the self. His contribution to the dialogue between Christianity and

Hinduism could be a paradigm for the personal commitment to a spiritual and contemplative search in the case of Christianity and Buddhism, without the ultimate fear: not to attain eternal life within Christianity or reincarnation in the Hindu *samsara*.

Abhishiktanada agonized over the possibility of not fitting into a dual religious life: Christian and Hindu. In the analysis of Shirley Du Boulay 'he had come to India to proclaim Christ, but he had found Christ in another form'.[93] In Abhishiktanada's words: 'It was You who made yourself known to me by means of them in the overwhelming features of Arunachala'.[94] After a severe heart attack he had to leave his hermitic life and he died at a nursing home run by sisters in Indore. He was buried 4 miles away at the cemetery of the Divine Word Missionaries and later transported back to Shantivanam, his first ashram.

Another example of this search for a Christian–Hindu dialogue was the Camaldolese Benedictine Bede Griffiths (Hindu name = Swami Dhayananda meaning the gift of prayer and later Swami Dayananda meaning the bliss of compassion).[95] Born in England on 17 December 1906, Alan Richard Griffiths studied at Oxford University (1925–9) and graduated as a journalist, having had C. S. Lewis as his tutor. In 1931 he converted from Anglicanism to Roman Catholicism, he was received into the Catholic Church and joined the Benedictine community of Prinknash Abbey. In December 1932 he became a novice and was given the name Bede (= prayer). In 1937 he took his final vows and was ordained as a Catholic priest in 1940. Later he was transferred to two French Benedictine foundations: Farnborough and later Pluscardin in Scotland, a place that he found very cold and where he wrote his autobiography.[96]

After returning to Prinknash Abbey Dom Bede asked his abbot to send him to India. While at Farnborough he had met a priest born in Europe but of Indian origin, Fr Benedict Alapott, and he had been introduced to Eastern thought, yoga and the Hindu scriptures by Tony Sussman, a therapist. His abbot rejected his request first but later allowed him to depart for India, but not as Benedictine; he was to serve as a priest under obedience to a local bishop. Thus, in 1955 Benedict Alapott and Bede Griffiths departed for Bombay. They settled in Kengeri, Bangalore until 1958 when Fr Bede departed for Kurisumala, an ashram in Kerala where he stayed for 10 years. At the ashram and together with Fr Francis Acharya he used the Syriac rite for the liturgy and developed a Hindu monastic life (*Sannyasa*) dressing in Kavi (orange robes). During these years Fr Bede studied Indian religions and society and he wrote his seminal work *Christ in India*.[97]

His influence started to be felt outside India and in 1963 while the council was on its way he was invited to New Mexico to speak on East–West dialogue, he was interviewed in the CBS station and spoke to 500 missionary sisters at Maryknoll, New York. In 1968 he moved to Shantivanam, the ashram that had been started by Monchanin and Le Saux where he remained until his death in May 1993.[98]

These three pioneers offered not only the possibility of dialogue between Christianity and Hinduism by their example, but they also offered a diversity of personal dialogic theologies that could be emulated by others in a pluralistic manner. Michael Barnes described their differences as follows: 'If Monchanin was remarkable for an austere theological wisdom and Bede [Griffiths] famous for the warmth of his hospitality, Abhishiktananda was an energetic explorer who committed himself to an ever-deeper engagement with the riches of classical Hinduism'.[99] The example of these three Benedictines moved other priests and nuns, Indian and expatriate alike, to seek a life of meditation and prayer that connected Christianity and Hinduism. On the side of Hinduism Mahatma Gandhi remains as the greatest example of dialogue and pluralistic inclusion. The violence that followed the announcement of the partition of India between Hindus and Muslims that triggered Gandhi's fast and strong words for unity remain among the most important efforts for dialogue in the twentieth century.[100]

Post-Conciliar Reflections

It is difficult to know if the seeds of this kind of dialogue through a life of contemplation was already flourishing and the council reaffirmed the possibility of a life of inter-faith dialogue or if the challenges of the 1960s and the advent of the council triggered many others to live a Christian life immersed within another religious tradition particularly in places of meditation and silence such as ashrams in India. Nevertheless, it is clear that those examples of holy Christian men and women searching for further religious experiences abounded.

There was no doubt that the newly described servant church post-Vatican II longed for the possibility of serving the poor and the marginalized in the world, a fact that came to the fore through leading pastoral changes in Latin America. It is in Latin America that words such as 'suffering' and 'liberation' started to become central to the church's existence, words that also were used by Hinduism and Buddhism and within Islam connotating in a very strong sense the offering alms to the poor. Thus, the necessity of exploring commonality in theoretical and doctrinal practice in a concrete crosscultural manner arises out of the possibility expressed and opened up by the fathers of the council, the subject of the next chapter.

Notes

1. For a reflection on this moment 50 years later see Joseph A Komonchak, 'Convening Vatican II: John XXIII Calls for a Council', *Commonwealth*, 12 February 1999.
2. For an overview of these councils see Michael J. Walsh, 'Councils in Christian History', in Adrian Hastings, ed. *Modern Catholicism: Vatican II and After*, London: SPCK and New York: Oxford University Press, 1991, pp. 14–19.
3. Peter Hebblethwaite, *John XXIII: Pope of the Council*, London: Geoffrey Chapman, 1984, p. 196; cf. *John XXIII: Shepherd of the Modern World*, New York: Doubleday, 1984 and 'John XXIII', in Adrian Hastings, ed. *Modern Catholicism: Vatican II and After*, London: SPCK and New York: Oxford University Press, 1991, pp. 27–34 at p. 27.
4. John XXIII, 'Opening Speech of the Second Vatican Council' 11 October 1962.
5. Robert J. Schreiter, 'The Impact of Vatican II', in Gregory Baum, ed. *The Twentieth Century: A Theological Overview*, Maryknoll, NY: Orbis, Ottawa, Ontario: Novalis and London: Geoffrey Chapman, 1999, pp. 158–72 at p. 159.
6. See the role of the bishop in *The Code of Canon Law in English Translation*, London and Sydney: Collins, 1983, § 375–430.
7. For a portrait of John Paul II see among others Peter Hebblethwaite, *Introducing John Paul II: The Populist Pope*, London: Collins, 1982.
8. Rose Drew, *Buddhist and Christian? An Exploration of Dual Belonging*, London: Routledge, 2011 and Paul F. Knitter, *Without Buddha I Could Not Be a Christian*, London: Oneworld, 2009.
9. *Dignitatis Humanae* § 1–2; cf. John Paul II, *Essays on Religious Freedom*, Milwaukee: Catholic League on Religious and Civil Rights, 1984.
10. For a fuller commentary on *Dignitatis Humanae* see James Tunstead Burtchaell CSC, 'Religious Freedom (*Dignitatis Humanae*)', in Adrian Hastings, ed. *Modern Catholicism: Vatican II and After*, London: SPCK and New York: Oxford University Press, 1991, pp. 118–25.
11. *Dignitatis Humanae* § 6.
12. Owen Chadwick, *Catholicism and History: The Opening of the Vatican Archives*, Cambridge: Cambridge University Press, 1978.
13. *Dignitatis Humanae* § 4–7.
14. *Dignitatis Humanae* § 3.
15. Burtchaell, 'Religious Freedom (*Dignitatis Humanae*)', p. 120.
16. For the history of the document and a critical analysis see Donald Nicholl, 'Other Religions (Nostra Aetate)', in Adrian Hastings, ed. *Modern Catholicism: Vatican II and After*, London: SPCK and New York: Oxford University Press, 1991, pp. 126–34.
17. Joseph A. Komonchak, 'Toward and Ecclesiology of Communion', in Giuseppe Alberigo, ed. *History of Vatican II*, vol. IV *Church as Communion: Third Period and Intercession September 1964 – September 1965*, Maryknoll, NY: Orbis and Leuven: Peeters, 2003, pp. 1–93 at p. 135.
18. *Nostra Aetate* § 1.
19. *Nostra Aetate* § 2.
20. Ibid.
21. Ibid.
22. Ibid.

23 *Nostra Aetate* § 3.
24 Ibid.
25 *Nostra Aetate* § 4.
26 Ibid.
27 Ibid.
28 Ibid.
29 *Nostra Aetate* § 5.
30 Text available at www.vatican.va/holy_father/paul_vi/encyclicals/documents/hf_p-vi_enc_06081964_ecclesiam_en.html.
31 Ricardo Burigana and Giovanni Turbanti, 'The Intersession: Preparing the Conclusion of the Council', in Giuseppe Alberigo, ed. *History of Vatican II*, vol. IV *Church as Communion: Third Period and Intercession September 1964 – September 1965*, Maryknoll, NY: Orbis and Leuven: Peeters, 2003, pp. 453–615 at p. 610.
32 *Ecclessiam Suam* § 5.
33 *Ecclessiam Suam* § 18.
34 Ibid.
35 *Ecclessiam Suam* § 26.
36 Ibid.
37 Ibid.
38 *Ecclessiam Suam* § 30.
39 *Ecclessiam Suam* § 31.
40 *Ecclessiam Suam* § 35.
41 *Ecclessiam Suam* § 37.
42 *Ecclessiam Suam* § 39; for the meaning of baptism see § 39–40.
43 *Ecclessiam Suam* § 49.
44 *Ecclessiam Suam* § 50.
45 *Ecclessiam Suam* § 54.
46 Ibid.
47 Ibid.
48 *Ecclessiam Suam* § 55.
49 *Ecclessiam Suam* § 56.
50 Ibid.
51 It is important to recall here that the church and the world in Catholic theology are not opposed to means of grace as it has been assumed by some protestant theology following John Calvin but that God imparts grace on a world that is His creation and that is completely under His positive guidance, see Vatican II's Pastoral Constitution on the Church in the Modern World – *Gaudium et Spes* § 1.
52 *Ecclessiam Suam* § 59.
53 *Ecclessiam Suam* § 60.
54 *Ecclessiam Suam* § 63.
55 *Ecclessiam Suam* § 65.
56 *Ecclessiam Suam* § 68.
57 *Ecclessiam Suam* § 69.
58 *Ecclessiam Suam* § 70.
59 Ibid.
60 *Ecclessiam Suam* § 71.
61 *Ecclessiam Suam* § 72–3.
62 *Ecclessiam Suam* § 74–5.

63 *Ecclessiam Suam* § 76–8.
64 *Ecclessiam Suam* § 81 cf. § 79.
65 *Ecclessiam Suam* § 97.
66 *Ecclessiam Suam* § 99–104.
67 *Ecclessiam Suam* § 106–7.
68 *Ecclessiam Suam* § 108.
69 *Ecclessiam Suam* § 109.
70 Donald Nicholl, 'Other Religions (Nostra Aetate)', pp. 126–34 at p. 131.
71 Abraham J. Heschel, *The Prophets*, New York: Harper Collins, 1962.
72 Youakim Moubarac, *Bibliographie de Louis Massignon: Réunieel classéepar Y. Moubarac*, Damascus: Institut Français de Damas, 1956.
73 See Mary L. Gude, *Louis Massignon: The Crucible of Compassion*, Notre Dame, IN: University of Notre Dame Press, 1997.
74 A full English edition was edited by Herbert Mason, ed. *The Passion of al-Hallaj*. 4 volumes with a biographical introduction, Bollingen Series XCVIII. Princeton: Princeton University Press, 1983. An abridged edition was edited by Herbert Mason, ed. *Hallaj, Mystic and Martyr*, Mythos Series. Princeton: Princeton University Press, 1994.
75 Charles de Moiser – Jeremy Little Brother of Jesus, *Silent Pilgrimage to God: The Spirituality of Charles de Foucault*, London: Darton, Longman and Todd, 1974.
76 Donald Nicholl, 'Other Religions (Nostra Aetate)', pp. 126–34 at p. 126.
77 Shirley Du Boulay, *The Cave of the Heart: The Life of Swami Abhishiktananda*, Maryknoll, NY: Orbis, 2005, pp. 110, 189.
78 For the relationship of Le Saux and Mahieu see Shirley Du Boulay, *The Cave of the Heart*, pp. 154–5.
79 Harry Oldmeadow, *A Christian Pilgrim in India: The Spiritual Journey of Swami Abhishiktananda (Henri Le Saux)*, Bloomington, Indiana; World Wisdom, 2008, p. 9.
80 Shirley Du Boulay, *The Cave of the Heart*, p. 206.
81 It has been the Jesuit Michael Barnes that has named Mahieu as one of 'the three founders of Shantivanam', see Michael Barnes SJ, 'From Ashrams to Dalits: The Four Seasons of Inculturation', *The Tablet*, January 2001.
82 Abbé Jules Monchanin and Dom Henri Le Saux, *A Benedictine Ashram*, Isle of Man: Times Press, 1964; and Jules Monchanin (1895–1957), *As Seen from East and West*, 2 vols, Dehli: ISPCK and Saccidananda Ashram, 2001.
83 For a short biography see Harry Olmeadow, *A Christian Pilgrim in India*, pp. 6–17.
84 *The Bhagavad Gita*, Oxford: Oxford University Press, 2008.
85 For a biographical profile of his contemplative life see J. C. Weber, *In Quest of the Absolute: The Life and Work of Jules Monchanin*, Kalamazoo: Cistercian Publications, 1977.
86 Harry Oldmeadow, *A Christian Pilgrim in India*, pp. 7–8.
87 J. C. Weber, *In Quest of the Absolute*, p. 73.
88 For his biography and influence on Christianity in India see Harry Oldmeadow, *A Christian Pilgrim in India*; William Skudlarek OSB, *God's Harp String: The Life and Legacy of the Benedictine Monk Swami Abhishiktananda*, Brooklyn, NY: Lantern Books, 2010; William Skudlarek OSB and Bettina Baümer, eds. *Witness to the Fullness of Light: The Vision and Relevance of the Benedictine Monk Swami Abhishiktananda*, Brooklyn, NY: Lantern Books, 2011.

89 See Abhishiktanada, *The Church in India: An Essay in Christian Self-Criticism*, Madras, India: Christian Literature Society, 1969 and Abhishiktanada with Father Monchanin, *Ermites du Saccidânanda: Un Essai d'intégration Chrétienne de la Tradition de l'Inde*, Tournai/Paris: Casterman, 1956.
90 Abhishiktanada, *Saccidananda: A Christian Approach to Advaitic Experience*, Delhi: ISPCK, 1997, *Hindu-Christian Meeting Point: Within the Cave of the Heart*, Delhi: ISPCK, 1983 and *Initiation à la Spiritualité des Upanishads: 'Vers l'autre rive'*, Sisteron: Editions Présence, 1979.
91 Abhishiktanada, *The Secret of Arunachala: A Christian Hermit on Shiva's Holy Mountain*, Delhi: ISPCK, 1979.
92 Harry Oldmeadow, *A Christian Pilgrim in India*, p. 137.
93 Shirley Du Boulay, *The Cave of the Heart*, p. 142.
94 Abhishiktanada, Letter to Marc Chaduc 29 September 1969 in *Swami Abhishiktanada: His Life Told through His Letters*, ed. James Stuart, Delhi: ISPCK, 1989.
95 For a biography see Shirley du Boulay, *Beyond the Darkness: A Biography of Bede Griffiths*, London: Rider, 1998.
96 Bede Griffiths, *The Golden String: An Autobiography*, Tucson, AZ: Medio Media, 2003.
97 Bede Griffiths, *Christ in India: Essays towards a Hindu-Christian Dialogue*, Springfield, IL: Templegate Publishers, 1984. A selection can be found in *Bede Griffiths: Essential Writings*, with an introduction by Thomas Matus, Maryknoll, NY: Orbis, 2004.
98 An account of life at Shantivanam in the 1980s and 1990s can be found in Thomas Matus, *Ashram Diary: In India with Bede Griffiths*, Winchester, UK and Washington: O Books, 2009.
99 Michael Barnes SJ, 'From Ashrams to Dalits', cited in Shirley Du Boulay, *The Cave of the Heart*, p. 154; see also Michael Barnes SJ, *Theology and the Dialogue of Religions*, Cambridge: Cambridge University Press, 2002.
100 For an overview see K. L. Seshagiri Rao, 'Mahatma Gandhi: A Prophet of Pluralism', in Paul F. Knitter, ed. *The Myth of Religious Superiority: A Multifaith Exploration*, Maryknoll, NY: Orbis, 2005, pp. 45–55.

Chapter 2

LATIN AMERICAN PRAXIS

The effects of an initial dialogue with the world that had been emphasized and systematized by Vatican II had a deep impact in Latin America, a continent where the majority of Christians of the world live.[1] The impact of the aggiornamento that took place in Latin America did not impact conferences or world meetings on dialogue but very quickly shaped a refreshed mode of being Church, a model from below in which everybody was able to feel at home in the church and the world, particularly through the so-called Based Ecclesial Communities (CEB).[2] The first characteristics of dialogue with the world that *Gaudium et Spes* had emphasized were realized in the 1968 meeting of Latin American bishops in Medellín (Colombia) and the subsequent 'preferential option for the poor' declared by the Latin American bishops against all pressures by the Vatican in Puebla de los Angeles (Mexico) in 1979.[3]

The main thrust of this renewal, of what I have somewhere else called 'a new reformation' in Latin America came through a rethinking of theological paradigms associated with dogmatic statements and a new reading of history.[4] Within this new theological reading effected by a materialistic reading of history the 'people of God', in their majority poor, and their history became closer to the people of Israel and the Israelites at the time of Jesus, living in societies full of conflicts, violence, poverty and suffering.[5] I have argued for the acknowledgement of this theological leap for the poor and within history in other contexts, and particularly within a situation of extreme violence such as the Rwanda genocide of 1994.[6] In that work I emphasize the place of justice in dialogue, rather than reconciliation and forgetting, arguing that the dialogue with the world religions starts from the realization that human beings living in poverty and uncertainty, that is 'the victims of globalization are part of larger symbolic globalized communities; namely, the world religions'.[7] Thus, this chapter deals with the change in the process of the theologizing while Chapter 6 returns to the human subject, the common humanity and the poor of the world, a world of Christians and Buddhists alike.

Theology as a Second Act

For Gutiérrez, theology is a second act and a narrative that uses language in order to understand God's presence in the world. Thus, for Gutiérrez: 'Theology is a language. It attempts to speak a word about the mysterious reality that believers call God. It is a *logos* about *theos*'.[8]

Theology is not a first act for a theologian; the first act is clearly faith, expressed in prayer and commitment within the Christian community.[9] However, that clear statement had been the product of many years of theological disputes, doctrinal misunderstandings, interpretative projects and engagement with Marxists and neo-liberals, and all within a changing Latin American Church that became fully engaged with the world of politics, economics and development.[10] In other words, for Gutiérrez theology is a textual narrative that arises out of a practice within a particular context of a Christian community engaged with the world, and particularly within the world of the poor and the disadvantaged of society.

This chapter explores ideas of religion and politics within the writings of Gustavo Gutiérrez and his own contribution to a dialogue between the Church and others. In its first part it outlines greater ecclesial and social influences within his early theological period, in its second part it focuses on the centrality of human history in the theological framework of his second theological period and in its third part it examines some of Gutiérrez' post 1992 writings in relation to religion and politics in a wider social context.[11] It is clear that Gutiérrez' treatment of religion and politics presupposes God's presence in human history through a Church engaged with the world, in which it is necessary to participate actively in the political in order to act religiously. Religion as the ritual and social practices of a rule of life (*religio*) produces theology as a narrative. That narrative as a text allows practitioners (and others) to follow historical interpretations of the rule of life and those interpretations also affect the way in which practitioners understand practices within that way of life. Therefore, and according to Gutiérrez, religion and politics are embodied in religious ritual and secular governance respectively through a constant dialectic of interaction, contradiction and solidarity.

It is in that response to religious practice in the contemporary world of the 1960s and within that framework of a *post idealist theology* that Metz and Gutiérrez articulated a theological narrative that described and challenged the possibility of theologizing outside the social structures of political governance and indeed of people's lives.[12] Metz' context is European and he develops a strong political theology while Gutiérrez' context is Latin American (and the third world) and he develops a theological framework known as liberation theology.[13] For both theologians religion and politics are not separate entities; instead they come out of actions carried out by Christians who involve themselves with those in need within society, involvement that arises from their religious selfhood and their Christian life in community. The place of the Church in history is not as an establishment but as people, and the place of theology is that of a narrative rather than as a doctrine.

The influence of those ideas were enormous in Catholic theological circles not because those were new ideas – it must be remembered that the social doctrine of the Church was already articulated since 1891 – but because they were the first theological fruits of the Second Vatican Council. The 'post-idealist' narrative of God's work in the world had returned to the biblical and doctrinal sources that had been confused by European philosophical epistemologies within European theology. The works of Metz in Europe and of Gutiérrez in Latin America became catalysts for pastoral models centred on the concept of the 'people of God' rather than on the Church as the only place where God could or should intervene within the contemporary world.

Gutiérrez' talk to a group of priests in Chimbote, Peru, in 1968 and the subsequent publication of his seminal work did not end theological discussions on pastoral matters related to the implementation of Vatican II but activated a clear theological exploration of the place of religious practitioners within society.[14] The European context of secularism and atheism was changed into a theological narrative that explored the religious practices and beliefs of Christians within a heavily religious environment that questioned the political governance offered within their own societies. Theological works spoke of the 'irruption of the poor', of oppressors and oppressed and of liberation from personal sin as well as from sinful structures of governance.

The impact of Gutiérrez' work was enormous because he relocated a majestic God with a triumphant Church into an anthropomorphic and incarnate deity closer to the Hebrew Scriptures than to Greek thought and platonic ideals. The rediscovery of the Scriptures as authority within the Catholic Church at Vatican II helped to question the possible dichotomies of the neo-scholastics by returning to the Old Testament where relations within society were part of a social practice in which there was no clear separation between religion and politics. North American and European theologians took the challenge of Gutiérrez and organized conferences and seminars in order to examine their own theological presuppositions and the diversified contexts in which those theological statements were being made. The students of the University of Chicago, for example organized a conference in 1979 where the new Shailer Matthews Professor of Divinity, Langdon Gilkey, addressed their concerns with the following statement:

> Surely there can be no doubt that the important later symbols of the New Covenant people, the messianic reign, and even the Kingdom itself repeat and develop, rather than abrogate this union of the social and the religious,

the historical and the ideal, which begins here in the original calling and establishment of the people of God. This interrelation and interdependence of the religious and the social, the individual and the communal – and the providential constitution of both – was re-expressed in classical, Hellenistic form in Augustine's *De Civitate Dei*, and variously – and often unfortunately – in the subsequent concepts of Holy Christendom and in the Calvinistic views of the Holy Community.[15]

Within Latin America, Africa and Asia theologians explored their commitment, their religious practices and the political world in which they lived in. Within North America the oppressed of the past and of the present asked questions about their role in society (their religion), God's involvement in the world (their theology) and their politicians governance of society (their politics).

However, while most theologians, academics and politicians have explored some of Gutiérrez' ideas related to his first period of work, he continued his practice of religion and his ministry as a priest in a slum of Lima, where the politics of Peruvian society required him to reflect on his practice through two other research periods: one on the place of history in God's plan of salvation, and another one on the place of political events and the teaching of the Church as its response. Gutiérrez found a companion in the anthropologist, novelist and poet José María Arguedas (1911–69), who wrote about the poor and challenged the oppression towards the poor within Peruvian society. They met at Chimbote, a coastal fishing port to the north of Lima, while Gutiérrez was giving conferences and Arguedas was finishing his novel *El zorro de arriba y el zorro de abajo*.[16] Arguedas was influential to Gutiérrez and vice versa because both found that God was present in the poor of Peru, either in Chimbote or in Rimac, a Lima slum where Gutiérrez ministered through a parish and through his Las Casas Institute.[17] It is difficult to imagine but it was at the Rimac slum that Gutiérrez wrote most of his theology, teaching only part-time at the university.[18]

Theology as History

If during his first theological period Gutiérrez asked questions about social and divine processes of underdevelopment and poverty during his second period of research Gutiérrez asked questions about God's involvement in human history.[19] Gutiérrez' understanding of human history followed the Second Vatican Council in its document on the Church in the Modern World, where the Council Fathers assert that 'The Lord is the goal of human history, the focal point of the desires of history and civilization, the centre of mankind, the joy of all hearts, and the fulfilment of all aspirations'.[20] Those thoughts had been applied to the Latin American pastoral reality in his seminal talk to the meeting of the National Office for Social Research in Chimbote (July 1968) when he stated that,

> If there is a finality inscribed in history, then the essence of Christian faith is to believe in Christ, that is to believe that God is irreversibly committed to human history. To believe in Christ, then, is to believe that God has made a commitment to the historical development of the human race. To have faith in Christ is to see the history in which we are living as the progressive revelation of the human face of God.[21]

His main source for this second period was the Bible and he argued for one major theological presupposition: God became human through the Incarnation and is therefore one of us. The outcome of such theological presupposition is that God acts through human history in order to save and He administers graces for human beings in order to interact in the world and be part of it. As a result religious practice (religion) takes place within a particular society that is governed not by others but by the same 'people of God' with the Church as a community immersed in a particular society. However, that Incarnation as theological principle was relevant to the people of Israel in the Old Testament. Yahweh led his people out of oppression at an early stage of their history, he gave them the land and he asked them to keep a covenant that included just and equal relations between all. Within those just relations the prophets reminded Israel of her obligations towards the poor, the needy, the widows, the orphans and the stranger.[22] The demands by God in the history of Israel point to the fact that 'the history from which biblical faith springs is an open-ended history, a history open to the future'.[23]

Gutiérrez moved to a re-reading of Latin American history by assuming God's involvement in human history throughout the Hebrew Scriptures. The history of Latin America was no different than that of Israel because within that human history there were God-fearing people who asked questions about history in order to understand questions about God. If the liberation of Israel through the Exodus made a people, Gutiérrez explored the 'encounter' between Europeans and indigenous peoples in 1492. Christians led a colonial conquest based initially on ideals of civilization and evangelization but that subsequently was driven by human greed and an ongoing strife for riches and power.[24] Those who suffered poverty and social annihilation under the conquistadors became part of a society that proclaimed itself Christian and in the name of an unjust Christian relation between colonizers and colonized subjected indigenous peoples to slavery, genocide, forced conversion and inhuman conditions of life.[25] Nevertheless, for Gutiérrez, God was in Latin America in pre-Columbian times and he remained with the suffering indigenous peoples while many atrocities were taking place.

In reading Latin American history Gutiérrez isolated the example of some Christians who did not comply with the *status quo* of colonialism and degradation and became themselves defenders of the poor for the sake of the Gospel. One of them, Bartolomé de Las Casas, was an example of a full conversion to the poor in colonial Latin America that allowed their voice to be heard within the Spanish courts and the learned universities of Europe.[26] Las Casas's own attitude and his Christian attitude made a difference in God's action in history because he defended the poor and the needy, and in return he became a sign of contradiction that had to suffer attacks from philosophers, theologians and conquistadors alike.[27] Those attacks came upon him because Las Casas not only exercised Christian charity towards the indigenous population but constructed a theologically informed defence of their human rights because of their condition as children of God made in His own image.[28]

In his defence of the indigenous populations Las Casas resembled Job, another biblical figure important for Gutiérrez. If Gutiérrez dwells on the suffering of the innocent by examining the book of Job he does so by associating the person of Job not with a passive sufferer but with an example of suffering-trust in God and his love for all.[29] Job in the Bible and Bartolomé de las Casas in the Latin American context become prototypes of Christian history because they are able not only to empathize with those suffering but because in enduring physical and emotional suffering themselves they see God not through a general depersonalized historical narrative but they see the poor as protagonists of that history. Thus, they develop a theology that speaks once and again of the love of God in a human history in need of liberation and not in a theology ridden with clauses, argumentations and intellectual discourses attached to the learned and to the philosophers. In the case of Las Casas,

> Bartolomé welds faith to what we today would call social analysis. This enables him to unmask the 'social sin' of his time. That, doubtless, was his forte – and also the difference between him and the great majority of those in Spain who were concerned with the affairs of the Indies. . . . Those who had not seen the abuse and contempt to which the Indians were subjected, those who had not suffered in their own flesh the aggression of the mighty ones of the Indies, those who had not counted dead bodies, had other priorities in theology.[30]

During this period of biblical and theological reflection Gutiérrez brings together the concept of the God of history, already present in his *A Theology of Liberation*, with a shift in Latin American ecclesial history towards the place where the God of history makes his presence felt: the world of the poor. The 'irruption of the poor' within Latin America suggests that the centrality of the poor within the practice of religion should bring a change in the political understanding of social, economic and power relations. If the Christian communities of Latin America, and therefore the Latin American Church, decided to strive for the world of the poor because it was among the poor that the incarnate Son of God decided to dwell then the political world should do the same, particularly in a continent where most politicians declared themselves Christians and are part of that servant Church of the poor. The 'preferential option for the poor' forwarded by Gutiérrez and others and sanctioned within the pastoral options of the Latin American Church constitutes not a change in pastoral orientation but 'is nothing short of a Copernican revolution for the Church'.[31]

Gutiérrez explores God's involvement in human history through the religious practice of His Church in the past but in doing so he moves with theological, religious and political questions that take place in the present scenario in Latin America. The publication of *A Theology of Liberation* takes place after the implementation of the Second Vatican Council in Latin America through the second meeting of all Latin American Bishops in Medellín (Colombia), while Gutiérrez' second period of theological reflection coincides with the third meeting of Latin American Bishops in Puebla de Los Angeles (Mexico) in 1979. It is at Puebla that the 'preferential option for the poor' is publicly declared by the meeting of bishops within the political climate of a number of military coups, including those in Chile (1973) and Argentina (1976), while the force of Medellín remains the crucial impact for Gutiérrez' theology. It is at Medellín in 1968 that the theological movement of a Latin America driven by lay unpublished theologians began.[32] The Church in Latin America had to ask questions about their religious practice within difficult political circumstances and aided by the theological reflection of Gutiérrez the bishops did not separate religion and politics, but provided a political response of commitment to political change and the defence of human rights. However, the subsequent pastoral implementation of Medellín was very different so that in the case of Chile the bishops challenged the military regime while there was an avoidance of any prophetic denunciation in the case of Argentina.[33]

Gutiérrez provides a clear biblical and theological reflection that does not differentiate between religion and politics because those processes are neither separated in the Hebrew Scriptures nor in the history of the Church in Latin America. The politics of religion that a local church decides to implement cannot be influenced by theology as a second step but it reflects the first step of commitment and practice with the poor in the case of Gutiérrez, and to the wealthy and powerful in the case of many clergymen and bishops of Argentina. For Gutiérrez' return to the biblical sources follows from his own commitment to the poor, his own involvement with the reading of contemporary history in Latin America, and his own involvement with important ecclesiastical figures such as Helder Camara, Pedro Casaldáliga, Oscar Romero, Evaristo Arns and Manuel Larraín.

Religio *and the* Polis *in Postmodernity*

During a third period of action, reflection, and writing Gutiérrez asked questions about the response to God's actions in history by the Latin American poor and marginalized. They, after all, are the majority of theologians because they reflect on the Scriptures together allowing for narratives on the action of God in the world to be articulated. Their religious response through their Christian life produces different localized ways of responding to the work of the Holy Spirit, thus producing new spiritualities.

Spirituality for Gutiérrez does not relate to a pious individual response to God in order to acquire security; on the contrary, an honest response to God creates insecurity, persecution, misunderstanding and suffering. The actions of those who respond to the Holy Spirit do not always please the powerful and the rich; thus the poor become ever more dependent on God, not on their own means. Religion as a way of life based on the Spirit produces men and women who trust and wait for God's promises while sharing solidarity with the poor and the marginalized within communities. Thus, Gutiérrez challenges the idea of a self-sufficient individualistic spirituality that creates prosperity and security. On the contrary, he systematizes the possibility of a distinct Latin American spirituality closer to the values of the Kingdom and distant from the security of riches, power and social acceptance.[34]

Spirituality, for Gutiérrez, is a way of life that moves towards the poor because the poor are the ones who show more trust and need of God, not because they are better than other human beings. Spirituality becomes a method for theology because a way of life close to the poor comes before any theological thinking or theological writing. Thus, religion as a practice informs the involvement of Christians within politics because all actions that precede theology are enacted within society, within the *polis* and therefore they are all political. Even those who practice a spirituality that agrees with the *status quo* express opinions within society, and therefore within the realm of political governance; they elect politicians and professional governors according to their beliefs, their spirituality, their theology and their preferences that cannot be rationally contrary to their way of life.

For Gutiérrez, God is at the centre of that social and religious change that allows human beings to be liberated from their own personal sin, but most importantly from sinful structures that do not allow them to be fully human and in God's image. Thus, in his later work Gutiérrez who so far has not allowed for a separation between religion and politics returns to the theme of liberation by returning to reflections on the action of God in the Bible as liberator within a particular history. God is the God of life because he liberates. However, Gutiérrez makes very clear distinctions about the fact that God is a liberator when he writes:

> God is not a liberator because God liberates; rather God liberates because God is a liberator. God is not just because he establishes justice, or faithful because God enters into a covenant, but the other way around. I am not playing with words here, but trying to bring out the primacy and transcendence of God and to remind ourselves that God's being gives meaning to God's action. According to the Bible, God's interventions in the life of God's people do not imply any kind of immanentism or any dissolution of God into history; rather they emphasize that God is the absolute and transcendent sort of being.[35]

In this late reflection on God and his work Gutiérrez synthesizes his theology by integrating the Latin American context and the action of the absolute being much preferred within European discourses on transcendence and immanence. The difference in his discourse in relation to other theologians is that any discourse about God arises out of a communal practice of social justice within the *polis* and not in isolation from those social realities. For Gutiérrez is not making an attempt to integrate two separate realities, that is religion and politics; the separation is in the mind while the practice indicates that theological discourses and the act of contemplation constitute a political act of prophetic solidarity, defiance and a social pronouncement. It is at the end of his theological book on God that Gutiérrez discloses the possibility of a relation between aesthetics, poetics and God's option for the poor by outlining the hope that comes out of suffering in the poetic works of César Vallejo.[36] He does not return to theological aesthetics and instead continues an exploration of history within a Latin American postmodernity.

Gutiérrez' later theological work, always a reflection on his pastoral work, is influenced by the preparations for the five hundredth anniversary of the encounter between indigenous peoples and Europeans. As the Latin American Church prepared for the fourth General Meeting of Latin American Bishops in Santo Domingo, Gutiérrez, as a theological expert, realized that for some 1492 meant a great moment of discovery, for others a great moment of evangelization but for the indigenous peoples of Latin America it meant an encounter with a colonial machine that destroyed, enslaved and did not differentiate between religion and the politics of the empire. While historians such as Enrique Dussel explored the chronological periods and changes of the Church in Latin America Gutiérrez delivered an uncompromising Christian manifesto for solidarity with the indigenous peoples of Latin America, but within the context of the Church.

The context of the Latin American Church at Santo Domingo was already postmodern and post-romantic. The military regimes in Latin America had ceased to exist, civil wars in Guatemala and El Salvador were coming to an end and the influence of a neo-liberal economic system that fostered individualism, economic prosperity and personal salvation was felt throughout the continent. The rise of Protestantism pointed to a refreshed Christianity for Latin America but in many cases the individual salvation supported by those Christian groups coming from North America undermined the pastoral aims and objectives of the Christian Communities. The violence of the military regimes had ended but the violent protests by indigenous peoples against the state had brought new challenges associated with indigenous rights, international laws of cultural protection and the recovery of indigenous sacred landscapes and political spaces.

Gutiérrez took active part in the 1992 meeting of bishops in Santo Domingo and together with others he challenged the neo-conservatism coming out of the Vatican and of the newly appointed bishops, most of them of a more neo-scholastic way of thinking. If for some of them religion and politics could be separated Gutiérrez returned in his theological writings to the social doctrine of the Church and to the pastoral achievements of Medellín and Puebla. If Vatican II had prepared the way for a clear engagement of the Church with the contemporary world, it was the reflection on ecclesial praxis at Medellín and Puebla that had provided the theory and method for being religious in Latin America. The epistemology of Medellín, particularly, had indicated that it was not possible to do theology without a commitment to the poor and that to be committed to the poor a religious practitioner had to engage with the political in order to influence it for the sake of the poor. Thus, democratic or non-democratic institutions did not perceive the poor as the recipients of Good News but as a social and political problem. Economic growth and successful economic policies did not take into account the human value of the poor but were geared to maximize profit in order to implement successful economic models of development that benefited few and punished the majority that did not have resources for economic growth or investment.

For Gutiérrez, the newly centred reflections on the religious, the social and the political stem from the centrality of the human person. Political systems that are not person centred fail to understand the beauty of God's creation of man and woman in His own image. For example, on the subject of work and coinciding with John Paul II's encyclical letter *Laborem Exercens* Gutiérrez argues that the dignity of the person who works comes from the fact that a human being is recreating the earth and not from the type of work undertaken, a clear break from the Spanish colonial understanding that there was a higher type of work, a more intellectual one, that left a lower type of manual work to slaves and servants.[37] However, Gutiérrez recognizes that for some commentators the Pope seems to be speaking about the third world only and that is not the case. The encyclical recalls the dignity of every human being everywhere and the absolute primacy of the human over technological discoveries, economic and political systems that place profit over workers and economic growth over human dignity. As already argued at Medellín the call of the Church is to denounce poverty but also to show through material poverty that human beings remain at the centre of passing systems, policies and social structures, be they just or unjust. Thus, Gutiérrez argues forcefully that,

> The encyclical clearly describes the universality of the social problem, the depth of the injustice and the abandonment suffered by the poor today, the responsibility of leaders of socio-economic systems which violate the rights of workers, and the urgent need for the whole Church to make the cause of the dispossessed her own.[38]

To be religious within a society that violates human dignity and favours markets over people requires a return to the body of social teaching of the Church in order not to foster solely academic study, but in order to give further authority to the already plentiful commitment by Christian communities towards the poor. It requires a return to the idea articulated by the Church Fathers that a Christian life needed a style of life that visibly spoke of the religious. Therefore words and confessions do not match a style of life in solidarity with the poor, in which what is given is not only the excess gained but the goods acquired by human and divine right. A style of life and a spirituality of poverty do not become an exception to ordinary life but the norm of the life of all Christians and of the Church. Thus, Gregory the Great wrote that,

> The earth is common to all men, and therefore the food it provides is produced by all in common. Thus they are wrong to believe themselves innocent who demand for their private use the gift that God gave to all ... when we give what is indispensable to the needy, we do not do them a favour from our personal generosity, but we return to them what is theirs. More than an act of charity, what we are doing is fulfilling an obligation of justice.[39]

It is that theology of the daily life, of a style of life, of a social morality of connection with other human beings that makes Gutiérrez' theological agenda meaningful as well as central within a post-socialist world. Those who understood his agenda as a religious commitment to socialist ideas rather than to Christian's ideas saw an end to liberation theology after the collapse of socialist states in Eastern Europe during the 1990s. However, the religious preoccupation for the poor and the oppressed can only end when there is no more poverty. Until then the voice of the poor in theology, in the practice of religion and in politics is to be heard as a central commitment to the building of the Kingdom of God now and for the future. The Church as the body of believers and as a signifier of God's presence altered the role of the poor at Medellín, where they became theological and political actors in society. The task remains, according to Jon Sobrino, to make the Church of the poor a reality in order to continue challenging the centrality of wealth and profit in the running of society.[40] Sobrino, as well as Gutiérrez, points to the fact that the Christian utopia of religion and politics has not been realized; however, both of them remain committed to bridge any separation between religious practice and governance between the world of the poor and the neo-liberal world that dominates Latin America at the beginning of the twenty-first century.[41]

Theological Solidarity

As already argued, within Gutiérrez' writings there is no clear separation between the religious and the political. Theological narratives about God textually recreate understandings of a divine history that it is expressed through human history, following Nicholas Lash' theological dictum: 'All human utterances occur in a context. And the contexts in which they occur modify their meaning'.[42] Thus, Gutiérrez provides a challenge to any privatization of theological reflection concentrated in academia but he also assumes that a few within the theological community and the Christian community exercise their Christian mission within universities and theological colleges through an ongoing ministry of teaching and research.

For Gutiérrez, the relation between the practice of religion and the practice of politics needs to be articulated through the Christian faith. Within that relation commitment to the poor and the marginalized in the name of God provides the first step of involvement by Christians in the world, and particularly within the social context of Latin America. The commitment to justice and to the poor is the first step in any theological reflection about the world and its relation with God. Faith comes first, and reason follows because 'theology is an understanding of the faith. It is a rereading of the word of God as that word is lived in the Christian community' so that 'we can separate theological reflection neither from the Christian community nor from the world in which that community lives'.[43]

Gutiérrez' reflection on the relation between religion and politics presupposes an ongoing commitment to God through the poor of society that is inscribed much later in theological narratives about the love of God for human beings and the need for the theologian to immerse himself in that extension of the incarnation in contemporary human history. Thus, his theologizing differs from political theology, theologies of development and theologies of revolution because in all those theological movements the articulation of ideas and writings comes first, the practice of religion and politics comes second. What unites all those theological models is a Christian response to individualistic models related to romantic movements, post-enlightenment ideas and the postmodern condition.

Religion as the practice of faith becomes politics because Christians involve themselves in their own contexts in solidarity with the poor and the marginalized. If the response to modernity had been to reject the world and to establish immanent truths with the help of reason and philosophy, Gutiérrez provides continuity to Bonhoeffer's theological commitment by assuming that at the root of a Christian response to modernity is the search for a life in Christ that is lived 'irreligiously' by expressing solidarity with others.[44] For Bonhoeffer to practice religion was to assume the life of the weak and suffering God of the Cross; for Gutiérrez to practice religion is to assume the politics of the weak and the suffering human beings who represent the face of God.[45] Thus, solidarity with the oppressed presumes a critique to the political establishment that in most cases has failed to protect the poor and where Christians had failed to practice the ethical values of religion within the social spheres of political influence. If initially Gutiérrez could have followed some of the Latin American theologians calling for a socialist-oriented society his methodological critique of the possibility of a single political model and a continuous solidarity with the poor have made Gutiérrez' forceful assessment of the religious and the political even more important in understanding the involvement of Christians within the contemporary world in a post-Soviet Union and post-9/11 world.[46] In the words of Gutiérrez,

> We shall not have our great leap forward, into a whole new theological perspective, until the marginalized and exploited have begun to become the artisans of their own liberation – until their voice makes itself heard directly, without mediation, without interpreters – until they themselves take account, in the light of their own values, of their own experience of the Lord in their efforts to liberate themselves. We shall not have our quantum theological leap until the oppressed themselves theologise, until 'the others' themselves personally reflect on their hope of a total liberation in Christ. For they are the bearers of this hope for all humanity.[47]

The conclusion is simple: the sole practice and advancement of theology depends on the right relation between religion and politics; thus, the theological project is to be realized as a second act of solidarity rather than as the only possible intellectual response to human solidarity – and therefore becoming a selfish individual act. Thus, 'in searching for this meaning, the theologian knows that, as Clodovis Boff says, everything is politics but politics is not everything'.[48]

It is with the world of the poor and the marginalized and within the world of sociopolitics that acts of dialogue take place. Theology as a theology of dialogue follows. In the next chapter the story of the dialogue between a Trappist community in Algeria and local Muslims is told. The Trappists make a first choice of dialogue and a dialogue of Christian presence among Muslims and finally they are assassinated by their kidnappers in the midst of the Algerian civil war. Their theological thinking on dialogue only follows their actions of dialogue, actions that led them to remain in Algeria and face death and martyrdom for dialogue.

Notes

1 For an overview of Vatican II's impact on Latin America see Enrique Dussel, 'Latin America', in Adrian Hastings, ed. *Modern Catholicism: Vatican II and After*, London: SPCK and New York: Oxford University Press, 1991, pp. 319–25; see also Enrique Dussel, *Historia de la Iglesia en América Latina: Coloniaje y Liberación (1492–1983)*, Madrid: Esquela Misional, 1983 and *Los últimos 50 años (1930–1985) en la historia de la Iglesia en América Latina*, Bogota: Indo American Press, 1986.

2 Among the many works that cover the genesis and development of the CEBs see Leonardo Boff, *Eclesiogênese: As comunidades eclesiais de base reinventam a Igreja*, Petrópolis: Editora Vozes, 1977 and 'Comunidades eclesiais de base: povo oprimido que se organiza para a libertaçao', *Revista Eclesiástica Brasileira*, 41 (June 1981), 312–30. English translation of both Portuguese works published as Leonardo Boff, *Ecclesiogenesis: The Base Communities Reinvent the Church*, Maryknoll, NY: Orbis, 1986; Thomas C. Bruneau, *The Political Transformation of the Brazilian Catholic Church*, New York: Cambridge University Press, 1974 and *The Church in Brazil*, Austin: University of Texas Press, 1982; W. E. Hewitt, *Base Christian Communities and Social Change in Brazil*, Lincoln and London: University of Nebraska Press, 1991; Cardinal Aloísio Lorscheider, 'Fifty Years of the CNBB: A Bishop's Conference Based on the Council – Evangelization Projects, Political and Ecclesiastical Tensions and Challenges', in José Oscar Beozzo and Luiz Carlos Susin, eds. *Brazil: People and Church(es)* (*Concilium* 2002), pp. 25–30; Scott Mainwaring *The Catholic Church and Politics in Brazil 1916–1985*, Stanford: Stanford University Press, 1986; Maria Helena Moreira Alves, *Estado e oposição no Brasil 1964–1984*, Petrópolis: Editora Vozes, 1984.

3 For an overview of these 10 years see Enrique Dussel, *De Medellín a Puebla: una década de sangre y esperanza (1968–1979)*. Mexico City: CEE-Edicol, 1979.

4 This ecclesial renewal of Latin America also affected the reformed churches in Latin America, see Guillermo Cook, *The Expectation of the Poor: Latin American Basic*

Ecclesial Communities in Protestant Perspectives. Maryknoll, NY: Orbis, 1985; see also Mario I. Aguilar, 'The Kairos of Medellin: Towards a Movement for Liberation and New Mission After Vatican II', in Patrick Claffey and Joe Egan, eds. *Movement or Moment: Assessing Liberation Theology Forty Years after Medellín*, Bern: Peter Lang, 2009, pp. 9–28 and '1968: A historiography of a New Reformation in Latin America', *Schweizerische Zeitschrift für Religions – und Kulturgeschichte*, 2010, 104, pp. 201–11.

5 Leonardo Boff, 'A Theological Examination of the Terms "People of God" and "Popular Church"', in Leonardo Boff and Virgil Elizondo, eds. *La Iglesia Popular: Between Fear and Hope* (Concilium, 1984/6, 176), pp. 89–97.

6 Mario I. Aguilar, *Theology, Liberation and Genocide: A Theology of the Periphery*, London: SCM Press, 2009.

7 Ibid., p. 69.

8 Gustavo Gutiérrez, 'Theological Language: Fullness of Silence', in Gustavo Gutiérrez, *The Density of the Present: Selected Writings*, Maryknoll, NY: Orbis, 1999, p. 186; from 'Address on the occasion of his induction to the Peruvian Academy of Spanish Language 1995', full original in *Páginas*, 1996, 137, pp. 66–87.

9 Gustavo Gutiérrez, 'Mirar lejos: Introducción a la decimocuarta edición', in *Teología de la liberación: Perspectivas*, Salamanca: Ediciones Sígueme, 16th edn. Lima: Centro de Estudios y Publicaciones 1999[1971], p. 38.

10 Theology as a poetic narrative on God's presence and action in the world presupposes a changing paradigm, thus it is no longer possible to write about Gutiérrez' theological work by just focusing on his major initial work *Teología de la liberación*.

11 The theological periods within the original Spanish texts are clearly chronological and they follow theological reflections that arise out of preparations for the meeting of Latin American Bishops at Medellín, Puebla and Santo Domingo. These periods are more difficult to isolate within the published works in English due to the fact that Gutiérrez has not published everything he has ever written and that not everything published in other languages has been translated into the English language. Frei Betto has suggested that, 'It is quite likely that he is the author of more unpublished texts, known only to a small circle of readers, than of published works. Usually he does not even sign the mimeographed texts, which include an excellent introduction to the ideas of Marx and Engels and their relationship to Christianity', Frei Betto, 'Gustavo Gutiérrez – A Friendly Profile', in Marc H. Ellis and Otto Maduro, eds. *The Future of Liberation Theology: Essays in Honor of Gustavo Gutiérrez*, Maryknoll, NY: Orbis, 1989, pp. 31–7, at p. 35.

12 Gutiérrez has been criticized for having been influenced by modernity and its romantic idealism; however, it is clear that the thought of Gutiérrez was in the 1960s and 1970s influenced by the Latin American context in which the Pauline vision of the 'new man' was also used by socialist discourses associated with the Cuban revolution and with a socialist conception of revolution led by the icon of Ché Guevara, see Mariano Delgado, '"Esperanza plañe entre algodones": Cuando Gustavo Gutiérrez habla de dios', in *Teología de la liberación: Cruce de miradas*, Coloquio de Friburgo, April 1999, Lima: Instituto Bartolomé de Las Casas-Rímac and Centro de Estudios y Publicaciones, 2000, pp. 101–32, at pp. 102–3, cf. Michael Sievernich, 'Von der Utopie zur Ethik. Zur Theologie von Gustavo Gutiérrez', *Theologie und Philosophie*, 1996, 71, pp. 33–46.

13 Gutiérrez gave the name to an ecclesial reflection that had already taken place, thus 'liberation theology is not a new growth of Christian theological reflection, but rather an outgrowth of long years of such reflection', William Boteler MM, 'Greetings', in Marc H. Ellis and Otto Maduro, eds. *The Future of Liberation Theology: Essays in Honor of Gustavo Gutiérrez*, Maryknoll, NY: Orbis, 1989, pp. 13–15 at p. 13.

14 It is clear that 'the influence of Gustavo [Gutiérrez] on theological method and praxis began in Peru long before the concretisation of that influence took place in books and at high-level church conferences. Taking time to work with groups of persons – delegates of the word, pastoral agents, local religious, students groups, missionaries – became the modus operandi of these young Peruvian priests', see Luise Ahrens MM and Barbara Hendricks MM in Marc H. Ellis and Otto Maduro, eds. *The Future of Liberation Theology: Essays in Honor of Gustavo Gutiérrez*, Maryknoll, NY: Orbis, 1989, pp. 3–4.

15 Langdon Gilkey, 'The Political Dimensions of Theology', in Brian Mahan and L. Dale Richesin, eds. *The Challenge of Liberation Theology: A First World Response*, Maryknoll, NY: Orbis, 1981, p. 117; Inaugural Lecture as the Shailer Mathews Professor in the Divinity School of the University of Chicago, pp. 113–26.

16 Chimbote is described as 'a coastal fishing port to the north of Lima noted for its astounding stench and pollution produced by local fishmeal factories and steel mills. A small version of Lima, Chimbote harbors masses of exploited, impoverished workers who have come from the Peruvian sierra in search of work, only to find themselves unemployed and living in hellish, concentric circles of mat houses that surround the city', see Curt Cadorette, 'Peru and the Mystery of Liberation: The Nexus and Logic of Gustavo Gutiérrez' Theology', in Marc H. Ellis and Otto Maduro, eds. *The Future of Liberation Theology: Essays in Honor of Gustavo Gutiérrez*, Maryknoll, NY: Orbis, 1989, pp. 49–58, at p. 53.

17 Gutiérrez, *A Theology of Liberation* is dedicated to Arguedas, Gutiérrez close friend and fellow writer, both influenced by Peru's socialist thinker José Carlos Mariátegui (1895–1930), and to the Brazilian priest Henrique Pereira Neto, assassinated in Recife on 26 May 1969; see Freí Betto, 'Gustavo Gutiérrez – A Friendly Profile', pp. 31–7, pp. 32, 37, and Stephen Judd MM, 'Gustavo Gutiérrez and the Originality of the Peruvian Experience', in Marc H. Ellis and Otto Maduro, eds. *The Future of Liberation Theology: Essays in Honor of Gustavo Gutiérrez*, Maryknoll, NY: Orbis, 1989, pp. 65–76 at pp. 66–7.

18 Since 2001 Gutiérrez held the John Cardinal O'Hara Chair in Theology at the University of Notre Dame. Otherwise he lived in Rimac, 'a gray, dirty, noisy slum where residents are frantically trying to survive, to find or keep a job, to feed and clothe their children. It is a place where struggle is a common denominator and hope, however tenuous, is a thin thread that holds human lives together', Curt Cadorette, 'Peru and the Mystery of Liberation', pp. 49–58 at p. 49.

19 Gustavo Gutiérrez, *La fuerza histórica de los pobres*, Lima: Centro de Estudios y Publicaciones, 1979, English translation, *The Power of the Poor in History*, Maryknoll, NY: Orbis, 1983.

20 *Gaudium et Spes* § 45.

21 Gustavo Gutiérrez, 'Toward a Theology of Liberation', in James B. Nickoloff, ed. *Gustavo Gutiérrez: Essential Writings*, London: SCM Press, 1996, p. 27.

22 Juan Alfaro, 'God protects and liberates the poor – O.T.', *Concilium*, 1986, 187 pp. 27–35; Leonardo Boff and Virgil Elizondo, eds. *Option for the Poor: Challenge to the Rich Countries*, Edinburgh: T&T Clark, 1986.
23 Gustavo Gutiérrez, 'God's Revelation and Proclamation in History', in *The Power of the Poor in History: Selected Writings*, London: SCM Press, 1983, p. 6.
24 Gutiérrez prefers the term 'encounter' or 'collision' while those reading history from a European viewpoint term it 'discovery' or 'conquest' and others even term it 'invasion' or 'covering'; Gustavo Gutiérrez, *Las Casas: In Search of the Poor of Jesus Christ*, Maryknoll, NY: Orbis, 1993, p. 2.
25 It was in that context that the Jesuits developed safe places around the borders of current Argentina, Paraguay and Brazil, for indigenous peoples to live in well-bounded territories where they learned about Christianity, toiled the land, lived communally and escaped the enslaving mechanisms of the Portuguese slavers. The Jesuits were expelled from the Portuguese colonies in 1759, from France in 1762, and from the Spanish colonies in 1767. On the 21 July 1773 Pope Clement XIV suspended the mere existence of the Society of Jesus; Michel Clévenot, 'The Kingdom of God on Earth? The Jesuit Reductions of Paraguay', *Concilium*, 1986, 187, pp. 70–7; Boff and Elizondo, eds. *Option for the Poor*.
26 Gustavo Gutiérrez, *En busca de los pobres de Jesucristo*, Lima: Instituto Bartolomé de las Casas-Rimac and Centro de Estudios y Publicaciones, 1992.
27 However, Las Casas was not, according to Gutiérrez, an isolated prophetic voice but he was part of a minority group that included missionaries, bishops, civil servants and event members of the royal court who expressed their concern about the fate of the Indians under the conquistadors, Gutiérrez, *Las Casas*, p. 5.
28 Lewis Hanke, *Aristotle and the American Indians: A Study in Race Prejudice in the Modern World*, London: Hollis & Carter, Chicago: Henry Regnery, 1959; *All the Peoples of the World Are Men: The Disputation between Bartolomé de Las Casas and Juan Ginés de Sepúlveda in 1550 on the Intellectual and Religious Capacity of the American Indians*, Minneapolis: University of Minnesota Press, 1970; *All Mankind is One: A Study of the Disputation between Bartolomé de Las Casas and Juan Ginés de Sepúlveda in 1550 on the Intellectual and Religious Capacity of the American Indians*, Dekalb: Northern Illinois University Press, 1974.
29 Gustavo Gutiérrez, *On Job: God-Talk and the Suffering of the Innocent*, Maryknoll, NY: Orbis, 1987.
30 Gutiérrez, *Las Casas*, pp. 6–7. Gutiérrez refers to Las Casas' account of the atrocities done by the conquistadors, *A Short Account of the Destruction of the Indies*, London: Penguin, with chronology and further reading 2004 [1992].
31 Virgil Elizondo and Leonardo Boff, 'Editorial: Theology from the viewpoint of the poor', *Concilium*, 1986, 187, p. ix; Boff and Elizondo, eds. *Option for the Poor*.
32 Virgilio Elizondo has argued, for example that 'the transformative impact of the Medellín Conference on the church's pastoral practice and theology was far greater than that exercised by any other council of the church. No dogmas or confessions of faith were questioned or challenged – Protestant or Catholic. Instead, the whole edifice of Constantinian Christian thought, imagery, and symbolism was radically challenged in the name of Christianity itself. What was initiated was not a new academic or philosophical theology, but rather the transformation of the very structures and methods of doing theology. To be faithful and authentic, Christian theology will have to emerge out of the spiritual experience of the believing

community grappling with its history and responding to its contemporary situation'; See 'Emergence of a World Church and the irruption of the poor', in Gregory Baum, ed. *The Twentieth Century: A Theological Overview*, Maryknoll, NY: Orbis, 1999, p. 108.
33 See Mario I. Aguilar, *A Social History of the Catholic Church in Chile*, vol. I *The First Period of the Pinochet Government 1973–1980*, Lewiston, Queenston, and Lampeter: Edwin Mellen Press, 2004.
34 Gustavo Gutiérrez, *Beber en su propio pozo: En el itinerario de un pueblo*, Lima: Centro de Estudios y Publicaciones, 1983, English translation *We Drink from Our Own Wells: The Spiritual Journey of a People*, Maryknoll, NY: Orbis, 1984, twentieth Anniversary Edition 2003.
35 Gustavo Gutiérrez, *The God of Life*, London: SCM, 1991, p. 2. Spanish original *El Dios de la vida*, Lima: Centro de Estudios y Publicaciones, 1982 (shorter version); Lima: Instituto Bartolomé de Las Casas-Rimac and Centro de Estudios y Publicaciones, 1989 (longer version).
36 Gutiérrez does not dwell on issues of contemplation but those who did, for example Ernesto Cardenal and Pedro Casaldáliga associated mysticism, aesthetics and poetics with a political commitment to social change inspired by their Christian commitment to the poor and the marginalized, see Ernesto Cardenal, *El Evangelio en Solentiname*, Salamanca: Ediciones Sígueme, 1976, and *El Evangelio en Solentiname: Volumen Segundo*, Salamanca: Ediciones Sígueme, 1978.
37 Paper presented at the first Hugo Echegaray University Seminar, organized by UNEC, in G. Gutiérrez, R. Ames, J. Iguíñez and C. Chipoco, *Sobre el trabajo humano: Comentarios a la Encíclica Laborem Exercens*, Lima: Centro de Estudios y Publicaciones, 1982.
38 Gustavo Gutiérrez, 'The Gospel of Work: Reflections on *Laborem Exercens*', in Gustavo Gutiérrez, *The Density of the Present: Selected Writings*, Maryknoll, NY: Orbis, 1999, p. 37.
39 Gregory the Great, Pastoral Rule, 3, 21, in Gustavo Gutiérrez, 'New Things Today: A Rereading of Rerum Novarum', in Gustavo Gutiérrez, *The Density of the Present: Selected Writings*, Maryknoll, NY: Orbis, 1999, p. 51, n. 14. Most of these ideas were given by Gutiérrez at the Catholic University of Lima during the 'Jornadas de Teología' in February 1991.
40 Jon Sobrino SJ, 'El Cristianismo ante el siglo XXI en América Latina: Una reflexión desde las víctimas', in *Teología de la liberación: Cruce de miradas*, Coloquio de Friburgo, April 1999, Lima: Instituto Bartolomé de Las Casas-Rímac and Centro de Estudios y Publicaciones, 2000, pp. 207–38.
41 In 1999 Gutiérrez argued that 'Estamos ante una estimulante y prometedora tarea en la que la teología de la liberación tiene mucho que hacer, y sobre todo por aprender' (We are faced with a challenging and promising task in which the theology of liberation has much to do, and especially to learning), in 'Situaciones y tareas de la teología de la liberación', *Teología de la liberación: Cruce de miradas*, Coloquio de Friburgo, April 1999, Lima: Instituto Bartolomé de Las Casas-Rímac and Centro de Estudios y Publicaciones, 2000, pp. 239–64 at p. 264.
42 Nicholas Lash, 'Theologies at the Service of a Common Tradition', *Concilium*, 1984, 171, p. 74; Claude Geffré, Gustavo Gutiérrez and Virgil Elizondo, eds. *Different Theologies, Common Responsibility: Babel or Pentecost?*, Edinburgh: T&T Clark, 1984.

43 Gustavo Gutiérrez, 'Liberation Praxis and Christian Faith', in *The Power of the Poor in History: Selected Writings*, London: SCM Press, 1983, p. 36.
44 'The vanguard of Protestant theology would become the great Christian theology of modernity, for it was a current that would lend an attentive ear to the questions asked by critical reason and individual liberty in this society forged by the bourgeoisie. For a number of historical reasons, this theology would centre in Germany, the land of the Reformation', Gustavo Gutiérrez, 'Theology from the Underside of History', in *The Power of the Poor in History: Selected Writings*, London: SCM Press, 1983, p. 178.
45 On Bonhoeffer see Gustavo Gutiérrez, 'Theology from the Underside of History', pp. 179–81.
46 'It [the revolutionary struggle] insists on a society in which private ownership of the means of production is eliminated, because private ownership of the means of production allows a few to appropriate the fruits of the labour of many, and generates the division of society into classes, whereupon one class exploits another', Gustavo Gutiérrez, 'Liberation Praxis and Christian Faith', pp. 37–8.
47 Gustavo Gutiérrez, 'Liberation Praxis and Christian Faith', p. 65.
48 Frei Betto, 'Gustavo Gutiérrez – A Friendly Profile', pp. 31–7 at p. 36.

Chapter 3

CONTEMPORARY DIALOGUES: THE TRAPPISTS OF ALGERIA

As outlined in the previous chapter, praxis as a Latin American recovery devise for ecclesiological purposes becomes a common trend in the development of third world theologies.[1] Already in December 1986 the Ecumenical Association of Third World Theologians had outlined the need of theological praxis as dialogue with other religions stating in its final document agreed at the end of their meeting in Mexico: 'Dialogue with other religions as God's partners and ours in the human-religious task of liberating the oppressed and constructing a new world is a felt need at all levels of EATWOT.'[2] Moreover, all over the southern hemisphere, the option for the poor, an option for others rather than me as a selfish human centred individual, has always been associated with the monastic choice of fleeing from the world.[3] Such flight that eventually marks the arrival of the monk within contemporary society provides the monastery and the monk as challenges to the possible absence of dialogue between those involved in the world and those who seem to be absent from the world. Monks and monasteries by their very presence in the contemporary landscape proclaim as symbolic signifiers a challenge to the primacy of violence, greed and the absence of the divine. In fact, they constitute a spiritual presence within the human realm in general and within daily human existence in particular. This presence was affirmed by the Trappist John Bamberger commenting on Thomas Merton's prophetic contribution. He wrote: Merton 'presents contemplation as the activity of a person who becomes whole in his humanity through seeking ultimate union with God'.[4]

One of those examples of a liberating praxis from within, of a monastic theology as a second step, was that of the Cistercians (Trappists) in Algeria during the civil war. For Trappists dialogue and hospitality become grounded on the basic rule of St Benedict that exhorts its fellow monks in the following manner: 'Let all guests who arrive be received like Christ, for He is going to say, "I came as a guest, and you received Me".'[5] In fact, Benedict exercised a liberating praxis of action – prayer first, monastic theological thinking came later – and the Trappists of Algeria discerned their spiritual journey and their passage into eternity in the same way. Their sense of hospitality as a common trait to Islam and Christianity led to a compatible search for the divine and the possibility of questioning war, violence and division in Algeria.

The Praxis of Hospitality

On the night of 26/27 March 1996 seven monks of the Trappist Monastery of Thibirine in Algeria were abducted.[6] The seven monks assassinated were: Dom Christian de Chergé (1937–96), Br Luc Dochier (1914–96), Fr Christophe Lebreton (1950–96), Br Michel Fleury (1944–96), Fr Bruno Lemarchand (1930–96), Fr Celestin Ringeard (1939–96) and Br Paul Favre-Miville (1939–96). Almost 2 months later their captors announced their death: they had been shot and their heads severed from their bodies. Their bodies were never found while their heads were found on 21 May 1996 looking mummified as they had been buried and then disinterred before being left beside a tree in Algeria. Their burial took place at their own monastery on 4 June 1996 after a solemn funeral Mass at the Cathedral of Algiers.

As members of the Cistercian Order of the Strict Observance (Trappists) they professed a vow of stability as contemplatives within one monastery to which they belonged for life and they had consciously and after much reflection decided not to leave Algeria in a violent period of civil war.[7]

The importance of this event was similar to other tragic events provided by witnesses and martyrs who decided to give their lives without immediate consent and without ownership of their lives for the Gospel. Their killing as a mass event against a religious community was similar to that of the killing of the Jesuit community in El Salvador in 1989, an occasion triggered by the choice of the Jesuit Ignacio Ellacuría and companions to remain in El Salvador throughout El Salvador's civil war and to share their students' and parishioner's lives.

Ignacio Ellacuría (1930–89), a Jesuit and rector of the José Simeón Cañas University of Central America (UCA) of El Salvador, 59 years of age, was murdered by members of the Atlacatl regiment of the Salvadorian Army, the unit that entered the compound of the Jesuit residence at the UCA at 1.00 am on 16 November 1989.[8] The soldiers fired into the air and as they reached the Jesuit residence one of them threw a grenade into the building where the Jesuits were sleeping. Soldiers entered the building and shot two of the priests, Joaquín López y López and Juan Ramón Moreno, while they were sleeping. They also killed the Jesuits' cook Julia Elba Ramos and her daughter Celina, who had requested permission to spend the night at the Jesuit residence due to the military curfew and the uncertain situation within San Salvador. Three other priests, Amando López, Ignacio Martín-Baró and Segundo Montes, were dragged outside onto the lawn and were joined by Ignacio Ellacuria who slept in a separate quarter. The soldiers forced them to lie face down on the ground. According to a witness Martín-Baró shouted at the soldiers and accused them of committing an injustice; however, four Jesuits were quickly shot dead.[9] Other accounts suggest that 'their brains were spilled out on the ground by their murderers', interpreted by Joseph O'Hare, president at that time of the Jesuit-run Fordham University in New York, as 'a chilling symbol of the contempt shown by men of violence for the power of truth'.[10] The soldiers burned university archives and threw grenades into the school of theology before painting rebel slogans on the walls accusing the rebels of murdering the Jesuits. On the following morning, a military truck with a loud speaker went around the archdiocesan offices announcing that Ellacuría and Martín-Baró had already been killed and that they would continue killing Communists.

The difference between the Trappists and the Jesuits, if differences are possible in death, is that the Jesuits remained in communion with other Christians while the Trappists remained together among Muslims. In El Salvador Jesuits exercised the predicament of a missionary presence; in Algeria Trappists exercised the predicament of a *contemplative presence as dialogue* with Muslims, treated by them as equals, as sons and daughters of God, as their brothers and sisters rather than as 'non-Christians'. It is a fact that much less is known of the Trappists' death than of the Jesuits but both groups were killed in order to terrorize others.

This chapter outlines the history of the Trappist community of Our Lady of Atlas, the history of the killings and the original contribution of Dom Christian, the prior of the monastery, and the other Trappists to an inter-faith dialogue based on love and presence rather than proclamation. This departure from Vatican guidance in documents on inter-faith provides a very fruitful ground for further dialogue with Islam and particularly with those who do not believe in a God such as atheists/agnostics and Buddhists.

Thibirine Monastery and the Civil War

The monastery of Thiribine with the name of Our Lady of Atlas was founded in 1934 as a Trappist foundation from the Yugoslavian Abbey of Our Lady of Liberation. It was an oasis of dialogue and peace for neighbouring peoples and even at the height of the troubles the Trappists rejected the protection offered by armed guerrilla groups or their transfer to the town of Medea, located nearby, by government forces representing the town's major.

The Trappists found themselves in the middle of the period known as the Algerian Civil War.[11] During this conflict that started in 1991 the Algerian government fought several Islamist rebel groups with casualties estimated between

100,000 and 200,000 people. At the end the Algerian government won the war after the surrender of the Islamic Salvation Army and the defeat in 2002 of the Armed Islamic Group.

The conflict started in December 1991 when the Islamic Salvation Front (FIS) party gained enormous popularity and the National Liberation Front (NFL) cancelled the national elections fearing after a first round of voting that the FIS would gain executive power. Following this election cancellation the army took control of the country and President Chadli Bnjedid was thrown out of office. The FIS was banned from public life and armed rebel groups started to emerge in order to fight the Algerian government. Among those groups the Islamic Armed Movement (MIA) was located in the mountains and the Armed Islamic Group (GIA) located itself in the towns. The first rebel operations were against the army and the police but quickly the conflict escalated and the rebel groups started attacking civilian populations. In 1994 while there were peace negotiations between the government and the FIS the GIA declared war on the FIS and supporter groups while the MIA and other smaller groups regrouped in the FIS-loyalist Islamic Salvation Army (AIS).

In 1994 there were presidential elections and General Liamine Zéroual, the army candidate, was elected. The conflict between the GIA and the IAS intensified and resulted in some civilian massacres by the GIA and by some government forces. In 1997 there were parliamentary elections won for the most part by a newly created pro-army party the National Democratic Rally (RND). By then the AIS, fought by the other two sides, opted for a ceasefire while the GIA continued the fight against the government. In 1999 a new president, Abdelaziz Bouteflika, was elected and an amnesty for all rebel fighters was offered so that if they refrained from violence they could reintegrate into Algerian life. This amnesty marked the triumph of the government and only pockets of GIA fighters continued fighting the government until they were fully defeated in 2002.

Witnesses to Dialogue

During these years of civil war in Algeria 18 Christian missionaries (among these the seven Trappists), witnesses to dialogue, who had remained in Algeria were killed. While all historical attention has been centred on the Trappists because of their choice of staying among Muslims and their choice of sharing the gift of hospitality that led to their deaths, it is worth mentioning these other 11 witnesses to dialogue between Christianity and Islam.

Brother Henri Vergès, a Marist Brother, was born on 15 July 1930 in the East Pyrenees, France. At 22 years of age, he took his final vows as a Little Brother of Mary. From 1958 to 1966 he was sub-master of novices in Corrèze

(Notre-Dame de Lacabane). However, on 6 August 1969 he arrived in Algeria. From 1969 to 1976 he was Director of the St Bonaventure School in Algiers, from 1976 to 1988 he was a teacher of mathematics at the Sour-El-Ghozlane and from 1988 onwards he worked in Algiers and was responsible for the diocesan library that more than a 1,000 young people from the neighbourhood of the Casbah used. He was murdered at his work place together with Sister Paul-Hélène on 8 May 1994 in the early afternoon. During his funeral on Thursday 12 May Cardinal Duval stated: 'Dear Brother Henri was an authentic witness to the love of Christ, to the absolute self-denial of the Church and to fidelity to the Algerian people.' In his letters Brother Henri expressed his commitment to Muslims in Algeria as part of his own Christian commitment: '. . . It is my Marist commitment that has allowed me, despite my limitations, to harmoniously be part of the Moslem environment, and my life in this environment, in its turn, has made me more profoundly a Marist Christian. May God be praised!'

Sister Paul-Hélène Saint-Raymond was a Little Sister of the Assumption. She was born in Paris on 24 January 1927. She was an engineer who in 1952 entered the community of the Little Sisters of the Assumption where she took final vows in 1960. From 1954 to 1957 she worked with working families at Creil; then she studied nursing and through her new profession served in working-class areas of Paris. In 1963, she was sent to Algiers where she stayed until 1974. These years in Algeria were followed by 1 year at Tunis, 9 years at Casablanca and her return to Algiers in 1984. During her first stay in Algiers, she worked at the medical and social centre of the Little Sisters of the Assumption. The centre offered nursing care, family guidance to the poor and it had a private dispensary. In 1988 she rejoined the community at Belcourt in Algiers and worked in the library of the Casbah with Brother Henri Vergès. It was there that she was murdered together with Brother Henri Vergès, on 8 May 1994. When Father Teissier warned the community as to the risks of staying in Algeria she responded: 'Father, in any way our lives are already given.' Another sister described her as follows: 'Her life was given, delivered to the little ones and to the poor, whom she passionately loved, welcomed and from whom she would say she received so much. Her way of "announcing Jesus Christ" in the Moslem society was for her the respect for the beliefs of others, a deeply personal aspect of her Christian faith, demanded in life by the Gospel.'

Sister Esther Paniagua Alonso, an Augustinian Missionary Sister, was born at Izagre (León, Spain), on 7 June 1949. At 18 years of age, she entered the Novitiate of the Congregation of the Augustinian Missionary Sisters and in August 1970 she took her final vows. After qualifying as a nurse she was sent to Algeria where she was deeply touched by the Arab culture and the practice of Islam and she gave herself without reserve. She worked in hospitals where she gave herself totally to the sick, especially to handicapped children for whom she did not keep to a timetable. They used to call her 'their angel' and when asked about her possible fear of staying in Algeria she replied: 'No one can take our life because we have already given it . . . Nothing will happen to us since we are in the hands of God . . . and if something does happen, we are still in his hands'. Her preferred book was the Bible but she also read the Koran to better understand the faith of the people she served; she also liked to read the mystics and the Sufis of the Islamic world. On 23 October 1994 she was killed, together with Sr Caridad, on her way to Sunday Mass.

Sister Caridad Álvarez Martín, an Augustinian Missionary Sister, was born at Santa Cruz de la Salceda (Burgos), Spain, on 9 May 1933. In 1955 she entered the Congregation of the Augustinian Missionary Sisters and she was sent to Algeria having taken final vows on 3 May 1960. She lived in Algeria for more than 30 years, only interrupted by medical treatment in Spain because of her weak health. In Algeria she looked after the elderly and the poor and when the violence started she had no doubt that she wanted to accompany the Algerian poor who had given her so much hospitality and acceptance. On 23 October 1994 she was killed, together with Sr Esther, on her way to Sunday Mass.

Jean Chevillard, a Missionary of Africa (White Father), was born in Angers (France) on 27 August 1925. He took his vows on 29 June 1949 and was ordained a priest on 1 July 1950 at Carthage. Appointed to Algeria, he stayed there nearly all his life being responsible for centres of formation, serving as regional superior and regional bursar. He was murdered on 27 December 1994 at Tizi-Ouzou while he was in his office, attending to people and answering mail. Towards midday he was kidnapped by four armed men. Chevillard was aware that he was in serious danger and stated it as follows: 'I know that I can die murdered. Our vocation is to witness to the Christian faith on Moslem land. For the rest, "in sha Allah!".' When asked why he was returning to Algeria in September 1994 he answered: 'I am returning there to give witness. My home is there, near my Berber friends. If I die, I want to be buried there.'

Alain Dieulangard, a Missionary of Africa (White Father), was born on 21 May 1919 at St-Brieuc (France). He studied law and qualified as a lawyer in 1943. During the same year he joined the White Fathers and he took his vows at Thibar on 29 June 1949 and was ordained as a priest on 1 February 1950. Appointed to Algeria, he spent all his missionary life there, especially in Kabylie, working in administration and teaching. Before his death he wrote: 'As the apostles on the lake, we have only to cry towards the Lord to wake him . . . The future is in the hands of God.' He was murdered in the mission courtyard on 27 December 1994.

Charles Deckers, a Missionary of Africa (White Fathers), was born at Anvers (Belgium) on 26 December 1924. He took his vows on 21 July 1949 and was ordained a priest on 8 April 1950. He studied Arabic in Tunis and later in 1955 he learnt Berber at Tizi-Ouzou and became responsible for a youth hostel. For 3 years he directed the El Kalima Centre in Brussels, a centre of documentation and of dialogue between Christians and Muslim immigrants. In 1982 he went to Yemen and in 1987 he returned to Algeria as parish priest of the parish of Our Lady of Africa. He was aware of the dangers he was encountering when he wrote: 'I know that my activities are dangerous for my life. Here is my vocation, I remain . . . Our Lady of Africa remains at the mercy of an insane act. In the diocese, we think that the maintenance of the presence of the Church is important, as much for the Church itself as for the country.' On 27 December 1994, he set on his way to celebrate Mass with his friend Jean Chevillard. A few minutes after his arrival, he was killed in the mission courtyard.

Christian Chessel, a Missionary of Africa (White Father), was born in Digne (France) on 27 October 1958. After having obtained his engineering diploma in 1981 he worked as a volunteer in Ivory Coast for 2 years and in 1985 he entered the White Fathers. It was in Rome that Chessel took his vows on 26 November 1991; his right hand placed on the pages of a Gospel of Saint Luke in the Arabic language that has been found on the remains of Father Richard, murdered in the Sahara in 1881. He was ordained a priest on 28 June 1992 and on return to Tizi-Ouzou he worked on a library project for the students. A young Algerian woman wrote after his death: 'To the parents of our young Father Christian . . . I would say: know that during his last days, Christian was very happy . . . He had started the project, so dear to his heart, of building a library for all the young people of Tizi-Ouzou.' In November 1994, Chessel had gone to the monastery of Tibhirine to be with the group Ribât-es-Salam (Link of Peace). He wrote: 'I feel the necessity of balancing my life with a more spiritual dimension and something more simple and lived.' He was machine-gunned on 27 December 1994 in the Tizi-Ouzou courtyard.

Jeanne Littlejohn, Sister Angèle-Marie, a Sister of Our Lady of the Apostles was born in Tunis on 22 November 1933. In 1957 she entered the postulancy of the Sisters of Our Lady of the Apostles and received the name of Angèle-Marie. She took her first vows on 8 September 1959 and left for Bouzarea where the Sisters ran an orphanage and boarding school for young girls. She stayed there from 1959 to 1964 as an embroidery teacher. However, in 1964 when the Algiers School of Art opened in Belcourt she went there as an embroidery teacher, where she stayed until her death. Sister Angèle-Marie was profoundly attached to Algeria, to its inhabitants, to her mission, sharing with this people their joys and their sufferings. When Father Bonamour, the parish priest, mentioned the impeding danger and invited the sisters to be ready they responded: 'We are ready.' When leaving Mass during the afternoon of Sunday 3 September 1995 one of the sisters shared her fear of violence with her. Angèle-Marie told her: 'We must not be afraid. We must only live the present moment well . . . the rest does not belong to us'. About 10 minutes later, on their way to the house, Sister Angèle Marie was killed with Sister Bibiane, her companion.

Denise Leclercq, Sister Bibiane, a Sister of Our Lady of The Apostles was born on 8 January 1930 at Gazerau, France. She entered the Sisters of Our Lady of the Apostles on 4 March 1959 and took her first vows on 8 March 1961 and she was sent to Algeria to the maternity ward of Constantine. She shared her life with the newly born and their mothers and in 1964 she was posted to a sewing and embroidery centre for young people without studies in Algiers. Through this work she discovered the shocking realities of poor Algerian women. In 1994 she had to take the decision of whether to stay or to leave and she was very clear: 'It is the people themselves who have asked for the Sisters. Actually they have asked that we stay. I am very saddened, I feel powerless before so much suffering, but I know, God loves these people and I have great confidence in Our Lady of Africa. Jesus said, "the Father will give you all that you ask for in my name" . . . His light helps me to discover marvels that are hidden, surprising solidarities, generosities, superhuman courage; the Spirit is in their heart who works. The Word of God helps me to stay attentive to be a ray of hope: I choose to stay'. When leaving Mass on 3 September 1995, only about 100 metres from their house, Sister Bibiane was killed together with Sister Angèle-Marie.

Sister Odette Prévost, a Little Sister of the Sacred Heart, was born on 17 July 1932 in Champagne, France. In 1950 she qualified as a teacher and worked as a teacher for 3 years. In 1953, at the age of 21, she entered the Little Sisters of the Sacred Heart of Charles de Foucauld and in 1959 she took her final vows. From 1958 she worked in the mission at Kbab in Morocco and later she was transferred to Argenteuil (France) where she worked among the Maghrebines. In 1968 she was sent to Algiers and she tried to enter into the great spiritual adventure of understanding others at the interior of their own religious tradition. She read the Koran and prayed in groups where Christians and Muslims prayed together. She lived very close to the people of her poor neighbourhood and became very aware of the dangerous situation that was building up in Algeria. She was machine gunned in Algiers while she was going to Mass on 10 November 1995.

The Assassination

The seven Trappists were victims of the violence against foreigners that was so much part of the Algerian civil war.[12] The conflict started in 1991 after a first round in the Algerian presidential election showed that the FIS had a lead given by the voters. Immediately after, the Algerian government cancelled the next round of presidential elections and the armed conflict started in December 1991. The army took over the government and ousted President Chadli Benjedid. As the FIS was banned and thousands of its members were arrested Islamic groups began an armed struggle against the military government. The main groups were the MIA based in the mountains and the GIA based in the towns.

The human cost of the conflict was huge and between 100,000 and 200,000 casualties. Seven journalists as well as several Christian missionaries died until the surrender of the FIS and the 2002 victory of the government forces against the GIA.

The Trappists were kidnapped by members of the GIA and their severed heads were found at Medea, a place not too far from the monastery. After the assassination, the Thibirine Monastery continued to be open with the presence of a French priest called Jean Marie Lassausse who toiled the land helped by the same people who helped the assassinated Trappists.

An Example of Dialogue

From the start of the Civil War the monks made arrangements to reduce their number within the community, to reject the admission of any novices, to be ready to evacuate to Morocco instead of France as to return quickly if it was needed and to offer medical help to all parties involved in the violence – taking into account that most people wounded were civilians. Once again they rejected an offer from the Apostolic Nuncio who offered to move the monastery within protected Vatican premises. They voted year after year to remain in the monastery as signs to God's love, living simply, working the land and helping the poorest of the poor.[13] Their lives and death started to be known later in France and Algeria because of their witness to dialogue and cooperation with Muslims and because through a process of discernment they decided to remain in Algeria during troubled and violent times in order to support their Muslim brothers and sisters.[14]

The Testament written by Dom Christian De Cherge OCSO bore testimony to the enormous sense of presence among Muslims that the Trappists felt was needed in order to respond to God's call to journey with Muslims in Algeria.[15] Dom Christian, prior of the community of Thibirine, wrote his testament (*Quand un à-Dieu s'envisage*) in Algiers on 1 December 1993 and it was completed at Thibirine on 1 January 1994. It was opened shortly after the monks' death on Pentecost Sunday 1996. The short text reads as follows:

> If it should happen one day – and it could be today – that I become a victim of the terrorism which now seems ready to encompass all the foreigners in

Algeria, I would like my community, my Church, my family, to remember that my life was given to God and to this country. To accept that the One Master of all life was not a stranger to this brutal departure. I would like them to pray for me: how worthy would I be found of such an offering? I would like them to be able to associate this death with so many other equally violent ones allowed to fall into the indifference of anonymity. My life has no more value than any other. Nor any less value. In any case, it has not the innocence of childhood. I have lived long enough to know that I share in the evil which seems, alas, to prevail in the world, and even in that which would strike me blindly. I should like, when the time comes, to have a space of lucidity which would enable me to beg forgiveness of God and of my fellow human beings, and at the same time to forgive with all my heart the one who would strike me down. I could not desire such a death. It seems to me important to state this. I don't see, in fact, how I could rejoice if the people I love were indiscriminately accused of my murder. It would be too high a price to pay for what will be called, perhaps, the 'grace of martyrdom' to owe this to an Algerian, whoever he may be, especially if he says he is acting in fidelity to what he believes to be Islam. I know the contempt in which Algerians taken as a whole can be engulfed. I know, too, the caricatures of Islam which encourage a certain idealism. It is too easy to give oneself a good conscience in identifying this religious way with the fundamentalist ideology of its extremists. For me, Algeria and Islam are something different. It is a body and a soul. I have proclaimed it often enough, I think, in view of and in the knowledge of what I have received from it, finding there so often that true strand of the Gospel learned at my mother's knee, my very first Church, precisely in Algeria, and already respecting believing Muslims. My death, obviously, will appear to confirm those who hastily judged me naive or idealistic: 'Let him tell us now what he thinks of it!' But these must know that my insistent curiosity will then be set free. This is what I shall be able to do, if God wills: Immerse my gaze in that of the Father, to contemplate with Him His children of Islam as He sees them, all shining with the glory of Christ, fruit of His Passion, filled with the Gift of the Spirit whose secret joy will always be to establish communion and to refashion the likeness, playing with the differences. This life lost, totally mine and totally theirs, I thank God who seems to have wished it entirely for the sake of that JOY in and in spite of everything. In this THANK YOU which is said for everything in my life, from now on, I certainly include you, friends of yesterday and today, and you, O my friends of this place, besides my mother and father, my sisters and brothers and their families, a hundredfold as was promised! And you too, my last minute friend, who will not know what you are doing, Yes, for you too I say this THANK YOU AND THIS 'A-DIEU' – to commend you to this God in whose face I see yours. And may we find each other, happy 'good thieves' in Paradise, if it pleases God, the Father of us both . . . AMEN![16]

Dom Christian's testament gives witness to a complete trust in God and the fulfilment of a vocation, Christian and monastic, within a Muslim world, knowing that he could be assassinated soon. Dialogue and simplicity as presence were the mark of the life of Dom Christian and the other Trappists. As he had suggested in his testament no human life is more worthy than another; however, as he was the prior he had the opportunity at international meetings to share this particular way of Christian presence among Muslims in Algeria. Due to the fact that he gave conferences and wrote his testament the attention of the outside world was focused on him and the names of the other Trappists remained in the shadow.

In a conference given to the General Chapter of the Trappist Order Dom Christian shared some of their Cistercian life in Algeria and gave some insights into their motivation as follows:

> This is a call to learn to dialogue on the very level of the spiritual experiences which these religions awaken while, at the same time, to be summoned to a humility dependent on God's forgiveness for the unfeeling and sometimes shameful response given by the believer (monks included) to the Lord's inmost promptings. In practice, we have hardly begun the inter-religious monastic dialogue with Islam.[17]

Throughout all other writings Dom Christian explored the possibilities of inter-religious dialogue as centred in God, a God common to Muslims and Christians.[18]

Theological Markers of Dialogue

Lawrence Cunningham has suggested that the monks' pattern of Christian life and hope in the face of death 'contains within its story many elements of martyrdom in our days'.[19] They chose to become martyrs because they felt that they needed to remain in Algeria as a sign of God's love. It must be noted that at no time they wanted to accept converts to Christianity or new members of their community. It is clear that theologically Dom Christian has managed to interpret the voice of the community as grounded in Christian love, showing due respect to other human beings and showing that Muslims were following a good path towards God. While most dialogue with other religions has shown love, acceptance and respect it has also overemphasized the non-Christian nature of other people's lives.

Dom Christian shows in his writings an innovation in dialogue that according to Christian Salenson, a researcher from Lyon who forms part of a group preparing writings from Thibirine for publication, 'is innovative and likely to be of interest to the whole Church in the matter of interreligious dialogue'.[20]

The grounding of this dialogue as presence is the friendship and openness with Mohammed, a field-guard, a Muslim who according to Dom Christian brought freedom to his faith.[21] One day, when Dom Christian was attacked on the street, Mohammed defended him against his aggressor and got killed. Dom Christian saw this as a sign of God, as a sign that if a Muslim was willing to give his life for a monk and a Christian foreigner the Trappists should be willing to do the same.[22] Thus, according to Salenson Dom Christian understood the giving of Mohammed life as Eucharist, as communion with another person, as the shedding of blood for another. However, Dom Christian inversed the meaning of the Eucharist where one receives in order to give, one's giving is done in order to receive life. Mohammed had asked him to pray for him remarking that Christians did not know how to pray; thus, Dom Christian offered his own life for Algeria through a constant prayer for the land that had offered him his own life which in that particular assault could have been taken away.

Dom Christian's theology started moving from an intellectual dialogue and a presence in a land without Christ to the need to give his life completely for a land that had given life in full. Further, he understood that the monastic fourth vow of stability meant stability among a people rather than within the walls of a monastery. On 1 October 1976 when he made his solemn profession he offered his stability to Algeria and to the dialogue with Muslims addressing the community of the monastery at Atlas to receive him with that intention. He made clear that his intention was of a full giving to Algeria rather than to his own sole sanctification within the monastery.

Dom Christian had the experience before his solemn profession of being alone in the church at night time when somebody else sat beside him and asked him to pray. They prayed together the main Christian prayers and the main Muslim prayers for 3 hours; then when the person praying left him Dom Christian noticed that he was accompanied by a Muslim who went around the church and chanted in happiness for those hours spent together in prayer. This happened sometime before his solemn profession and he did not speak about this event until that day as to say that he had felt that within those 3 hours that the encounter between the world religions had taken place based on a common eschatology and a new and renewed theology of hope.

In 1979 Dom Christian left the community for 3 months and lived in Assekrem. When he returned to Thibirine the Christian–Muslim dialogue had already been

Contemporary Dialogues

established through the Rabat es-Salâm (the Link of Peace) founded by Claude Rault. A group of Trappists was already sharing prayers with a Sufi community in Medea. It is clear that inter-religious dialogue for Dom Christian was not a theological or intellectual matter but a matter of interior conversion, an interior path and a deep spiritual attitude within one's life.

Inter-Faith Innovations

Dom Christian departed from the four types of dialogue outlined in the Roman documents *Mission and Dialogue* and *Dialogue and Proclamation*.[23] For as previously examined in this work the Vatican documents centred inter-faith dialogue within the church's mission and within the issue of a Christ-centred proclamation by the Church rather than by the individual in dialogue. Within *Dialogue and Mission* five elements are central to mission: presence and witness; commitment to social development and human liberation; liturgical life, prayer and contemplation; interreligious dialogue and proclamation and catechesis. This document, published in 1984, constituted the first encouragement for inter-faith dialogue since Vatican II.

The document *Dialogue and Proclamation* was to be followed by the document *Mission and Dialogue* which was published by the Pontifical Council for Dialogue in 1990 shortly after the encyclical of John Paul II *Redemptoris Missio* (RM). For John Paul II it was very clear that mission cannot be reduced to dialogue as if all religions were of equal value but that dialogue with other religions is part of a proclamation of Christ (RM). *Dialogue and Proclamation* has three parts: one on dialogue, one on proclamation and a third on the relation between dialogue and proclamation. The document makes clear that dialogue comes first in the document because it is a document prepared by the Pontifical Council for Dialogue; however, dialogue and proclamation go together in a constant tension. The model offered by the document is that of a God who works and offers salvation to the world but works in dialogue, never forcing, always persuading (DP 38). It is in this document that four types of inter-religious dialogue are outlined: the dialogue of life where people simply live together and appreciate each other on a human level; the dialogue of action where members of different religions unite around some particular cause for the betterment of humanity; the dialogue of theological exchange where, especially, experts and church leaders share perspectives and study one another's traditions and the dialogue of religious experience in which members share the richness of one another's spiritual traditions and personal spirituality and perhaps – as in Assisi in 1986 and 2002 – pray in one another's presence (DP 42).[24]

Christian Salenson in his own hermeneutics of Dom Christian's writings has isolated the following main characteristics of the Trappist Prior's dialogue and encounter with Muslims: Dialogue is a necessity based on the spiritual bonds that brings us together; dialogue is theological not political so that peace is not the goal of dialogue but a fruit; dialogue is a theological necessity; dialogue takes us out of our securities, we don't know what to expect; dialogue is profoundly existential; dialogue is an interior attitude so that whoever does not meet a Hindu or a Buddhist can also enter in dialogue through prayer. The conditions of dialogue are humility, the respect for other faiths, and the possibility of being part of another school in order not to intellectually compare but to search for God, the ultimate goal of all dialogue. The foundations of dialogue are the mercy of God, the Oneness of God and the eschatological 'hereafter'.

Dom Christian compared dialogue between Christians and Muslims as two ladders linked to each other – divine ladders to be climbed not counting the steps but ascending knowing that others are doing the same through a parallel, united and different ladder. Thus, the fruit of dialogue is a deeper penetration into the mystery of God. Islam for Dom Christian is a question not about a religious system but about God and therefore he asserted that he would only know the answer after his death; thus, when asked about Islam *vis-à-vis* Christianity he constantly said that only God knew the answer to those human questions about a divine truth. Islam remained for him a question about possible paths in order to understand God. That searching for the answer leads to dialogue because it connects with questions about God, answers that are given in a different manner by different religious practitioners.

Finally, Dom Christian wrote in his testament and some four homilies on martyrdom as something that was quite imminent in his own life.[25] Theologically, martyrdom served the purpose of dialogue with Muslims because the monks were also in danger of being assassinated in Algeria, a situation that they shared with most Algerians at that time.[26] The incident that triggered those writings and homilies on martyrdom that Dom Christian wrote about and delivered to the community took place on 24 December 1993. On Christmas Eve an armed group of three arrived at the Monastery asking for Fr Luc, who was a medical doctor, as they had wounded men without medical help up in the mountains. Fr Paul opened the door and after an initial request called Dom Christian who spoke to the armed men. At about 8.00 pm Dom Christian dialogued with Sayah Attiyah, the local emir of the GIA who had led the killing of some Croats on 14 December 1993. Despite this dangerous presentation card Dom Christian advised Attiyah that nobody armed could enter the monastery because the monastery was a place of peace. Thus, he gave the visitors the choice of disarming or stepping outside to talk about their needs. They talked outside and Attiyah requested money, medicines and a doctor emphasizing that the prior did not have any other choice but helping them. However, Dom Christian told them he had a choice and that it was to refuse their demands because they were preparing to celebrate the arrival of the Prince of Peace and he did not like the fact that the visitors were armed. The armed men left promising to return after appearing moved by the words of Dom Christian. Years later they returned to kill them all.

Issues of Community and Dialogue

In the understanding of Dom Christian and the Trappists killed, the community of Muslims and the community of Christians would be united with the arrival of the Kingdom not on this life but after. Thus, martyrdom as part of a dialogue of presence was not for the Trappists martyrdom for the Christian faith but a martyrdom of love. In the words of Christian Salenson: 'The gift of "the martyrdom of love" is a "gift" of life, and not a "taking" of life; one receives, one does not take'.[27] This, is probably the task of dialogue in an ongoing daily martyrdom in which one gives one's life for others knowing that the intellectual responses to other religions do not matter but what does matter is the love of journeying together not having all the answers to the questions, questions that only God can answer.

This perspective provided by the Trappists in Algeria challenges the static sense that dialogue and proclamation provide a tension. Instead, dialogue proclaims a larger reality than the Church, the Kingdom of God where all believers are united in that 'ladder' of Dom Christian, facing God in a dialogue of love, presence and togetherness. This perspective on dialogue brings an opening on the perspectives of dialogue for the sake of communion with God and a spiritual journey towards God rather than as a process of dialogue with an objective of achieving peace. Dialogue for the Trappist martyrs became a way of encountering God rather than a way of proclaiming God to others without knowledge of the Christian God. Their giving of themselves has given dialogue a new authority departing from the proposals found in the Vatican documents of the past 50 years.

One of the clear impacts of dialogue is the possibility that the actual action of dialogue creates the possibility of human unity and the empathy of others with the aims of dialogue. In a secularized Europe and a France in which religious symbols are not lawful within public places the witness to dialogue of the Trappists, by then known as the Trappists of Algeria, had an impact in a secularized European world. An example of this impact was the making of a film about their lives, premiered in 2010 with the title *Of Gods and Men*. Directed by Xavier Beauvois the film in the original French (*Des homes et des dieux*) won the Grand Prix prize at the 2010 Cannes Festival. Later it won the Lumière Award and the César Award for Best Film.

The film was also nominated for the 2011 foreign film of the year award given by BBC4 and it was remarked by the jury that the impressive part of the film was the very human way in which the monks through long deliberations remained in Algeria suspecting that they could get killed. This issue of communal discussions and their own acceptance of Muslims in Algeria make a central contribution to dialogue because it provides the necessary foundation for dialogue: human commonness and openness to the other.

For it is a historical fact that the monks did not die because they were Christians; instead, they were killed because they did not leave their Muslim friends. Martyrdom does not lead to dialogue but it is dialogue as the discovery of the commonality of others that leads to martyrdom. In a world that defines good relations as relations of power between factions and groups any cooperation and dialogue between people of symbolic difference such as Christians and Muslims.

There are many occasions when Christians can foster dialogue in situations of war and the next chapter explores the dialogue that arose between Christians and Buddhists in the context of the arrival of the Jesuits in Tibet during the eighteenth century and the dialogues that took place in Paris during the period of the Vietnam War in the early 1970s.

Notes

1 For an overview of the concept of 'praxis' see Clodovis Boff, 'Epistemology and Method of the Theology of Liberation', in Ignacio Ellacuría SJ and Jon Sobrino SJ, *Mysterium Liberationis: Fundamental Concepts of Liberation Theology*, Maryknoll, NY: Orbis and North Blackburn, Victoria: CollinsDove, 1993, pp. 57–85.
2 'Commonalities, Divergences, and Cross-fertilization among Third World Theologies: A Document Based on the Seventh International Conference of the Ecumenical Association of Third World Theologians', Oaxtepec, Mexico, 7–14 December, 1986, § 92. Document available in K. C. Abraham, *Third World Theologies: Commonalities & Divergencies*, Papers and Reflections from the Second General Assembly of the Ecumenical Association of Third World Theologians, December 1986, Oaxtepec, Mexico and Maryknoll, NY: Orbis, 1990, pp. 195–213.
3 See for example the contemplative life and prophetic action of the Amazonian bishop Pedro Casaldáliga in Mario I. Aguilar, *The History and Politics of Latin American Theology*, vol. 2: *Theology and Civil Society*, London: SCM Press, 2008, pp. 135–49.
4 John Eudes Bamberger OCSO, *Thomas Merton: Prophet of Renewal*, Kalamazoo, MI: Cistercian Publications, 2005, p. 78.

5 The Rule of Saint Benedict, Collegeville, Minnesota: The Liturgical Press, 2001, chapter 53. Cf. Mt 25.35.
6 For a full account of their lives, abduction and the discovery of their heads see John Kiser, *The Monks of Thibirine: Faith, Love and Terror in Algeria*, New York: St. Martin's Press, 2002; Donald McGlyn, *A Heritage Too Big For Us: The Atlas Martyrs*, Nunraw, Scotland: Nunraw Abbey, 1977; Bernardo Olivera, *How Far To Follow? The Martyrs of Atlas*, Bel Air, CA: Non Basic Stock Line, 1997 and M. Basil Pennington, *Twentieth Century Martyrs of the Cistercian Order of the Strict Observance: Martyrs of Algeria, Martyrs of the Spanish Civil War, Martyrs of the Chinese Communists: Their Story*, Spencer, MA: St. Joseph's Abbey, 1997.
7 *History of the Cistercians/Trappists* – Monastic reforms throughout the years arose out of the search for further ways of becoming detached from the world and worldly affairs so that monastic reformers were once again individuals who went on their own, searching for a more ascetic life challenging the monastic status quo and later were followed by others forming new monastic communities. Thus, before the completion of the first Christian millennium new developments took place in the Abbey of Cluny in France that embraced other monasteries in a monastic confederation of strict observance that eventually became too powerful for the lords of the land and was criticized for being too large, too communal and too financially established. Monastic reactions against Cluny soon arose in the form of the foundation of the Camaldolese by St Romuald in 1012, a group of hermits that while united in the spirit of solitude lived the Egyptian monastic ideal by remaining in single cells without community life. That monastic foundation was followed by one of the most significant monastic foundations and the only one that has never been reformed, the Carthusians by St Bruno in 1084 at the Grande Chartreuse near Grenoble. Finally, the third order that differed from the communal life, the study and the liturgical emphasis of the Benedictines was founded in Cîteaux near Dijon with the name of the Cistercians by St Robert of Molesme in 1098. The difference of the Cistercian Order from Cluny was that every monastery was autonomous but united within the same rule and way of life with the Abbott of Cîteaux as a primus inter pares.
8 El Salvador had a civil war from 1979 to 1992 in which the military committed atrocities against peasants in order to exterminate the guerrilla movement (Farabundo Martí National Liberation Front (FMNL)) that had been active since the halting of the agrarian reform programme in 1976; a military coup took place in 1979 carried out by reformist army officers led by Colonel Adolfo Majano and by a conservative group of officers led by Colonels Jaime Abdul Gutiérrez and José Guillermo García, with links and support from the American Embassy and with the recognition of the military governments of Chile, Argentina, Brazil and Panama, see Hugh Byrne, *El Salvador's Civil War: A Study of Revolution*, Boulder and London: Lynne Rienner Publishers, 1996, pp. 53–4.
9 Martha Doggett, *Death Foretold: The Jesuit Murders in El Salvador*, Washington, DC: Georgetown University Press, 1993; Jon Sobrino, Ignacio Ellacuría et al., *Companions of Jesus: The Jesuit Martyrs of El Salvador*, Maryknoll, NY: Orbis, 1990 and Teresa Whitfield, *Paying the Price: Ignacio Ellacuría and the Murdered Jesuits of El Salvador*, Philadelphia, PA: Temple University Press, 1995.

10 Joseph O'Hare SJ, 'Six Slain Jesuits', in Jon Sobrino, Ignacio Ellacuría et al., *Companions of Jesus: The Jesuit Martyrs of El Salvador*, Maryknoll, NY: Orbis, 1990, p. 177.
11 See Luis Martinez, *The Algerian Civil War 1990–98*, New York: Columbia University Press, 2000.
12 For the history of the Algerian Civil War and related issues see Luis Martínez, *The Algerian Civil War 1990–98*, London: C Hurst & Co, 2000; Khalida Messaoudi and Elisabeth Schemla, *Unbowed: An Algerian Woman Confronts Islamic Fundamentalism*, PA: University of Pennsylvania Press, 1998; Frederic P. Miller, Agnes F. Vandome and John McBrewster, eds. *Algerian Civil War*, Beau Bassin, Mauritius: Alphascript Publishing; and Isabelle Werenfells, *Managing Instability in Algeria Since 1995: Elites and Political Change*, London: Routledge, 2007.
13 The monks' process of communal discernment has been portrayed very well in the film *Des hommes et des dieux* ('Of Men and Gods', 2010), a film that won the Grand Prix Award at the Cannes Film Festival.
14 A personal analysis of the monks' abduction and death and their process of discernment has been outlined and critically assessed by Dom Armand Veilleux OCSO, the abbot of Scourmont in Belgium, at that time assistant to the Abbot General of the Trappists, who on 31 December 2002 wrote 'The death of the monks of Thibirine: Facts, questions and hypotheses', available at http://users.skynet.be/bs775533/Armand/wri/hypothesis.htm.
15 Christophe Lebreton, *Le souffle du don, journal de frère Christophe, moine de Tibhirine, 8 août 1993 – 19 mars 1996*, Paris: Bayard/Centurion, 1999.
16 Text taken from the *Bulletin of the North American Monastic Interreligious Dialogue*, May 1996, 55.
17 Dom Christian de Chergé OCSO, 'Conference given to the General Chapter of the Trappist Order', *Bulletin of the North American Monastic Interreligious Dialogue*, May 1996, 55, available at http://monasticdialog.com/a.php?id=492.
18 For writings by Dom Christian see Christian de Chergé, *L'invincible espérance, Textes recueillis et présentés par Bruno Chenu*, Paris: Bayard/Centurion, 1997; *Dieu pour tout jour, Chapitres de Père Christian de Chergé à la communauté de Tibhirine (1986–96)*. Bonjoyer, France: Abbaye d'Aiguebelle, 2004; *Jusqu'à l'extrême* (forthcoming) and Bruno Chenu, *Sept vies pour Dieu et pour l'Algérie, Textes recueillis et présentés par . . . avec la collaboration amicale des moines de Tamié et de Bellefontaine*, Paris: Bayard/Centurion, 1996.
19 Lawrence S. Cunningham, *A Brief History of Saints*, Oxford: Blackwell, 2005, p. 142.
20 Christian Salenson, 'The Spiritual and Theological Itinerary in the Writings of Christian de Chergé, *Dialogue Interreligieux Monastique 76, January 2006*.
21 Salenson, 'The Spiritual and Theological Itinerary'.
22 Dom Christian de Chergé OCSO, *Journées Romaines: Chrétiens et Musulmans, pour un projet commun de société*, Bonjoyer, France: Abbaye d'Aiguebelle, 1989.
23 Secretariat for Non-Christian Religions, *The Attitude of the Church Towards the Followers of Other Religions: Reflections and Orientations on Dialogue and Mission* (DM), 1984, AAS 75, pp. 816–28; see also *Bulletin Secretariatus pro non Christianis*, 1984/2, 56(13).

24 Critical commentary of these documents available in Stephen Bevans SVD, 'Church Teaching on Mission: Ad Gentes, Evangelii Nuntiandi, Redemptoris Missio and Dialogue and Proclamation', n.d. at www.maryknollvocations.com/mission.pdf.
25 The 'martyrdom of love' (Holy Thursday, 31 March 1994); The 'martyrdom of innocence' (Good Friday, 1 April 1994); The 'martyrdom of hope' (Easter Vigil, 2–3 April 1994); and The 'martyrdom' of the Holy Spirit (Pentecost, 22 May 1994).
26 Christian de Chergé, *L'invincible espérance, Textes recueillis et présentés par Bruno Chenu*, Paris: Bayard/Centurion, 1997, chs 12–15.
27 Salenson, 'The Spiritual and Theological Itinerary'.

Chapter 4

BUDDHISM AND A SECULARIZED DIALOGUE

The previous chapters of this book explored the positive practical developments towards dialogue outlined as church policy by the Second Vatican Council. This dialogue, I would argue, not only comes out of documents, commissions and meetings but it arises out of a commitment to explore one another's traditions and the actual daily practical ways in which they are not only implemented but lived. Thus, the theological change proposed by the council was not necessarily a relocation of the Christ within the church but the opening of the church's vision of the world, the acknowledgment that people had the right to believe without coercion and that the church was to serve all human beings rather than control their movements, thoughts and actions. This service to others and the search for a common human understanding was lived in a fuller manner by those who in their own lives applied the principles of dialogue and found human commonality and personal affection for other religious traditions. Those who found a complete solace in religious dialogue such as the Trappists in Algeria became also the target of those who did not want this dialogue to take place at all. As a result the Trappists were killed.

This chapter explores two instances of Christian–Buddhist encounter and dialogue: the arrival of the Jesuits in Tibet and the role of the Jesuit Dan Berrigan in a practical and conversational dialogue with Buddhism within the period of violence created by the Vietnam War. It is in the realm of the secular that Christianity and Buddhism encounter each other because what they have in common in the emptied voids of society without religious statements is the common search for a meaningful role within the hopes and fears of humanity in the case of Christians and within the realm of a totally equal common humanity in the case of Buddhists.

Colonial Encounters

The encounter between a previously Christian Europe and an Asian Buddhist world has been limited. Buddhism did not engage itself with Christian missionaries and the fact that both religions were perceived as intrinsically different did not provide the historical ground for an encounter or a deep dialogue. *Propaganda Fide*, the Roman agency in charge of evangelization, became increasingly concerned with missionary work in Latin America after the arrival of Christopher Columbus to the Americas and with missionary work in Africa, both territories dominated by the Spanish and Portuguese empires.

However, the Jesuits, a Roman Catholic congregation, experienced not only the encounter of Francis Xavier and companions with other religions in China and Japan but also sent missionaries to the territories known today as encompassing an ethnic (if not a political) Tibet. The Jesuits sent personnel to Tibet during the seventeenth and eighteenth centuries in order to convert Tibetans to Christianity. Very quickly their aims of Tibetan conversion became a process of learning Tibetan Buddhism and Tibetan religion. Highly influenced by the methods and life of St Francis Xavier, missionary to Japan and China, who established the first Christian communities at Goa, Jesuits established small Christian settlements in Eastern Tibet and at the same time developed the first study of Tibetan civilization within Europe. The Jesuit mission in Tibet lasted only from 1625 to 1721; however, the Jesuits left after having established instances of dialogue with the Tibetan monks of Lhasa. In fact, the Jesuit withdrawal from Tibet was a forceful one that coincided with the suppression of the Jesuits from the Spanish and Portuguese empires due to political reasons.

The Jesuits in Tibet

The most complete historical source for the period of Jesuit presence in Tibet is the account of the travels of Fr Ippolito Desideri, an Italian Jesuit, born at Pistoia in 1684 and ordained as a Catholic priest on 28 August 1712.[1] On 27 September 1712 he left for India, made his way to Tibet and lived and worked in Lhasa, the Tibetan capital.[2] On 4 November 1727 he returned to Europe from India and worked in Rome after the mission territories of Tibet were given to the Capuchin Fathers.[3] He died on 14 April 1733 at the age of 48.

The Jesuits had established the first Christian missions to Tibet almost a century earlier. Thus in 1625 Fr Antonio de Andrade founded the first Catholic mission in Tibet at Tsaparang. Together with Brother Manuel Marques, Andrade had journeyed from Delhi to Kashmir where he joined a group of Hindu pilgrims. After negotiating the mountain path at Mana (altitude 18,390 feet) they arrived at Charapangue or Tsaparang, the capital of the Kingdom of Guge, in the valley of the Langtchen-Kamba or Upper Sutlej. The king allowed him to teach and considered him a high lama. In April 1626 and after the arrival of other three Jesuits the king authorized the building of a church and a house for the missionaries. On Easter Sunday, 12 April 1626, the first foundation of the first Catholic church was laid in Tibet with the name of Our Lady of Hope.

Later, another centre was opened 100 miles away from Tsaparang. In total 12 people were baptized including the queen. However, the king's revenue taken from his brother in order to support the Jesuits created animosity and trouble started to flair. Matters became out of hand because Fr Andrade was appointed to run the Jesuit province of Goa and left Tibet before 1630. In February 1630 enemies of the king arose and the king was taken prisoner to Leh. The Jesuit churches were ransacked and the missionaries arrested and sent to Leh. Later, they were released and Fr Azevedo returned to Tsaparang on 25 August 1631 finding everything destroyed beyond repair. It was decided then to end the mission at Tsaparang and the Jesuits pursued their missionary work back at Leh.

By 1632 five Jesuits were back at Tsaparang but were kept as virtual house prisoners by the local army commander. Thus by 1635 all Jesuit missionaries returned to Goa feeling that the mission had been an utter failure. In 1640 a new attempt at returning to Tsaparang was made, as there was still a Jesuit brother there, but on crossing the mountains the Jesuits were arrested and on their release they sent news to Rome that Tibet had been permanently closed. In 1626 another mission attempt had been carried out at Utsang but it also failed. Thus, the first attempt of establishing the Church in Western and Central Tibet ended in failure.

In November 1713 Fr Desideri, at that time studying in Rome, was appointed to open a new mission in Tibet. Fr Desideri journeyed with Fr Emanuel Freyre who had been in India for 20 years already and they arrived in Leh on 26 June 1715. They reached Lhasa on 18 March 1716. In April 1716 Freyre returned to Hindustan via Nepal and Desideri was left in Lhasa as the only European resident in the city of the Dalai Lamas. Previously, a capuchin missionary had arrived in Lhasa in 1707 but due to the hard climate had left Lhasa later. Desideri stayed in Lhasa for 5 years after he got permission on 1 May 1716 to buy a house in Lhasa, an activity that was forbidden to foreigners at that time.

Desideri studied the Tibetan language day and night and on 6 January 1717 he delivered a public lecture on the Christian religion at the king's court. The king advised that he study the religion of the lamas and Desideri stayed at Ramocce monastery from 25 March to the end of July of 1717. Later, he moved to the monastic school of Sera where he had his private room and discussed Tibetan Buddhism with many teachers. His aim was to write a comparative work of Christianity and Buddhism following the apologetic and argumentative methods of that time but on 3 December 1717 the Tartars took Lhasa and murdered the king and ministers of his government. Desideri fled the city and stayed at Takpo Khier where he finished his book and lived until April 1721.

Desideri gave his work on Christianity and Buddhism in three volumes to one of his former teachers and there was great discussion all over Lhasa by many people who wanted to discuss his understanding of Buddhism and the ideas related to 'the migration of souls', 'the Godhead within Christianity' and the 'exposition of Christian doctrine' Many scholars from Sera and Breebung discussed the book with him as well.

In December 1718 conversations in Rome settled the matter of the missions in Tibet and all Jesuits were recalled. Desideri received a letter with this disappointing news in 1721 and after translating the Tibetan work *lam rim chenmo* into Italian returned to Lhasa from Takpo-Khier and on 28 April 1721 left Lhasa for Nepal. His journey back to Europe meant in practice the end of the Jesuit missions in Tibet.

What made the Jesuit attempt at converting Tibetans to Christianity a failure was the lack of grounding by the first missionaries on Tibetan Buddhism. What made Desideri so successful in his dialogue with Tibetans was his study of the language and the religion of Tibetans as well as his spirituality grounded on the Ignatian Exercises. It was the Exercises that made Jesuit missionaries aware of the need to discern God's path in many different ways and as the Jesuits did in China and South America to respect the fact that God could act in many different ways. In their understanding God could provide the human soul with different paths towards the final awareness of the power and glory of Jesus as Saviour, the leader of the Jesuits in their official name: the Society of Jesus.

Dialogue and the Vietnam War

Another example of Christian–Buddhist dialogue was the encounter between the Jesuit Dan Berrigan and the Buddhist monk Thich Nhat Hanh. At the time when Vatican II was unfolding a change in the close allegiance between the church and the established order a former European colonial territory, Vietnam, became the centre of international attention. The initial defence of a pro-Western regime in Vietnam became a full-blown war in which the United States became fully involved. While bombs and troops were flown from the United States, dialogue and diplomatic talks took place in Paris.[4]

Among the Christian presence on the Vietnam War there were thousands of Christians who did not support the war in Vietnam, a conflict already too close to the memories of World War II and the Korean War. However, the Vietnam War also provided an opportunity for a Christian awareness of the common task for peace that was embraced by Christians and Buddhists. This awareness arose out of the Buddhist protest by Vietnamese monks against the attack on their country and the support of a cessation of hostilities by Christian groups in Europe and the United States. This awareness created the conditions for an inter-faith dialogue centred on the work of the Berrigan brothers, the Fellowship of Reconciliation, the writings of Thomas Merton and the actions by Dorothy Day.

The American Jesuit Dan Berrigan impacted the world of contemplation and politics because of his gift as writer and poet as well as his role of political activist, particularly within the non-violent movement against the Vietnam War, nuclear weapons and all aggressive actions by the United States against other countries and other conflicts. For those who resented his involvement in the political world he was a criminal and indeed for a while he was among the ten most wanted people by the FBI. For those who saw the connections between an honest response to the Gospel values of peace, justice and solidarity he has been an inspiration.[5]

Together with his brother Philip he became very active in the opposition to the Vietnam War and the drafting of young Americans in order to fight the Communist forces of North Vietnam.[6] There is no doubt that Thomas Merton, the Cistercian monk, influenced some of his activities by discussing particular developments within the Vietnam campaign. For example, on 3 June 1965 Dan Berrigan, Jim Douglass and Bob McDole visited Merton at the abbey of Gethsemani in Kentucky in order to discuss Schema 13 and the alterations that were made in the article on war that discussed particularly the use of the nuclear bomb by the US military.[7] In 1948 Dan Berrigan had written to Thomas Merton praising Merton's *The Seven Storey Mountain*, however Merton never replied because his abbot had forbidden him to reply to so many letters.[8] By 1962 Dan Berrigan and Merton were again exchanging regular correspondence and the lack of freedom given by Dan's superiors for his involvement in the civil rights movement of the South had been discussed. Dan was ready to leave the Jesuits and it was Merton who advised him against it arguing that if he left many of his followers would not continue striving for civil rights, justice and peace in American society. Due to those tensions Dan Berrigan was sent to France on sabbatical during 1964 and when he returned he had changed from the well-behaved Jesuit he was before into a self-assertive, conscious objector to social injustice and violence of any kind – military, economic, social or racial.

In November 1964 Merton invited Dan Berrigan and others for a three-day retreat at Gethsemani Abbey with the theme 'Spiritual Roots of Protest'. Those in attendance on 17 November were A. J. Muste, W. H. Ferry (Center for the Study of Democratic Institutions and the Fellowship of Reconciliation – FOR), Anthony Walsh of the Montreal Catholic Worker House, the Mennonite theologian John H. Yoder, John Oliver Nelson (previously national chair of FOR and professor at Yale Divinity School) and the Catholic activists Robert Cunnane, John Peter Grady, Tom Cornell, Jim Forest, Dan and Philip Berrigan.[9]

On Merton's suggestion there was to be no rigid agenda and he gave a talk on 'The Monastic Protest: The Voice in the Wilderness'.[10] Dan Berrigan celebrated Mass in English, a novelty at that time of customary Latin liturgies, and he gave communion to Protestants present at the liturgy, a fact that Merton deemed 'uncanonical' but 'simple and impressive'.[11]

Throughout the United States a whole generation of youth, mostly fresher ranks at colleges and universities were questioning the rationality of war and they were reading Merton's essays. Many of those protestors and activists for peace corresponded with Merton and went on retreat to Merton's hermitage because 'Merton and his fellow retreatants believed that humanity was at a historic moment. A fundamental re-examination of existing values and radical actions were needed. Though Merton declined to participate in person in the revolutionary forces at work in the world, he continued to encourage Ghandian non-violent action'.[12]

The escalation of hostilities against North Vietnam took place in August 1965 when after confusing reports of an attack by Communist boat patrols against the US destroyer *Maddox* in the South China Sea's Gulf of Tolkin President Johnson got a Congress resolution that allowed him all necessary measures to prevent further aggressions. US jets escalated the bombardment of North Vietnam. Most of the US voters still supported the war despite the fact that by the end of 1965 6,000 respected academics had requested the end of the war to the US Department, a body that dismissed the academic cry. The political climate in the United States was challenging as the civil rights movement was also changing tactics from peaceful demonstrations to further actions after the shooting of Malcom X in February 1965 and the students staged a mass demonstration in Washington DC against the Vietnam War. In March 1965 the Quaker Alice Herz, 82 year old German–born, set fire to herself in the streets of Detroit emulating the actions of the Vietnamese monks in order to protest against the bombardment of Vietnam; by the end of 1965 another protestor Norman Morrison who was holding his 1-year old daughter burned himself in front of the Pentagon.[13] On 9 November 1965 Roger La Porte, a Catholic volunteer at the Catholic Worker House of Hospitality on Chrystie Street in Manhattan set himself on fire in front of the United Nations Building. Dan and other non-violent activists had to regain a peaceful momentum as public opinion was going against those who burned themselves and in the words of Merton: 'Certainly the sign was powerful because incontestable and final in itself (and how frightful!). It broke through the undifferentiated, uninterpetable noises, and it certainly must have hit many people awful hard. But in three days it becomes again contestable and in ten it is forgotten'.[14] Dan's words at La Porte's funeral spoke of a sacrifice so that others could have life and those words ignited Cardinal Spellman's pressure on the New York Jesuits to get rid of him.

As part of the staff of the magazine *Jesuit Missions* Dan was forcefully sent to Latin America in order to report and write about the work of the Jesuits. In November 1965 Dan went to Cuernavaca (Mexico) in what was to be a 4 month tour of the Jesuit missions while students' protests at Fordham University and many other forms of support showed US public opinion that Dan Berrigan had struck a chord among ordinary American Catholics. Berrigan's exile was even more controversial because it happened during the year when the Second Vatican Council ended proclaiming a new atmosphere of change and dialogue between the Church and the contemporary world. In the meantime and coinciding with Christmas Cardinal Spellman flew to Vietnam to minister to the US troops and to assure them that the Vietnam War was a war to keep Western civilization going. Finally, and after enormous pressure on the Jesuits, Dan Berrigan returned to the United States on 8 March 1966 and on 11 March he spoke to a large crowd of reporters at New York's Biltmore Hotel stating that he was back to oppose the Vietnam War and that his trip to Latin America had shown him that the resources used in Vietnam were needed to relieve poverty and suffering in Latin America.

Dan continued his affiliation with the peace movement by taking new duties as councillor on religious matters at Cornell University and on February 1968 had the opportunity to visit Vietnam. The North Vietnamese government had decided to honour the Buddhist Tet holiday by releasing three prisoners, three American fighter pilots, and they were asking for a representative of the peace movement to collect them. Those chosen were Howard Zinn, historian and formerly World War II army air force bombardier and Dan Berrigan who flew into Hanoi. The three prisoners were delivered to the hotel where Zinn and Berrigan were staying. They were Major Norris Overly, Captain John Black and Lieutenant JG David Methany who flew back to Laos with Zinn and Berrigan. US Ambassador William Sullivan met them and insisted that the men were members of the US Armed Forces and therefore should return to the US by military carriers – the original idea was to give a boost to the peace movement and bring them back in a commercial airline accompanied by Zinn and Berrigan. However, Berrigan appreciated the opportunity to visit Indochina and to have sheltered from the bombs with so many defenceless children.

By March 1968 General William Westmoreland requested 206,000 more troops while the opinion polls showed that half of the US population felt that their involvement in Vietnam was wrong and the first trial of Phil Berrigan and others who had destroyed federal property started.[15] They were left free on bail after the trial was over pending a further appeal. Phil travelled to Cornell University to teach a course on non-violent resistance with Dan and the plans started for another strong action of protest that this time was to involve Dan Berrigan.

At 12.30 pm on 17 May 1968 nine protesters, seven men and two women, all Catholics went to the Knights of Columbus Hall on 1010 Frederick Road, Catonsville, a suburb of Baltimore and burned 378 files (1-A, 2A and 1Y) related to the Selective Service Board number 33 after storming the offices. It took them 10 minutes for the whole raid and the media that had already been alerted filmed the burning operation, the singing and the praying of the Lord's Prayer that had two central players: Dan and Phil Berrigan. Since 1965 the destruction of draft cards carried a penalty in cash and a possible sentencing to years in jail, however Dan Berrigan recognized that after long conversations with his brother Phil there was no way out. The change had taken place and Dan Berrigan who had challenged the ecclesiastical authorities with his discourse against Vietnam and against violence had changed into a citizen that was challenging the lawfulness of the state to draft into the army young Americans for the purpose of fighting in another country against forces that had not directly attacked US citizens. Those 'enemy forces' were instead allied with political systems not wanted by the United States and were fighting with the help of US enemies such as China and the Soviet Union. In the words of Patrick O'Brien:

> The actions were, and are, essentially sacramental, visible signs of invisible lives. The burning of draft cards to make real the burning of children; the pouring of blood over weapons to reveal their real intent; the digging of graves on the White House lawn to symbolize the earth as a cemetery of our best hopes; the use of hammers on the cones of nuclear weapons to awaken us to the urgent need of the world for ploughshares to feed the hungry.[16]

Dan and the Catonsville offenders stood trial on 7 October 1968. Phil and other three who were re-offending were already in prison having lost their bail, however a new phenomenon had taken place due to Dan Berrigan's involvement in violent protest and destruction of federal property as outlined by Polner and O'Grady: 'the Catholic Left and the secular antiwar movement had more or less converged, each with its own agenda but both with the identical aim of crippling the war effort'.[17] Hundreds of protesters were outside and a full rally of the peace movement gathered. Inside the Court Dan Berrigan spoke of his actions, prompted by the judge, in terms of trying to save the burning of children and the blood of the innocent on the American flag. At one point Dan Berrigan asked the judge if they could all recite the Lord's Prayer and so they did, all united in what Harvey Cox labelled 'a Pentecostal Moment'.[18] The judge convicted them all, Dan was given a custodial sentence of 3 years and left on bail pending an appeal. Phil Berrigan was given 3.5 years plus 6 years for his Baltimore raid. As always, their mother Freda Berrigan backed their cause.

Dan returned to Cornell to rest, to pray and to write troubled by the death of Merton and at the same time searching for further contemplation, for further visions of where God wanted him to go. His play on the Catonsville trial, *The Trial of the Catonsville Nine*, became one of the central literary events of his life and probably the most well-known of his writings as the play was staged time upon time by groups learning and discussing non-violence.[19] Cornell University restored Dan to his job despite his conviction and the support of many triggered in him the sense that he should delay his imprisonment by fleeing as Phil had done for 10 days. The FBI searched for the two priests who were in hiding and Dan appeared and reappeared within peace rallies and meetings as a fugitive and the FBI's most-wanted man from 9 April to 10 August 1970. On the 11 August 1970 Dan Berrigan was arrested at his hiding place in Block Island, Rhode Island. His arrest coincided with the expansion of the Indochina war, announced at the end of April 1970 by President Nixon who announced that US forces had bombed and invaded Cambodia. In the meantime Dan served time at the medium-security Federal Correctional Institute in Danbury, Connecticut, together with his brother Phil who by then was in and out of different prisons for ongoing destruction of federal property. While in prison Dan worked at the prison dental office, wrote liturgies, read and continued celebrating the Eucharist together with Phil.

However, there were also difficult moments as Dan almost died of an allergic reaction while on a dental chair and had to be rushed to an outside hospital to save his life. The incident triggered other illnesses and Dan became weak, with stomach problems and kidney ailments. In the summer of 1971 he became eligible for parole, however it was denied by the US Parole Board in Washington, DC. Dan went on a hunger and work strike. Dan's parole came through on 24 February 1972. As he left prison a group was there to meet him and he returned to his apartment at Fordham University to find it locked and all his possessions on a corridor.

Dan Berrigan and Thich Nhat Hanh

In 1974 the exiled Berrigan and the exiled Vietnamese monk Thich Nhat Hanh met in Paris. Both of them poets and peace activists found themselves in a conversation that was to mark some of the return of Christian–Buddhist conversations already influenced by the international presence of the Tibetans on exile, especially the fourteenth Dalai Lama, and the presence of more and more Vietnamese monks among the refugees arriving in Europe and the United States.

Thich Nhat Hanh was born in Vietnam on 11 October 1926 and lived since the 1960s in France. Born Nguyen Xuan Bao he joined a Zen monastery at the age of 16. In 1949 and after completing his studies he assumed Thich Nhat Hanh as his *dharma* name. Thich is an honorary name assumed by all Vietnamese monks and nuns stating that they are part of the Shakya clan (Shakyamuni Buddha). He is considered the most influential monk in the lineage of Lâm Té Thien and perhaps in Zen Buddhism as a whole.

In the 1960s he founded the School of Youth for Social Services (SYSS) in Saigon as a relief grass roots organization that rebuilt bombed villages, set up schools, medical centres and relocated families during the Vietnam War. He travelled to the United States where he tried to convince the US administration to withdraw from Vietnam; he asked Martin Luther King to help him to achieve this aim. King nominated Thich Nhat Hanh for the Nobel Peace Prize in January 1967. In 1966 Thich Nhat Hanh founded the Order of Interbeing that spread through centres and monasteries throughout the world. However, in 1973 he was denied permission to re-enter Vietnam and he remained on exile in France. From 1976 to 1977 he led efforts to rescue Vietnamese boat people in the Gulf of Siam.

Over the years he became an important influence in the development of Western Buddhism through 'mindful practices' applied and open to all religious practitioners of any political background. Based in a monastery at the Plum village in the Dordogne, southern France, he coined the phrase 'engaged Buddhism', a topic of conversation with Dan Berrigan.

The conversations between Berrigan and Thich Nhat Hanh can only be understood with the Vietnam War as a background in which both of them continued a conversation that had already started in practice. The Buddhist monk symbolized all those monks that had suffered together with their people at the hands of the Communists and at the hands of the invading US forces. Berrigan symbolized the Christian forces of change that were not able to accept any longer that war was just and that the church should be silent in situations of injustice. Dialogue was the way forward, not only between religions but also between citizens, peoples and states.

The conversations took place in an atmosphere of prayer. A candle was burned and silence was kept until the candle was consumed then vocal conversation followed and so forth. The themes were varied but in the textual edition published in 1975 they were summarized in eight sections: memory, Eucharist and death; religion in the world; exile; priests and prisoners; self-immolation; government and religion; economics and religion; Jesus and Buddha and communities of resistance.[20]

Within the conversation about Jesus and the Buddha Berrigan was the one who mostly listened while Nhat Hahn led the conversation.[21] How to see Jesus and the Buddha, one of the topics of conversation, led to their agreement that people who are not ready 'to see' the reality of the life and example of Jesus and the Buddha do not see the reality of them.[22] Jesus and the Buddha challenged the teachings and the life of their contemporaries who at that time had strayed somehow in the path of compassion and an attitude of immersion within their contemporary societies. Jesus challenged the integrity of Judaism but suggesting that he was the Messiah and he was killed by his contemporaries while the Buddha challenged the possibility of a non-duality existence through the atman (the soul) rejecting the teaching of the Vedas.[23] There was a certain rejection in that the followers of the Buddha while sharing some of the cultural practices of Hindus needed to search for new cultural and metaphysical forms as they became different from Hindus of their time. In fact, the Buddha challenged the very existence of a caste system, the control by Brahmans of other people's lives, the treatment of the untouchables and the monopoly of spiritual teaching.[24]

However, it was clear for Nhat Hahn that contemporary Buddhism (in the twentieth century) was a collective experience rather than a personal experience of non-self as he argued that 'our karma has come together, has become collective karma. Now the action of one group affects the other group. We must choose to suffer together or be happy together, be alive together or be destroyed together'.[25] Thus, in relation to the Vietnam War Nhat Hahn and Berrigan rejected the political interest of a single group and they rejected any solution that could come from only one quarter so that the solution to the conflict could not have been located within one group only. In Buddhist terms and as expressed by Nhat Hahn: 'the relationship between self and nonself is such that the self exists only when the nonself exists'.[26]

On religious 'truths' both Berrigan and Nhat Hahn were clear that principles and doctrines are not ends but means to an end. Particularly within Buddhism the moment that a person clings to Buddhist philosophy he is not a Buddhist any longer. Nhat Hahn cited the development of fewer rules by new Buddhist communities in the midst of conflict and he cited a particular Buddhist understanding that he could adhere to: 'One should not be idolatrous or bound to any doctrine, any theory, any ideology, including Buddhist ones.'[27]

This very fruitful dialogue between a Catholic priest and a Buddhist monk was the continuation of one of the most important conversations of the twentieth century: the conversation between the monk and activist Thomas Merton and the fourteenth Dalai Lama, the subject of the following chapter.

Notes

1 Filippo De Filippi, ed. *An Account of Tibet: The Travels of Ippolito Desideri 1712–1727*, New Dehli: Rupa and Co., 2005. For a commentary on Desideri's life and mission see Trent Pomplun, *Jesuit on the Roof of the World: Ippolito Desideri's Mission to Tibet*, New York: Oxford University Press, 2009.

2 For a historic and theological reading of this period of the history of Tibet see Mario I. Aguilar, 'The Jesuits in Tibet at the Time of the VI and VII Dalai Lamas', *The Tibet Journal*, 2010/3, 35, pp. 61–77.
3 Much later the Jesuit order was dissolved by an edict of Clement XIV in 1773, with a few Jesuits surviving in Poland and Russia under the protection of Empress Catherine II.
4 For a history of the Vietnam War see Stanley Karnow, *Vietnam: A History* (rev. edn), London: Pimlico, 1994.
5 Mario I. Aguilar, 'Daniel Berrigan SJ', in *Contemplating God, Changing the World*, London: SPCK, 2008, pp. 28–40.
6 It is possible to argue that a more thorough piece of research on contemplation and politics should include Daniel and Philip Berrigan side-by-side. However, I have chosen to deal mainly with Dan Berrigan's life because he shared with his brother Philip the same intense commitment to peace and justice but he was a writer, poet and contemplative in his own right and who remained a Jesuit and a priest, thus exercising a greater influence within twentieth-century American Catholicism. Philip Berrigan (1923–2002) was ordained as a Josephite priest in late spring 1955 at a liturgical celebration that took place at the Shrine of the Immaculate Conception in Washington, DC and immediately took up his ministry as assistant pastor at Our Lady of Perpetual Help parish in the Anacostia district working with poor Afro-Americans living in very poor housing, see Murray Polner and Jim O'Grady, *Disarmed and Dangerous: The Radical Lives and Times of Daniel and Philip Berrigan*, New York: Basic Books, p. 95. In 1970 Philip Berrigan married Elizabeth McAlister, an activist sister of the Sacred Heart of Mary. They had three children: Frida (born 1 April 1974), Jerry (born 17 April 1975) and Kate (5 November 1981), see Philip Berrigan and Elizabeth McAlister, *The Time's Discipline: The Beatitudes and Nuclear Resistance*, Baltimore: Fortkamp, 1989 and Philip Berrigan with Fred A. Wilcox, *Fighting the Lamb's War: Skirmishes with the American Empire*, Monroe, ME: Common Courage Press, 1996.
7 Robert E. Daggy, ed. *Dancing in the Water of Life: Seeking Peace in the Hermitage – The Journals of Thomas Merton Volume Five 1963–1965*, New York: Harper Collins and HarperSanFrancisco, 1997, p. 253.
8 Thomas Merton, *The Seven Storey Mountain*, London: SPCK, 2009.
9 Polner and O'Grady, *Disarmed and Dangerous*, p. 107. According to Merton's diary the retreat took place in November 1964 rather than March 1965 as reported by Polner and O'Grady, see entries for 17 and 19 November 1964 in Daggy, ed. *Dancing in the Water of Life*, pp. 167–8.
10 Michael Mott, *The Seven Mountains of Thomas Merton*, London: Sheldon Press, 1986, pp. 406–7.
11 Ibid., p. 407.
12 Paul R. Dekar, 'Thomas Merton, Ghandi, the "Uprising" of Youth in the '60s, and Building Non-Violent Movements Today', *The Merton Seasonal*, 2006, 31(4), pp. 16–23 at p. 21.
13 The first Buddhist monk to immolate himself was Quang Duc, a 62 year-old who immolated himself in the streets of Saigon in 1963 and left a note requesting 'charity and compassion' from the authorities.
14 Merton's diary entry for 7 November 1965, in Daggy, ed. *Dancing in the Water of Life*, p. 313.

15 Westmoreland requested three 'force packages': 108,000 for Vietnam to arrive on 1 May 1968, the rest could be assigned in September or December, even kept in the United States if there was a shortage of troops, see Stanley Karnow, *Vietnam: A History*, London: Pimlico, p. 564.
16 Patrick O'Brien, 'Introduction', in Daniel Berrigan, *Tulips in the Prison Yard: Selected Poems of Daniel Berrigan*, Dublin: Dedalus Press, 1992, pp. 7–11 at p. 9.
17 Polner and O'Grady, *Disarmed and Dangerous*, p. 202.
18 Harvey Cox, 'Tongues of Flame: The Trial of the Catonsville Nine', in Stephen Halpert and Tom Murray, eds. *The Witness of the Berrigans*, New York: Doubleday, 1972, pp. 22–3.
19 Daniel Berrigan, *The Trial of the Catonsville Nine*, Boston: Beacon Press, 1970.
20 Thich Nhat Hanh and Daniel Berrigan, *The Raft is not the Shore: Conversations toward a Buddhist-Christian Awareness*, Maryknoll, NY: Orbis, 2001.
21 Ibid., pp. 113–21.
22 Ibid., pp. 113–14.
23 Ibid., p. 117.
24 Ibid., p. 118.
25 Ibid., p. 119.
26 Ibid., p. 120.
27 Ibid., p. 127.

Chapter 5

THOMAS MERTON AND THE DALAI LAMA

This chapter outlines three aspects of an important moment in Christian–Buddhist dialogue, Merton's encounter with the Dalai Lama in 1968: (i) the commonality of the spiritual experience, (ii) the difference of context and path and (iii) the common call to kindness and love for the stranger as outlined in the Dalai Lama's opening remarks in his Nobel Prize Lecture of 1989:

> I am always reminded that we are all basically alike: we are all human beings. Maybe we have different clothes, our skin is of a different colour, or we speak different languages. This is on the surface. But basically, we are the same human beings. That is what binds us to each other.[1]

In its conclusions this chapter outlines the possibilities of inter-faith dialogue between faith communities of the so-called world religions through (i) common contemplation, (ii) daily study of other traditions and (iii) the common service to strangers.

It is important to remember that Merton's experience and perception of any stranger, understood as somebody not being a monk or a Christian, changed throughout his life. I refer to the stranger as the person whom Merton, as a student, a teacher, a convert and a monk did not know and therefore did not have any social obligations to fulfil. It is clear that Merton, having lost his mother and father at an early age, did not have the experience of the stranger in the streets until he moved to New York City and experienced the mass of human beings that he did not know. His schooling at Oakham School and at Clare College, Cambridge, made his life sheltered and secluded together with students who became in both cases his own extended family. In New York, and particularly at Columbia University he found others searching for God and his experience as a convert made him find a universal home in the Catholic Church and a particular home at the Abbey of Gethsemani in Kentucky where he became a Trappist. Within those changing circumstances and by the 1960s Merton found akin concerns towards 'the stranger' in the concerns for the church in the world discussed and ratified by Vatican II while the stranger in other religions, and particularly the world religions of the East, remained Merton's interest up to his death in December 1968. Dialogue became for him that mysterious encounter with strangers.

Merton's Monastic Experience of the Stranger

The 'monastic experience' of the stranger is rather different than others because monks do not have a daily contact with the passing crowds trying to get to underground stations or the homeless begging on a street corner. Indeed, the early experience of Merton as a visitor to the Abbey of Gethsemani made such an impression on him that he certainly found his Christian vocation in monasticism due to the immediacy of the experience of being a stranger. However, such a stranger was welcomed within a community that he did not know and by a monastic group that did not ask questions about his personal identity or his own likes or dislikes. Some of those strangers became monks, thus in turn they became strangers no more. Within the monastic setting all visitors, passers-by and those making retreats were welcomed by the fact that any of them and indeed all of them could represent the person of Christ as clearly stated in the Rule of St Benedict: 'Let all guests who arrive be received like Christ, for He is going to say, "I came as a guest and you received me".'[2]

Indeed, Merton's own personal anxiety came from the fact that he had been told by a confessor that he should not become a priest while his inner core longed for a family, a belonging to God and to a religious community. As he arrived for the first time at the abbey of Gethsemani the Trappist monk who opened the door for him asked him: 'Have you come here to stay?' Merton firmly replied in the negative even after the monk's second attempt by asking 'What's the matter? Why can't you stay? Are you married or something?'[3]

Merton's Ecclesial Experience of the Stranger

Much later and through his correspondence with other Catholics concerned with ecclesial reform Merton became one of the leaders of a new opening towards the stranger within the Catholic Church. Nevertheless, he also found himself sharing the same concerns of a large number of Council Fathers gathered in Rome for the Second Vatican Council who asked questions about the possible role of the church in the contemporary world.[4] One could argue that before Vatican II polemics and apologetics were central to the Catholic experience, thus any possible acceptance of other religious ways of life were considered detrimental to the Catholic truth, ways to be rejected as unholy. John XXIII in his speech calling a new council in 1959 opened the possibility of a 'Church of the poor' in which those who had been considered strangers could be considered part of God's mysterious plan of contemporary life and eternal salvation.[5] By the early 1960s Merton had already experienced the beauty of strangers who had visited the abbey and he had engaged with many non-Catholics who were writers, academics, mystics and public figures in their own right. Thus, the impatient Merton who complained about monastic structures and wanted desperately to live the life of a hermit was not troubled by diversity. Instead, he was very curious about other human and religious practices as well as other religious ways of practicing the love of God and neighbour or a human life of compassion and abstinence without a concept of God, for example Buddhism.

Very few passages concerning the uniqueness of truth, human or religious, are to be found in his writings, among those his reflections and meditations published in the mid-1960s.[6] One of them describes his possible cynicism towards truth as an absolute, as an obstacle to meet the stranger and those different than him, thoughts outlined within a whole section of thoughts about truth and violence:

> We are all convinced that we desire the truth above all. Nothing strange about this. It is natural to man, an intelligent being, to desire the truth. (I still dare to speak of man as 'an intelligent being'!) But actually, what we desire is not 'the truth' so much as 'to be in the right'. To seek the pure truth for its own sake may be natural to us, but we are not able to act always in this respect according to our nature. What we seek is not the pure truth, but the partial truth that justifies our prejudices, our limitations, our selfishness. This is not 'the truth'. It is only an argument strong enough to prove us 'right'. And usually our desire to be right is correlative to our conviction that somebody else (perhaps everybody else) is wrong.[7]

Merton's opening to the contemporary issues that challenged Catholicism during the 1960s was triggered by his avid spiritual and intellectual curiosity but was supported by the climate of opening to other religions discussed at the Second Vatican Council. There is no doubt that in exploring the stranger Merton found an affirmation to his own contentment towards monastic life; eventually, his solitary life and his search for other ways of encountering God or the monastic experience associated with Buddhism affirmed him in his own vocation. This monastic contentment on the part of Merton did not assume spiritual stagnation but a continuous challenge to the possibility of a non-changeable Cistercian way of life expressed in Merton's unfailing support for new ways of monasticism – among these the new monastic life suggested and later implemented by Merton's former novice, Ernesto Cardenal, in Nicaragua.[8]

Indeed, Merton disliked formality and even the formalism of new documents of renewal that were coming out of Vatican II. For example, during October 1964 the readings in the refectory of the Abbey of Gethsemani included the Bulletin of the Liturgical Commission and the Congregation of Rites related to liturgical changes for the 1965 season of Lent. Merton liked the liturgical changes but after the reading of such a formal liturgical document asked 'How can we have "renewal" with such elaborate formalities as this?'[9]

Regardless of Merton's anxieties the final documents of Vatican II included major changes in liturgical practice, the use of the vernacular and other new informal practices. However, the major shift incorporated by the Council was the immediate change of all strangers into human beings in relation with the Church, even all those not in communion with the Church. Thus, the opening of the Pastoral Constitution of the Church in the Modern World remains a clear statement, a clear blueprint that makes strangers into fellow human beings dear to God and dear to the Church when it proclaims that,

> The joy and hope, the grief and anguish of the men of our time, especially of those who are poor or afflicted in any way, are the joy and hope, the grief and anguish of the followers of Christ as well. Nothing that is genuinely human fails to find an echo in their hearts.[10]

On the area of inter-faith dialogue and relations with other world religions Vatican II produced a very forward-looking declaration stating that,

> The Catholic Church rejects nothing of what is true and holy in these religions. She has a high regard for the manner of life and conduct, the precepts and doctrines which, although differing in many ways from her own teaching, nevertheless often reflect a ray of that truth which enlightens all men.[11]

Vatican II made a particular positive description of Buddhism in the same document and in the following terms,

> Buddhism in its various forms testifies to the essential inadequacy of this changing world. It proposes a way of life by which men can, with confidence and trust, attain a state of perfect liberation and reach supreme illumination either through their own efforts or by the aid of divine help.[12]

Merton's trip to Asia became, in the spirit of the Council, a journey of love in which one of the most prominent Catholics in the United States journeyed to the only continent where Christianity was and still is a minority in order to learn about the joys and hopes of religious practitioners within Asia and to engage himself in dialogue with the strangers of the past, fellow pilgrims and fellow human beings of the present and the future. Merton assumed the challenges of the modern world stating very clearly that 'It is the peculiar office of the monk in the modern world to keep alive the contemplative experience and to keep the way open for modern technological man to recover the integrity of his own inner depths'.¹³

Merton's Tibetan Experience of the Stranger

Merton's trip to Asia came about due to an invitation extended by a Benedictine working group that was helping the possible implementation of renewal throughout the world as required by the Second Vatican Council. The idea was to gather in a conference all Asian monastic leaders, including Benedictines and Cistercians, in Bangkok (Thailand) in December 1968. Merton agreed to address the Spiritual Summit Conference in Calcutta and to give a series of talks at different monasteries in Asia. However, he also wanted to visit as many Buddhist monasteries as possible so that according to his secretary Brother Patrick Hart, 'Thomas Merton's pilgrimage to Asia was an effort on his part to deepen his own religious and monastic commitment'.¹⁴

It cannot be underestimated that Merton's position was unusual on three counts: dialogue with other world religions was not the norm in a pre-Vatican II climate of Catholicism, Cistercian monks did not undertake speaking tours for weeks without end and the Cold War and the Vietnam War created an ever more insular United States in which US citizens were certainly discouraged from visiting Asia, a continent that at that time was being swept by Chinese Communists and the influence of the Soviet Union in many emerging socialist-oriented regimes. However, and despite this international climate of war Merton had a sustained interest in Asian monasticism and had read extensively on Zen and Buddhism in general.¹⁵ If he had not died in December 1968 it is possible to argue that Merton would have done groundbreaking work in interfaith Christian–Buddhist relations. His Asian trip was authorized by his abbot so as to report back on the possibilities of a Cistercian expansion of monastic communities in Asia; this despite the fact that Merton's abbot had little confidence on the practicality of Merton as a decision-maker. It is a fact that on a previous occasion Merton had explored the possibilities of founding monastic communities in Alaska and due to the fact that he visited Alaska during summer he had missed the point that during winter the visibility due to bad weather and fog was nil. If the Cistercians had followed Merton's advice to push for a monastic foundation in Alaska it would have been quite a surprise to the founding monks that they could not have been able to see anything around them during winter.

Throughout his visit to Asia Merton kept a diary that was published later. The highlight of his visit was the visit to the fourteenth Dalai Lama in Dharamsala, India, and the addresses he gave to other Cistercians and Benedictines in Bangkok.[16] It is striking throughout his diary how conversant with Buddhist and Sanskrit terminology Merton was and how all his conversations related to monastic issues and his personal search for further solitude. Thus, after days of visiting places and people he could only think that he needed a few days of solitude. Maybe because of this personal reason the visit to Dharamsala where the headquarters of the Tibetan government on exile and the residence the fourteenth Dalai Lama are still located became the highlight of his Asian trip.[17]

Merton and the fourteenth Dalai Lama

Merton and the Dalai Lama met three times during November 1968.[18] The fourteenth Dalai Lama had fled Tibet, now the Tibet Autonomous Region of China, in March 1959 and had sought political asylum in India establishing over years his government in exile and a very large Tibetan community with temples and schools at the Himalayan town of Dharamsala in northern India. In 1968 'Little Lhasa', as the town is today known, was still small and the Dalai Lama had not had the publicity and world recognition that he was given after receiving the Nobel Prize for Peace in 1989. The prize was given to him because of 'his consistent opposition to the use of violence and his efforts to seek peaceful solutions, based on tolerance and mutual respect, in order to preserve the historical and cultural heritage of his people'.[19] Indeed, Tibetan Buddhism was less-known than today and over the 1960s Western seekers were more familiar with Zen Buddhism and the forms of self-enlightenment rather than the possibilities of enlightenment for all sentient beings through personal meditation as is the aim of Tibetan Buddhism.

Merton was brought to the Dalai Lama by Harold Talbott, an American student of Buddhism who at that time was studying with the Dalai Lama. Talbott had been a student at Harvard University and while studying there had become a Catholic. Talbott had made contact with Merton at Gethsemani and had been confirmed at the abbey. Merton stayed at the bungalow that the Dalai Lama had assigned to Talbott and after the scheduled meetings with the Dalai Lama Talbott accompanied Merton to Darjeeling where they parted on 24 November 1968.[20]

The meetings between Merton and the Dalai Lama took place at the Dalai Lama's quarters in McLeod Ganj, a small Himalayan enclave located on the hills above Dharamsala, described by Merton as 'admirably situated, high over the valley, with snow-covered mountains behind, all pine trees, with apes in them, and a vast view over the plains to the south'.[21] As Merton waited to enter the Dalai Lama's meeting room he noticed that there were shelves with Buddhist works presented to the Dalai Lama by his friend D. T. Suzuki.[22] Their first meeting on 4 November 1968 dealt with religion, philosophy and ways of meditating and Merton listened attentively to the importance of Tibetan Buddhism somehow criticized by other more traditional Buddhist schools of thought and practice.[23] Merton's knowledge of Tibetan Buddhism must have been good because they discussed *dzogchen*, the 'great perfection', the Great Way of All-inclusiveness and the esoteric tradition of the Nyingmapas order of Tibetan Buddhism, a tradition that goes back to the eighth century when great teachers such as Guru Padma Sambhava (Swat Valley) and Vimalamitra (India) visited Tibet. *Dzogchen* constitutes a very direct way to knowledge and the Dalai Lama told Merton 'not to misunderstand the simplicity of *dzogchen*'.[24]

Their second meeting took place on 6 November 1968 and they discussed epistemology and the mind, particularly Tibetan and Western-Thomist theories.[25] Later, they discussed meditation and the Dalai Lama showed Merton the essential position for meditation in Tibetan Buddhism whereby 'the right hand (discipline) is above the left (wisdom)', while in Zen Buddhism it is the other way around.[26] Merton commented on the Dalai Lama's way of thinking as follows: 'I like the solidity of the Dalai Lama's ideas. He is a very consecutive thinker and moves from step to step. His ideas of the interior life are built on very solid foundations and on a real awareness of practical problems'.[27]

Their third meeting took place on 8 November 1968 and they discussed Western monastic life, vows, dietary prohibitions, etc.[28] Merton raised the point of monasticism and Marxism, the topic he was to develop in his Bangkok lecture and the Dalai Lama, who admired Marxism, suggested that 'from a certain point of view it was impossible for monks and Communists to get along, but that perhaps it should not be entirely impossible *if* Marxism meant *only* the establishment of an equitable economic and social structure'.[29] It is clear that Merton's diaries only provide a short sketch of their conversations and that the actual sense of a personal conversation is missing for the readers and would have been expanded by Merton later in writings and conferences. However, it is possible to suggest that at the end of Merton's conversations with the Dalai Lama there was a natural closeness and a spiritual bond between them. Later, the Dalai Lama in his own autobiography recognized that the death of Merton had deprived the world of the possibility of a meaningful dialogue between Christians and Buddhists with all their ongoing similarities.[30] It is clear that the meetings between Merton and the Dalai Lama had provided a sign of Vatican II's clear statement to the effect that all human beings 'form but one community'.[31]

Merton's Destruction of the Stranger

When in 1995 the fourteenth Dalai Lama visited Merton's grave at Gethsemani he meditated in front of Merton's grave accompanied by Abbot Timothy Kelly OCSO.[32] In the eyes of those present, three decades later the conversation between Merton and the fourteenth Dalai Lama was resumed. In the words of Tenzin Gyatso (the fourteenth Dalai Lama): 'I am now in touch with his spirit'.[33] The fact is that the conversations about the spiritual path that had taken place between Merton and the Dalai Lama made them aware of *a common spiritual experience*. The commonality did not come from the possibility of discussing notions of a divine being, as Buddhists do not uphold creation out of an act by a divine being but from a notion of emptiness. The spiritual commonality of a Buddhist monk and that of a Cistercian monk lies in the act of self-emptying. For the Buddhist the emptying conduces to an awareness of the power of the mind in fostering enlightenment and in the particular case of Tibetan Buddhists such an emptying conduces to an attitude of compassion and communion with all sentient beings, human and animal alike. For the Cistercian monk the act of self-emptying comes from the giving of oneself to God and to a community with the monastic stability of not leaving a particular group of monks for the rest of one's life.

Tsong-Kha-Pa (1357–1419), founder of the Gelug school of Tibetan Buddhism, the order of the Dalai Lama, stated clearly within the instructions for daily meditation that the following supplication should be recited many times: 'Please bless all living beings'.[34] The daily reality of meditation which in Buddhism is not the sole realm of the celibate monk creates the possibility of an opening to others and indeed to all, even enemies who through their hostile actions teach the Buddhist practitioner about the realities of suffering, the causes and the remedies to all human suffering.[35] Unlike Zen Buddhism dear to Merton the practitioner locates herself in the realm of all sentient beings so that Soname Yangchen, a Tibetan singer on exile, asserts quite clearly the aim of her daily meditation as follows:

> I prayed for the end of suffering for all sentient beings. I visualised my family, my friends, my enemies and as many faceless strangers as I could sitting around me, and 'saw' the Buddha emanating streams of healing golden light, fillings us with love, compassion and wisdom.[36]

In this respect the experience of the contemplative Catholic, a Cistercian monk, is not different from a Buddhist as he seeks the love and manifestation of God through meditation. However, a common spiritual experience between a

Buddhist monk and a Catholic monk does not mean that their contexts and paths are identical. Merton and the Dalai Lama shared the common call of all human beings to acknowledge a spiritual path and a spiritual experience that makes all human beings share *a common path through different contexts*. This common call is expressed in the Buddhist compassion for all sentient beings and in the Christian love for all human beings – both realized through the hospitality shown by members of monastic communities to visitors – merely strangers in need of affirmation and in need of human examples of an ongoing appreciation of a spiritual world that becomes real and tangible through the experience of practitioners. Those practitioners such as Merton do not solely show *the kindness and compassion to strangers* but in doing so over a period of time minimized and finally destroyed the possibility of perceiving other human beings as 'strangers'.

The lessons of the encounter between Merton and the Dalai Lama remain central to contemporary life in that in a globalized society and a globalized spiritual experience there is an inherent danger: not to perceive other strangers kindly. Merton's challenge is to destroy once and for all that category of 'otherness' and to replace it with an ongoing commonality that surpasses all differences and that is dictated by a daily search for the spiritual and for the contemplative experience of a common 'otherness' in every stranger. It is Merton's example of study of other faiths and service to the stranger in our lives that remains a challenge for many contemporary Christians and Buddhists. This challenge becomes central to a globalized world to which the writings of Merton and his Asian journey have still a lot to offer. In Merton's words: 'attention must be concentrated on what is really essential to the monastic quest: this, I think, is to be sought in the area of true self-transcendence and enlightenment'.[37] These words and understanding remain central to contemporary reflections on relations between Christian and Buddhists as strangers today.

Thus, on 8 September 1966 he took a formal commitment to the hermitic life. This new path, much wanted by Merton over previous years, gave him the possibility of structuring his day around prayer, house activities, reading and writing. Immediately after taking up life as a hermit he studied and wrote significant essays on Albert Camus, published collectively after his death in the volume *Literary Essays of Thomas Merton*.[38]

The Bangkok Lecture

It was the day of his death in the retreat centre in Bangkok on 10 December 1968 that Merton delivered the last conference of his life with the title 'Marxism and

Monastic Activities'.[39] During 1968 Merton had been attending a conference at the Center for the study of Democratic Institutions in Santa Barbara, California, where the participants were revolutionary university leaders from France, Italy, Germany and the Low Countries.[40] In informal conversation with them Merton had discussed monasticism and Marxism and one of the French students told him: 'We are also monks'.[41] It is unclear to me why Merton thought that this student and others were saying to him: 'We are the true monks. You are not the true monks; we are the true monks' but this is the statement that Merton takes very seriously for his reflection on monks, Marxists and monasticism.[42] Merton opened the lecture by arguing that a young monk in a process of 'identity crisis' needs to ask about his identity in all contemporary contexts, including that of a dialogue and a challenge by a Marxist.[43] Merton concerned himself not with orthodox Marxism or the early writings by Karl Marx or with the political application of Marxism or the application of Marxist thought in the 1917 Soviet Revolution but with what he called 'a kind of mystique of Marxism'.[44] He relied heavily on a neo-Marxist interpretation of Marx by Herbert Marcuse, the 'father of the new left' in the United States, whom he regarded as 'a kind of monastic thinker' and with 'the monastic implications of Marcuse at the present moment'.[45]

Merton's shift from introducing the name of Marcuse to the text of his lecture is quite staggering. Merton is concerned with an author and a Marxist who was influential in the minds and lives of the youth and of the intellectuals in the West rather than the East within a common theme or social or theoretical problem: that of alienation in society.[46] Marcuse as a university professor made a tremendous impact by supporting and taking part in students' protests of the 1960s. Those young minds in the universities and Marxists alike influenced by Marcuse argued that the choices, 'significant choices', could no longer be made in organized societies led by capitalism or under Soviet influences but are made by individuals who escape a state of personal alienation.[47]

Merton's emphasis on the possibilities of changing a human being rather than institutions allowed him to deliver a lecture on a topic that could have seemed to be completely out of place within a conference attended by contemplative leaders. Merton's genius showed precisely the unexpected. It is the discipline of neo-Marxists to challenge structures that Merton was identifying himself with despite the fact that institutions were identified with social phenomena such as the Soviet Revolution and the reform of monasticism within mediaeval time as well as the social reforms fostered by the Second Vatican Council.

In delivering a lecture to the intellectual minds of Asia Merton, backed by Marcuse as 'a monastic thinker', made a formal address, a referential testament of his personal concerns that was very different in its form than Merton's writings and his style of addressing participants of his conferences. He told his audience:

> I am addressing myself to the monk who is potentially open to contact with the intellectual, the university student, the university professor, the people who are thinking along lines that are going to change both Western and Eastern society and create the world of the future, in which inevitably we are going to have to make our adaptation.[48]

If those were Merton's initial words the last words of the conference were 'so I will disappear', giving a dramatic exit from Merton's conference and an end to a life of spoken words. It was a fitting end to a lecture that was a kind of testament of contemplation and material–human activity, of Christianity and Marxism, of renewal and continuity, a truly dialectic conference.[49] I cannot help relating Merton's lecture and the farewell of another Marxist such as Marcuse, Salvador Allende, who exited a few years later on the day of the Chilean military coup. On 11 September 1973 Allende remained at the Chilean Presidential Palace of La Moneda as the plotting troops surrounded the palace and as the bombardment continued he addressed particular people as Merton did – in the formal way of a historical occasion that needs to be marked by formalized words, delivered for history.[50] In part of his final address through the Chilean Magallanes Radio Allende spoke thus:

> I am addressing myself to the humble woman of this land, to the female worker who worked harder, to the mother who understood our concern for children. I am addressing myself to professionals of this land, patriot professionals, those who until recently were challenging the fascist attitudes of the professional colleges [. . .] I am addressing myself to the youth, those who sang, those who offered their happiness and their fighting spirit [. . .] I am addressing myself to the Chilean man, to the worker, to the peasant, to the intellectual and those who will be persecuted [. . .].[51]

The form of public address used by Allende was so closed to that of Merton that one could only suggest that it follows the pattern of those who are about to die giving up their life for their ideals. Indeed, Merton's last conference has been discussed by Mertonean scholars who have suggested that it was a farewell to fellow contemplatives rather than a teaching moment by a wise teacher. As Marcuse and Allende did previously, Merton located himself in the place of the young looking for identity and felt that the professionals and intellectuals, despised by spiritualists, traditional Marxists and capitalists were the ones who could hear the words, who could 'listen' as in the beginning of the Rule of St Benedict and continue to carry the torch by changing themselves first and then the structures that sheltered them.

It is this possibility of removing 'alienation' from religious practice and academic life that united Merton and Marcuse. Merton's lecture outlined the particular contribution of the Jesuit Teilhard de Chardin, banned from publishing by the Vatican, because of his thought on the material world, studied and accepted by Marxist scholars.[52] For Marxism, with its emphasis on materialism, all knowledge and action are centred on matter. Thus, an understanding of economic processes is much needed in order to, in turn, understand the development of human beings.[53] This was a bold statement by Merton as Teilhard had been silenced because of the challenges that his non-linear reading of the book of Genesis had for the Catholic doctrine of original sin. However, Merton recognized in his lecture that there were three disciplines that were of Marxist conceptions of society's understanding because of their avoidance of the centrality of matter: religion, philosophy and politics.[54] Merton's dialogue with Marxism indicated that those disciplines were unified by a critique of the established and traditional Marxism and Christianity. Those establishments had made religion and politics oppressive for the aspirations of those who did not participate in a capitalistic world of profit, earnings and power/control over souls in a process of 'alienation' that once again unified neo-Marxists and progressive contemplatives within the church.

According to Merton the contribution that was important for a real movement towards Christian-Marxist dialogue was the contribution of Buddhist and Christian monks, contemplatives within religious traditions in which the building of monastic communities starts with the making of a person from the inside, indeed it starts 'with man's own consciousness'.[55] 'Ignorance' in Buddhism and 'alienation' in Marxism find their negative equivalent in the ignorance of 'myth' where everything is explained through 'myth', for example the case of 'original sin'.[56] Merton is clear in this point that he is not trying to discredit the doctrine of original sin but that this explanation has been used to explain all sorts of unexplained points of ignorance (Merton is afraid here that he could be labelled a heretic together with Teilhard de Chardin). Thus, the concept of ignorance of Christianity is very similar to ignorance in Buddhism as both traditions suggest an inability to seek enlightenment and a more solid explanation that arises out of the self. Merton argues very concretely that Christian and Buddhist monks share the same purpose of the traditional religions, religions that 'begin with the consciousness of the individual, seek to transform and liberate the truth in each person, with the idea that it will then communicate itself to others'.[57]

The monk, Christian or Buddhist, 'dwells in the centre of society as one who has attained realization', 'he has come to experience the ground of his own being in such a way that he knows the secret of liberation and can somehow or other communicate this to others'.[58] Ultimately, monastic life connects with Marxism because the way of monastic learning is a change, in traditional Augustinian terms, from *cupiditas* into *caritas*, from self-centred love into an outgoing selfish love.[59] In the case of Marxism and in Merton's analysis there is a change from capitalist greed to communal communism in a material order in which each one gives according to capacities and receives according to needs.[60] However, for Merton the only place where this communist sharing can be done and realized is in a monastery.[61]

Merton finally gets to some conclusions in his lecture and he argues very strongly that monasticism and the act of learning how to love remain central to human life despite monastic institutions because monastic institutions can fade away but the human inner longing for transformation and for a school of love remains.[62] For Merton this school of monasticism respects plurality, it learns from other traditions and asserts the possibility of a religious commitment based on compassion and not on ignorance. Religious diversity and the school of love become for Merton the path of monasticism and of Christian life. Marxism, and the work of Marcuse, even when poorly developed in Merton's lecture brings the materiality of love for others and for other religious traditions because it is in contact with others and with respect for the world religions that the call to contemplation takes place. In other words, it brings Christianity to appreciate dialogue with other religious traditions.

That call to love and to exercise a school of love becomes a Christian call that does not remain isolated in Christianity but it is a call for all other world religions. Thus, in another essay of his Asian journey Merton wrote about the Bhagavad-Gita, the sacred Hindu text, and concluded: 'The *Gita*, like the Gospels, teaches us to live in awareness of an inner truth that exceeds the grasp of our thought and cannot be subject to our own control'.[63] It is love that brings war to a dialectic materialist dialogue in the *Gita*, it is love that brings the Christian to learn and to cooperate with Marxists and practitioners of other world religions. Merton's prayer at the First Spiritual Summit Conference in Calcutta says it all. Merton prayed from a text saying 'I ask you to concentrate on the love that is in you, that is in us all' and later in his prayer *ad libidum* Merton asserted 'You witness to the ultimate reality that is love. Love has overcome. Love is victorious'.[64]

Contemplation and Dialogue

Merton's stress on Marxist theory in his Thailand lecture related not to a fashion but to his own engagement with philosophical thought that was central for the 1968 understanding of the world. French Marxism of the neo-Marxist strand of Louis Althusser had dominated a new kind of material understanding of political action in French and American society of that time.[65] The French Communist Party, still very strong, was keen to reactivate the power of the unions and a change of outlook in French institutions aided intellectuals and theoreticians. The 1968 discussions and consequent protests about the role of French universities pushed a certain immediacy for Marxist French theory. For it was clear that French Marxism was independent from the Soviet Union and that the Russian Revolution centralized political power. At the same time French Marxism opposed the American model of society based on antagonisms of the Cold War and a trickledown of economic benefits for the infrastructure of society through a private sense of the financial capital.

Political activity within French Marxism was people-centred and even challenged the power of the state by incorporating intellectuals and thinkers who by doing the same became parts of the infrastructure (in Marxist vocabulary) and not of the supra-structure. For it was knowledge given to all that changed the state and not the elimination of intellectuals who were being perceived as members of an oppressive structure. Once education was given to all intellectuals, thinkers and writers changed theoretically from the oppressive supra-structure into the liberating infrastructure. Thus, the change was theoretical within neo-Marxism and not pragmatic. Change was inherent in the realm of the imagination of social institutions rather than in the return to the original Marxist understandings of the nineteenth century or the hard applications based on the totalitarian experience of the Soviet Union and the People's Republic of China (aspect of French Marxism criticized by Althusser).

Merton's use of Marxism in a lecture to other contemplatives set a pace for dialogue that was rather different than solely a path of renewal stressed and normatively implemented by Vatican II. He referred to Marxism as a philosophical and materialistic view of the world that centred in 'matter'. Marxism did not outline a change of social structures as the only solution to society, to religion or to politics but a change in one's heart and experience: the des-alienation of the 'new man', a 'new man' fostered by socialist projects such as that of Salvador Allende in 1970s Chile as well as mentioned by the apostle Paul in relation to baptism and a new life in Christ. Thus, Merton's 'impressionistic treatment' of Marxism realized what others had not managed to accept: the correlation of the change of self over structures in Marxism, Christianity, Buddhism and Hinduism.[66]

In the same year and within the Latin American context a dialogue with Marxism and other religious traditions had taken place. The renewal of the Church fostered by Vatican II had influenced the possibilities of dialogue and liberation in Latin America through the implementation of a pastoral preference for the poor and the marginalized.

Notes

1 The fourteenth Dalai Lama, 'The Nobel Peace Prize Lecture, Oslo, Norway', in Sidney Piburn, ed. *The Dalai Lama: A Policy of Kindness – An Anthology of Writings by and about the Dalai Lama*, Ithaca, NY: Snow Lion Publications, 1990, pp. 15–25 at p. 15.
2 *The Rule of Saint Benedict*, 53, cf. Mt. 25.35.
3 Thomas Merton, *The Seven Storey Mountain*, London: SPCK, 1990, p. 321.
4 See Austin Flannery OP, ed. *Vatican Council II: The Conciliar and Post Conciliar Documents*, Northport, NY: Costello and Grand Rapids, MI: William B. Eerdmans, 1992.
5 See Pope John XXIII speech calling a council on 25 March 1959 when he spoke of 'the Church of the poor' and his own will under the section 'My last will concerning things which belong to me as patriarch of Venice' he wrote 'My crosses and rings likewise are to be sold so as to fetch the highest possible price and the proceeds from these also given to the poor in whatever seems the most suitable form', Castel Gandolfo, 12 September 1961, in Pope John XXIII, *Journal of a Soul*, London: Geoffrey Chapman, 1980, p. 370.
6 Thomas Merton, *Conjectures of a Guilty Bystander*, New York and London: Image Books Doubleday, 1989, part II 'Truth and Violence: An Interesting Era', pp. 63–128.
7 Thomas Merton, *Conjectures of a Guilty Bystander*, p. 78.
8 See ongoing correspondence between Cardenal and Merton in *Del Monasterio al Mundo: Correspondencia entre Ernesto Cardenal y Thomas Merton*, Santiago, Chile: Editorial Cuarto Propio, 1998 and materials related to the experimental lay contemplative community founded by Cardenal on the Nicaraguan island of Solentiname in Ernesto Cardenal, *El Evangelio en Solentiname*, Salamanca: Ediciones Sígueme, 1976 and *El Evangelio en Solentiname: Volumen Segundo*, Salamanca: Ediciones Sígueme, 1978, see also Mario I. Aguilar, *The History and Politics of Latin American Theology* I, London: SCM Press, 2007, chapter 5, pp. 91–104.
9 30 October 1964 in Robert E. Daggy, ed. *Dancing in the Water of Life: Seeking Peace in The Hermitage*, The Journals of Thomas Merton, vol. 5, 1963–1965, New York: HarperSanFrancisco, 1997, p. 159.
10 *Gaudium et Spes* 1.
11 *Nostra Aetate* § 2.
12 Ibid.
13 'Monastic Experience and East-West Dialogue: Notes for a paper to have been delivered at Calcutta, October 1968', see Appendix IV, *The Asian Journal of Thomas Merton*, New York: New Directions, 1975, pp. 309–17 at p. 317, cf. John Eudes Bamberger OCSO, *Thomas Merton: Prophet of Renewal*, Kalamazoo, MI: Cistercian Publications, 2005, p. 18.
14 Brother Patrick Hart, 'Foreword' in *The Asian Journal of Thomas Merton*, New York: New Directions, 1975, p. xxiii.
15 During the 1960s Merton had corresponded with many scholars of Hinduism and Buddhism, see for example William Apel, 'There Comes a Time: The Interfaith Letters of Thomas Merton and Dona Luisa Coomaraswamy', in *The Merton Journal*, 2006, 13(2), pp. 11–18 and *Signs of Peace: The Interfaith Letters of Thomas Merton*, Maryknoll, NY: Orbis, 2006.

16 Diary notes published as *The Asian Journal of Thomas Merton*, New York: New Directions, 1975.
17 The fourteenth Dalai Lama Tenzin Gyatso was born into a peasant family in Amdo, eastern Tibet in 1935 and after being identified as the incarnation of the previous Dalai Lama at the age of 2 he was moved to Lhasa at the age of 4. With the Chinese occupation of Tibet the political situation changed and after the Tibetan National Uprising on 10 March 1959 the Dalai Lama left Tibet and moved to India where he was granted refugee status. Over the years thousands of Tibetan refugees crossed into India and the Dalai Lama managed to establish monasteries as well as his government in a Dharamsala where he met Merton in 1968. For a detailed account of the Dalai Lama's life see Michael Harris Goodman, *The Last Dalai Lama: A Biography*, London: Sidgwick and Jackson, 1986.
18 See Thomas Merton, *November Circular Letter to Friends*, New Delhi, India, 9 November 1968, published as 'Appendix VI', in *The Asian Journal of Thomas Merton*, pp. 320–5; Merton's visit is also mentioned in Goodman, *The Last Dalai Lama*, p. 325.
19 William H. Shannon, Christine M. Bochen and Patrick F. O'Connell, *The Thomas Merton Encyclopedia*, Maryknoll, NY: Orbis, 2002, pp. 98–9 at p. 98.
20 See William H. Shannon, 'Talbott, Harold', in William H. Shannon, Christine M. Bochen and Patrick F. O'Connell, *The Thomas Merton Encyclopedia*, Maryknoll, NY: Orbis, 2002, p. 462.
21 *The Asian Journal of Thomas Merton*, p. 100. The same description of the meetings as published in Merton's *Asian Journal* has been also included in the last volume of Merton's personal diaries, see Patrick Hart OCSO, ed. *The Other Side of the Mountain: The End of the Journey*, The Journals of Thomas Merton VII 1967–1968, New York: HarperSanFrancisco, 1998, pp. 249–66.
22 Daisetz Teitaro Suzuki (1870–1966) was a Japanese scholar who interpreted Buddhism, and particularly Zen Buddhism, for the West and Christianity for the East. Merton met him in 1964 when Zuzuki lectured at Columbia University, see 'Zen', in William H. Shannon, Christine M. Bochen and Patrick F. O'Connell, *The Thomas Merton Encyclopedia*, Maryknoll, NY: Orbis, 2002, pp. 546–8.
23 'November 4/Afternoon', in *The Asian Journal of Thomas Merton*, pp. 100–2.
24 *The Asian Journal of Thomas Merton*, p. 102.
25 Ibid., pp. 112–13.
26 Ibid., p. 112.
27 Ibid., p. 113.
28 Ibid., pp. 124–5.
29 Ibid., p. 125. On the Dalai Lama and Marxism see The fourteenth Dalai Lama's, *Freedom in Exile: The Autobiography of His Holiness the Dalai Lama of Tibet*, London: Hodder & Stoughton, 1990, pp. 98–9, 251 and particularly p. 296 where he confesses that 'in as much as I have any political allegiance, I suppose I am still half Marxist' and 'the other attractive thing about Marxism for me is its assertion that man is ultimately responsible for his own destiny. This reflects Buddhist thought exactly'.
30 The Dalai Lama writes about 'Father Thomas Merton, the American Benedictine Monk', see The fourteenth Dalai Lama's, *Freedom in Exile*, pp. 207–8. See also Joseph Quinn Raab, 'Comrades for Peace: Thomas Merton, The Dalai Lama and the Preferential Option for Nonviolence', in Victor A. Kramer and David Belcastro, eds.

The Merton Annual: Studies in Culture, Spirituality and Social Concerns, vol. 19, Louisville, KY: Fons Vitae, 2006, pp. 255–66.
31 *Nostra Aetate* § 1, cf. Acts 17.26.
32 Photograph available in Shannon, Bochen and O'Connell, *The Thomas Merton Encyclopedia*, p. 99.
33 'Dalai Lama (Tenzin Gyatso)', in William H. Shannon, Christine M. Bochen and Patrick F. O'Connell, *The Thomas Merton Encyclopedia*, Maryknoll, NY: Orbis, 2002, pp. 98–9 at p. 99.
34 Tsong-Kha-Pa, Lam Rim Chen Mo – The Great Treatise on the Stages of the Path to Enlightenment, Volume I, IV A 2a, translation by The Lamrim Chenmo Translation Committee, Joshua E. C. Cutler, editor-in-chief, and Guy Newland, ed. Ithaca, NY: Snow Lion Publications, 2000, p. 99.
35 This daily practice is made clear in a recent autobiography of a Tibetan woman in exile in Britain when she writes: 'Whatever my work schedule, though, every day I woke up at 4 am to say my prayers and perform my meditation, as I had done since I lived with the Dalai Lama in Dharamsala', in Soname Yangchen with Vicki Mackenzie, *Child of Tibet: The Story of Soname's Flight to Freedom*, London: Portrait, 2007, p. 143.
36 Soname Yangchen with Vicki Mackenzie, *Child of Tibet*, p. 143.
37 Thomas Merton, 'Monastic Experience and East-West Dialogue: Notes for a paper to have been delivered at Calcutta, October 1968', see Appendix IV, *The Asian Journal of Thomas Merton*, pp. 309–17 at p. 316 § 9.
38 Thomas Merton, *The Literary Essays of Thomas Merton*, New York: New Directions, 1981.
39 Father Louis OCSO (Thomas Merton), 'Marxism and Monastic Activities', Talk delivered at Bangkok on 10 December 1968, in Naomi Burton, Br. Patrick Heart and James Laughlin, eds. *The Asian Journal of Thomas Merton*, New York: New Directions, 1975, pp. 326–43.
40 Burton, Heart and Laughlin, eds. *The Asian Journal of Thomas Merton*, pp. 328–9.
41 Ibid., p. 329.
42 Ibid.
43 Ibid., p. 326.
44 Ibid., p. 327.
45 Ibid.
46 Herbert Marcuse (1898–1978) was born in Berlin and completed his doctorate at the University of Freiburg in 1922. After a spell in Berlin he returned to Freiburg where he prepared his habitation with Martin Heidegger. As he could not complete his project under the Nazis he worked at the Frankfurt Institute for Social Research and immigrated to Switzerland in 1933 and later to the United States where he became a citizen in 1940. During World War II he worked for the US Office of Strategic Services. In 1952 he began his academic career as a political theorist at Columbia, Harvard, Brandeis and the University of California at San Diego. Marcuse engaged himself with the protests of the 1960s and was known as 'the Father of the New Left'. His main works of that time were his synthesis of Marx and Freud, *Eros and Civilization* (1955) and *One-Dimensional Man*, work used by Merton for his lecture.
47 Burton, Heart and Laughlin, eds. *The Asian Journal of Thomas Merton*, p. 335.
48 Ibid., p. 328.

49 Ibid., p. 343.
50 León Gómez Araneda, *Que el pueblo juzgue: Historia del Golpe de Estado*. Santiago, Chile: Terranova Editores, 1988; Ignacio González Camus, *El día en que murió Allende*, Santiago, Chile: CESOC Ediciones Chileamérica, 1988; Paz Rojas, Viviana Uribe, María Eugenia Rojas, Iris Largo, Isabel Ropert and Víctor Espinoza, *Páginas en Blanco: El 11 de septiembre en La Moneda*, Santiago, Chile: Ediciones B Chile, 2001; Robinson Rojas Sandford, *The Murder of Allende and the End of the Chilean Way to Socialism*, New York, Evanston, San Francisco and London: Harper & Row, 1976 and Oscar Soto, *El Ultimo Día de Salvador Allende*. Santiago, Chile: Aguilar Chilena de Ediciones, 1999.
51 Salvador Allende, Last words through Radio Magallanes, Santiago, Chile, 11 September 1973.
52 Burton, Heart and Laughlin, eds. *The Asian Journal of Thomas Merton*, p. 331. Teilhard de Chardin (1881–1955), Jesuit and trained palaeontologist, took part in the discovery of the Peking man in China. In his book *The Pehnomenon of Man Teilhard* he abandoned the strict narrative of Genesis as to account for the creation and unfolding of the cosmos and proposed a religious and scientific development of the atmosphere. Teilhard's work was banned by the Vatican because of the implications of his ideas against the doctrine of original sin and his condemnation was clear in the 1950 encyclical *Humani Generis*. In 2009 Pope Benedict XVI praised Teilhard's idea of the universe as a 'living host' but Teilhard's works still carried a warning about his ideas.
53 Burton, Heart and Laughlin, eds. *The Asian Journal of Thomas Merton*, p. 330.
54 Ibid., p. 331.
55 Ibid., p. 332.
56 Ibid.
57 Ibid., p. 333.
58 Ibid.
59 Ibid., p. 334.
60 Ibid.
61 Ibid.
62 Ibid., p. 340.
63 Thomas Merton, 'The Significance of the Bhagavad-Gita, Appendix IX', in *The Asian Journal of Thomas Merton*, New York: New Directions, 1975, pp. 348–53 at p. 353.
64 Thomas Merton, 'Special Closing Prayer' offered at the First Spiritual Summit Conference in Calcutta by Father Thomas Merton, Appendix V in *The Asian Journal of Thomas Merton*, New York: New Directions, 1975, pp. 318–19.
65 Louis Althusser (1818–1990) was born in Algeria and studied at the École Normal Supérieure in Paris where he became a Professor of Philosophy. He was a Marxist philosopher and a long-time member of the French Communist Party. A structuralist Marxist who challenged any humanism in Marx he was also critical of the over use of structures for personality cults and made an impassioned defence of the line exercised by the Chinese Communit Party. In 1980 he strangled his wife and was committed to a mental hospital for 3 years losing influence within the French political scene. His major works were on Marxism and on ideology, for example *Reading Capital* and *Ideology and Ideological State Apparatuses: Notes Towards an Investigation*.

66 At the start of his lecture Merton made a personal confession to avoid criticisms of his lack of formal study of Marxism in an age in which more people than now were conversant with Marxism because of its influence in the Soviet Union and the Cold War. He said: 'I must apologize for giving you what will inevitably be a rather impressionistic treatment of something I do not know very much about, because I cannot possibly pretend to be an authority in Marxism', see Burton, Heart and Laughlin, eds. *The Asian Journal of Thomas Merton*, p. 326.

Chapter 6

MEDELLIN AND THE SERVICE TO THE POOR

If the conversations between Thomas Merton and the fourteenth Dalai Lama could be considered theological it is because their encounter was filled with Merton's wonder and need to understand some of the main concepts of Buddhism that he was studying. Thus, Merton symbolized the Western preoccupation with theological knowledge, in a way, for the orderly correctness of the idea that brings subsequent action. In bringing ideas from Marcuse later in Bangkok Merton was following a theoretical exploration that was in practice making dialogue happen. For the most remarkable part of Merton's trip to Asia was that he showed publicly that Christian–Buddhist dialogue was possible and desirable and that on the other hand contemplatives within the church could not only engage themselves in inter-faith dialogue but in a dialogue with Marxists, with the secular and with those who did not find any religious faith important in their lives.

At the same time that those conversations were taking place (1968) the majority of Christians in the world were located in Latin America. Those Christians were establishing a renewed closeness with the poor and the marginalized, after all the majority of the Latin American population. As outlined in Chapter 2 a new way of theologizing was already emerging from the commitment to be close to those who in any case any world religion should protect: the poor, the vulnerable, the least of society and the marginalized.

Liberation and Poverty

While the conference of all Latin American Bishops met at Medellín (Colombia, 1968) there was a theological development that, I would argue, has marked and shaped the ecclesiological foundations for an ongoing dialogue with Buddhism. Issues of persecution and liberation, suffering and utopian solidarity important for theologians in Latin America at this time also became important for Tibetan Buddhists who became poorer, oppressed, exiled and vulnerable after the Chinese re-appropriation of Tibet after the Chinese Revolution of 1949.

While I shall return to these discussions later, it is important to clarify what the meaning of poverty and the poor was that arose out of a Latin American reflection in the 1960s and 1970s. Robert McAfee Brown has argued commenting on liberation theology and a theology of the poor that 'this is a people's theology, not a textbook theology'.[1] There is an inherent contradiction and a creative one within the life of the periphery and any life of poverty: poverty is not willed by God on any human being; however, when a person is out of poverty there is a need to remember poverty as a value because God opts for the poor and the marginalized.[2] In other words, there are further theological distinctions regarding the issue of poverty and the life of poverty: (i) There are those who do not choose material poverty, (ii) there are those who choose poverty as a Gospel value and follow a particular way of life such as monastic life or religious life, (iii) there are those who strive to do well but are satisfied with a simple style of life and (iv) there are those who strive to do better and never achieve a personal contentment with what they have, even when their situation is materially better than (i), (ii) or/and (iii).

The challenging theologizing of the periphery provides a challenge to all these groups of people in their common humanity because it allows the centrality of community and the centrality of the Gospel to mirror other possibilities of existence. There is no linear progression as within developmental economics between poverty and riches, between closeness to the Gospel and the hardening of hearts through riches but instead there is a circular reality, the reality of the Kingdom of God that embraces all those realities as centred within the values of the Kingdom of God. This creates a double principle: an ethical one to live according to the values of the Kingdom and a hermeneutical one that requires action in order to learn the values of the Kingdom.[3]

As a result of those ethical and hermeneutical considerations the contemporary process of theologizing in Latin America and elsewhere requires both an ethical and a hermeneutical response, both responses supported by spirituality. This spirituality forces a way of life in which the Spirit of God reinforces the necessary graces and understandings of history as to trigger theologizing at the periphery from the point of view of the poor and the marginalized.[4]

The Challenge of 1968

During the year 1968 the world seemed to have been an unhappy one despite the free culture of hedonism, music and celebration symbolized by the hippies and those who finally found their own freedom within society. Part of the unhappy and defiant world of 1968 expressed itself through the many protests and marches against the establishment that took place in Paris and in the United

States. In Paris, students and staff of the university protested against inequality and discrimination while the United States saw a full-blown social movement for peace and against the Vietnam War. These concerns dominated the life of university students involved in an ever-growing peace movement against the threat of nuclear weapons and the hegemony of the United States within the Cold War. Despite their passivity the other part of the population already lived in fear of self-destruction due to the proliferation of nuclear weapons and the experience of the Cuban missile crisis of 1962.

This chapter explores and stresses the ideological, social and religious changes triggered within Latin America at that time and particularly those that were the result of the 1968 meeting of bishops in Medellín, Colombia. That meeting included the papal visit of Paul VI to Colombia (the first papal visit to Latin America), the influential standby for the poor and the marginalized by the Jesuits of Latin America as well as the growing sense of a new process of 'revolution in freedom' that was taking place in Chile with the ever-growing support for the socialist project of the president-to-be Salvador Allende.[5]

A 'new reformation' was taking place in Latin America, triggered by religious values and concern for the poor. This religious reformation relocated and supported sociopolitical processes by left-wing coalitions that found their reason of existence in the Cuban Revolution and the figures of the Argentinean fighter Ernesto Ché Guevara and the Colombian Catholic priest Camilo Torres, both of them killed by the security forces of Bolivia and Colombia, respectively. This reformation relocated Catholic fundamentalism to the sacristies and opened a model of dialogue with the world, with the secular, with Marxists and with all religious traditions, including Protestantism and indigenous religions. The world of Buddhism was already present in Latin America through the Chinese and Japanese immigrants; however, it was absent from the written history of Latin America.

The Kairos of Medellín

Following the completion of Vatican II in 1965 the Latin American Bishops' Conference headed by the progressive Chilean Bishop Manuel Larraín scheduled a general meeting of Latin American Bishops at Medellín (Colombia) that took place in 1968. The meeting coincided with a time of questioning about poverty and injustice in Latin America and with the start of a period in which military regimes became more the norm rather than the exception.[6] The preparations at local diocesan level for Medellín were intense and those leading the deliberations at continental level were not the theologians but the Pastoral Bishops who in the case of Brazil were already experiencing a systematic violation of human rights since the military had taken charge of the Brazilian government in 1964.

Within this difficult political context the Latin American countries were responding to the implementation of Vatican II with enthusiasm and supported by a committed Catholic laity that had been heavily influenced by John XXIII's *Pacem in Terris* (1963) and Paul VI's *Populorum Progressio* (1967). The ideas contained in both encyclicals spoke of the possibility of a just order in society but an order that had to consider development rather than armed struggle as its core value for an economic stability that provided the possibility of restoring dignity to all nations and to all human beings.

The genesis of Latin American liberation theology coincided with developments within a theology of inculturation in Africa and the Christian dialogue with world religions in Asia.[7] However, within those globalized developments a Peruvian priest, Gustavo Gutiérrez, became the face of liberation theology and helped other priests' reflections *vis-à-vis* the implementation of Vatican II. Those priests were trying to develop a systematic framework that connected the life of the Latin American poor, development theory and a divine sense of history, all under an umbrella of theological and material liberation.[8] *A Theology of Liberation* (1971) became the classic theological monograph; however, many other theologians started working on Christology, ecclesiology, soteriology, the history of the Church and the role of the Basic Christian communities.[9] The final documents of Medellín supported that theological programme by reiterating the materiality of God's salvation and by encouraging an ecclesial immersion in the life of the materially poor, the marginalized and those who were the victims of social injustice due to the fact that societies had created unjust structures included by the Latin American Bishops under the umbrella of 'structural sin'.[10]

The development of Latin American theology has an enormous complexity but its genesis can be traced to the European reflection by Gustavo Gutiérrez and Juan Luis Segundo SJ in France, where both studied at the time when John XXIII (1959) had called the council and had spoken of 'a church of the poor'.[11] Juan Luis Segundo SJ and Gustavo Gutiérrez had a different pastoral experience and that experience shaped what Segundo called 'two kinds of liberation theology'.[12] Thus, for Gutiérrez and his life in the slums the poor and the marginalized were at the centre of God's work because they represented the incarnation of God while theology as a reflection was a 'second act'. A theological option for the poor meant for Gutiérrez that Jesus in his life expressed a real closeness to them and liberation theology arose out of 'our better understanding of the depth and complexity of the poverty and oppression experienced by most of humanity; it is due to our perception of the economic, social, and cultural mechanisms that produce that poverty; and before all else, it is due to the new light which the word of the Lord sheds on that poverty'.[13]

For Segundo, who had experienced pastoral work with the educated elites, liberation theology remained within the realm of the educated theologians who through their pastoral ministry passed some fresh ideas about the implementation of Vatican II to the laity and to the Catholic faithful in parishes. Those ideas reflected Segundo's own work with reflection groups, university students and young professionals and his own commitment to a systematic investigation of theological themes at the service of the Church.

There is no contradiction between the role of the theologian in Gutiérrez and Segundo's work but certainly Gutiérrez' work triggered numerous theological writings that used Marxism as a hermeneutical tool in order to explore social realities. Within the context of the 1970s Christians and Marxists had encountered each other in the same project of challenging unjust social structures: Christians following the values of the Kingdom of God, Marxists following the ideals of a revolution in which the people and the masses would be equal through further revolutions inspired by the Cuban Revolution (1959). The radicalization of the Latin American theologians coincided with the rising of Christians that equated the Gospel with a socialist political project, the so-called Christians for Socialism, and the consequent persecution of pastoral agents by the military in Brazil, Chile, Argentina, Uruguay, Paraguay, El Salvador and Guatemala.

The optimism of the Council Fathers, and the rich documents that reincorporated the Church into the contemporary world, created an optimistic and exciting atmosphere in Latin America. However, there was no way in which all the different pastoral agents were going to act and think in the same way. There was the need to renew the Christian communities but there was also the need to outline economic development and a better distribution of wealth within society. In this sense, the complexity of the task of the bishops' reflection in Medellín was enormous and the dissemination of their own pastoral ideas necessary and much wanted by religious sisters, lay people and particularly the grass roots communities.

The means to achieve that social and economic change were of concern to Christians and to Marxists alike, and therefore within a post-Cuban revolution period a few Christian communities and a few priests understood the 'signs of the times' as calling them to join Latin American groups that wanted to foster violent revolutions. That was the case of Fr Camilo Torres Restrepo, a Colombian priest who was to become a symbol of the possible Christian commitment to Latin American revolutions. Already at the time of the Council Camilo Torres had developed the idea that the revolutionary struggle could be a Christian and a priestly activity. His influence was large in Colombian society because he himself came from a well-to-do family but also because he was involved with students at the National University of Colombia. Cardinal Luis

Concha moved him from the university to a suburban parish where he started attacking the hierarchy of the Church by suggesting that they were part of the Colombian oligarchy, a group that according to him impeded the formation of a more just society in Colombia. In June 1965 he asked to be relieved from his priestly duties and in November 1965 he joined the Colombian guerrilla, the Ejército de Liberación Nacional. Torres was killed on 15 February 1966 and became an icon for many other Christians in Latin America.

Within that context of ongoing change and political challenges Paul VI travelled to Bogotá, Colombia in 1968, in order to open the thirty-ninth International Eucharistic Congress. The first visit by a Pope to Latin America was seen as a great moment for a growing Church. Thus, leading Latin American Bishops such as Cardinal Silva Henríquez of Chile felt excitement about the Pope's visit to Latin America and saw the visit as a service to all.[14] The 'continent of hope' was the best ground for the implementation of Vatican II and Silva Henríquez felt that finally the servant of the servants of God was arriving to visit the poor of Latin America as the leader of a servant Church. The meeting of Latin American Bishops in Colombia was to set the guidelines for the implementation of Vatican II in Latin America and the final document of Medellín was to vindicate the demands of those protesting against the pope's visit rather than to crush their pastoral dreams. It is possible to argue that without the arrival of Paul VI the meeting of all Latin American Bishops at Medellín would not have had the same strength and the same impact on the pastoral life of the Church in Latin America.

Paul VI during his visit to Colombia ratified the winds of change given by Vatican II, the support of the Church to the poor and their just causes, and he condemned any advocacy of violence in order to achieve a just society in Latin America. The visit by Paul VI coincided with the celebration of the International Congress in Bogotá between 18 and 25 August 1968. Unlike previous Eucharistic Congresses in Buenos Aires and Sao Paulo the Colombian one was a celebration of the Christian communities under the motto *Vinculum Caritatis*.[15] During the Eucharistic Congress the pope, addressing peasants, stressed his commitment and that of the whole church to defend the plight of the poor, to proclaim human and Christian dignities, to denounce injustices and abuses against peasants and to foster initiatives and programmes that supported peoples and their development.[16] In summary, the pope reaffirmed an ongoing ecclesial understanding in Latin America: the theme of the poor as a sacramental presence of Christ.[17] The pope warned those attending the celebrations about the danger of putting their trust in violence or revolution.[18] It cannot be underestimated that this was the first time that the pope had visited Latin America and that no previous pope had journeyed outside Europe in order to physically be with the sick and the orphans.[19]

Paul VI inaugurated the second general meeting of Latin American Bishops at Medellín at the cathedral in Bogotá on 24 August and returned to Rome. Those attending the Medellín conference were 137 bishops with right to vote and 112 delegates and observers.[20] Thus, the Medellín conference was a fruitful opportunity for renewal and many of the concepts outlined in the final document were new additions to the social doctrine of the Church, for example 'a truly human economics', 'institutionalised violence' and 'sinful structures'.

The Impact of Medellín

Thus, it is at Medellín in 1968 that the theological movement of a Latin America driven by lay, unpublished theologians began.[21] It is at Medellín that the possibility of a life of dialogue with other religious traditions started. The Church in Latin America had to ask questions about her religious practices within difficult political circumstances and aided by the theological reflection of Gutiérrez the bishops did not separate religion and politics, but provided a political response of commitment to political change, the defence of human rights and the implementation of dialogue with all. Virgilio Elizondo has argued, for example that the transformative impact of the Medellín Conference on the church's pastoral practice and theology was far greater than that exercised by any other council of the church. No particular dogmas or confessions of faith were questioned or challenged – Protestant or Catholic. Instead, the whole edifice of Constantinean Christian thought, imagery and symbolism was radically challenged in the name of Christianity itself. What was initiated was not a new academic or philosophical theology, but the transformation of the very structures and methods of doing theology. To be faithful and authentic, Christian theology would have to emerge out of the spiritual experience of the believing community grappling with its history and responding to its contemporary situation. The subsequent pastoral implementation of Medellín was very different in different Latin American countries but with the exception of Argentina and Colombia created the necessary pastoral and theological reflection as to challenge state oppression understood as 'structural sin'. For example, in the case of Chile the bishops, whenever needed, challenged the military regime of President Pinochet while in neighbouring Argentina there was an avoidance of any prophetic denunciation in the name of the Gospel.[22]

Among the groups that were going through a renewal and a Latin American reformation were religious men and women who already had been encouraged by the reflections and the 1968 public declaration by the Jesuits on their lifestyle and their pastoral work throughout Latin America. Thus, when the Provincials of all the Jesuit provinces of Latin America met in Rio de Janeiro, Brazil, from

6–14 May 1968 they reflected on their view of the mission and their positioning within Latin America. As a result of their deliberations they decided to reiterate their involvement 'in the temporal life of humankind'.[23] However, within the particular context of Latin America their statement for a larger involvement within a movement that could change unjust structures and to be with the people was very strong and very down to earth. There was no high theology within the document but a challenge to personal lives and community activities with an added social and religious utopia. In a central passage of that document they asserted:

> In all our activities, our goal should be the liberation of humankind from every sort of servitude that oppresses it: the lack of life's necessities, illiteracy, the weight of sociological structures which deprive it of personal responsibility over life itself, the materialistic conception of history. We want all our efforts to work together toward the construction of a society in which all persons will find their place, and in which they will enjoy political, economic, cultural, and religious equality and liberty.[24]

Within the document and in later educational practices the Jesuits addressed a usual criticism towards their academic institutions, particularly schools and universities: that Jesuit schools educated the children of the rich and that their universities reiterated that social paradigm. The document argued that all Jesuit institutions should foster the social gospel and that all students should be involved in practical activities in which they would experience different social realities.[25] The Jesuit Provincials called for a formation of consciences among those they taught and to use the media to foster those aims. However, the final call was aimed at all Jesuit superiors to implement those changes as soon as possible, even when some of those changes would take some time. Moreover, there was also a call for a personal conversion with deep questions to each individual Jesuit working in Latin America outlined in the following paragraph of the Jesuit document:

> Are we capable of responding to the world's expectations? Are our faith and charity equal to the anxiety-ridden appeals of the world around us? Do we practice self-denial sufficiently, so that God is able to flood us with light and energy? Does personal prayer have its proper place in our life, so that we are united with God in this great human task that cannot succeed without God? Can the Society keep within its ranks those members who do not want to pray or who do not have a real and personal prayer in life?[26]

The response to the tenets of Medellín by the Jesuit communities in Latin America was swift and sometimes unsettling for parents and teachers of those students involved. Parents were told about the revised Jesuit aims within their schools and were asked to adhere to them despite conservative parents' apprehensions towards the formation of their children outside the academic classroom. Despite the large number of Jesuits that left the Society of Jesus after Vatican II Jesuit secondary schools maintained their academic excellence with the addition of summer work or activities of a social nature for pupils in their last years of secondary school. Within universities it was easier to comply with practical activities of a social nature as most university students were affected by a political climate of change, political awareness and political questioning. Thus, the Jesuits not only affected the developments of theologies, pastoral or otherwise, but also became involved in many activities related to the defence of indigenous minorities, political refugees and migrants.

In the case of El Salvador, where over the years the prominent theologian Jon Sobrino SJ worked, the Jesuits decided to build and implement a university that was to be a reflection of the open spirit of Vatican II and at the same time became a model institution for a deep commitment to the poor and the marginalized. The challenges of Medellín assured the Jesuit community in El Salvador that Medellín was not only a *kairos* but also a movement that could not be stopped easily. A short outline of the influential educational Jesuit enterprise arising out of Medellín is in order here, particularly the contribution of the Jesuit University of Central America (UCA). For it is a fact that the educational reform and tertiary education led by the Jesuits in El Salvador was the cause of the assassination of several Jesuits by the Salvadorian Army and the death squads paid by Salvadorian landowners. The new reformation had a strong stance among Jesuits and the Jesuits, together with Monsignor Oscar Romero, shaped the application of such reformation within Central America in general and El Salvador in particular.

The UCA campus started to be built in 1970 through financial loans from the Inter-American Development Bank (Banco Interamericano del Desarrollo – BID). The UCA under Román Mayorga Quirós as rector moved quickly into a progressive line following changes within the Jesuits and by 1976 professor Ignacio Ellacuría SJ attracted the animosity of El Salvador's President Arturo Armando Molina after he wrote an editorial in the university's magazine criticizing the halting of the Salvadorian agrarian reform. The government withdrew educational subsidies to the UCA and the attacks on the Jesuits started with the assassination of the Jesuit Rutilio Grande in March 1977. From that moment the UCA supported all pastoral plans by Archbishop Romero through its department of theology, headed by Jon Sobrino. In 1979, Ellacuría became Rector of the UCA and moved the university into research programmes related to the national realities of El Salvador while immersing students, staff and the university community into the social realities of the poor of El Salvador. As the Salvadorean Civil War continued Ellacuría became very prominent within the mediation of peace accords and he spoke strongly against injustice and human rights abuses through television, UCA radio and UCA publications.

Ignacio Ellacuría SJ, rector of the university at the time of his assassination, articulated this particular ministry in the following words: 'the university should be present intellectually where it is needed: to provide science for those who have no science; to provide skills for the unskilled; to be a voice for those who have no voice; to give intellectual support for those who do not possess the academic qualifications to promote and legitimate their rights'.[27] Jon Sobrino SJ was less romantic about the possibilities of a university due to past experiences whereby Jesuit universities became top educational institutions but in doing so they compromised their possibilities of challenging unjust and sinful structures within society.

Sobrino advocated the option for the poor within a Christian university by arguing that it was unrealistic to suggest that a university should be located among the poor but that all activities and the central activities of a Christian university should look towards the poor. For him, one of the central activities within this kind of university was the dialogue between faith and science and therefore the importance of the teaching and research of theology as a discipline and as a reflection on the life of the poor and the marginalized from a Christian perspective. Sobrino's statement about theology within a university became central to understanding the challenges that the Jesuit posed to the powerful in El Salvador and the inspiration they provided to many of the communities linked to their extra-mural courses and training of leaders of Christian communities within El Salvador. Sobrino argued very strongly that 'theology must be turned, then, towards the people of God; it should be inserted effectively among them, draw its agenda from them and accompany them. In this sense, university theology should be a moment of theo-praxis for the whole people of God and should be considered as a theo-culture, a Christo-culture, an ecclesio-culture – that is, an instrument that cultivates and nurtures faith, hope, and love of God's people'.[28]

Impact on Dialogue and Religious Cooperation

The impact of the 1968 Conference of Bishops on Latin America cannot be underestimated. The conclusions of the conference followed a deep reflection on the role and existence of the Catholic Church in Latin America and triggered change within the church and also within the spheres of ecclesial influence in Latin America.

The Jesuit response to Medellín was crucial because the Jesuits were in charge of the best schools and best universities of Latin America; as a result, they had a timely influence on the Latin American intellectuals and professionals. The Jesuit response to the Medellín document was a communitarian act of love in which a theological response to liberation also entailed the possibility of questioning the Jesuit way of life at that time. Thus, the Jesuits reformed themselves as well as triggering challenges and winds of reform to the local churches in Latin America where the Jesuits played a central role in religious and political circles. Other religious congregations followed the same example and an exodus from well-to-do places of ministry took place whereby religious women left their teaching in well-to-do public schools in numbers and exited to poor shanty towns and deprived areas of Latin American cities. Missionary orders with foreign personnel also took very seriously the conclusions of Medellín and opened new parishes in locations where previously only Marxist activists and left-wing ideologists had any access.

It is a fact that the role of religious communities has been generally underplayed in the assessment of changes that took place in 1968 and after. Therefore it is particularly important to remember that religious congregations and communities with expatriate missionaries from Ireland, Spain, France and the United States expressed their own search for a closer follow-up of the Gospel within a movement from their convents and their religious houses to the periphery, to the shanty towns and to places where they were most needed. Their movement included a movement towards dialogue with other world religions.

This movement towards the periphery and the involvement of Christians within movements of liberation was to inbuild a golden pastoral moment to Latin America by which the period of the 1970s and 1980s could be called a true *kairos* arising of 1968 and at the same time the formation of a movement for liberation that was to shape the pastoral development of the universal church. In conclusion the year 1968 provided the beginning of a new reformation in and for Latin America.

Dialogues with the Secular

The impact of Vatican II at Medellín was also felt in the area of dialogue with other religious traditions, included those traditions that negated the existence of God, that is Marxists and atheists. Here it is important to remember that atheism as a non-theistic tradition stands together with Buddhism as a non-theistic religious tradition as well.[29]

One of those involved in the dialogue between Christianity and Marxism was the Argentinean theologian José Míguez Bonino. Míguez Bonino was aware that already by the mid-1970s many books on liberation theology had been written and that the conclusions of the Latin American Meeting of Latin American Bishops had been either deemed as a unique moment of Christian history or had been ignored by those who decided that Marxist-oriented bishops had lost their way. Therefore, in a more systematic but concise manner he assessed the new developments in Latin American theology through his seminal work *Revolutionary Theology comes of Age*.[30]

Míguez Bonino proposes the following actualizations of twentieth century theology as it moves forward, as unique developments and as beacons of hope for Christian practice and Christian life. First of all the context of theology has evolved from the study of religion or metaphysics. Secondly, there has been a closer alliance between the study of biblical research and human experience. Thirdly, the realm of history has mediated biblical research and human experience. Fourthly, theology has used a more political language through which experience, action and history have become prime movers of an ongoing theological reflection. Further, those theological developments were radicalized by Latin American theologians who asked questions about the social, political and religious realities of a particular context, that is Latin America.[31]

Christians and Marxists

One of his main concerns following from that context and its related theological reflection, not an intellectual but a practical concern, was the work that Christians and Marxists were pursuing within the Latin America of the early 1970s. Indeed, he was present in Santiago (Chile) during the international meeting on trade and commerce of those nations considered part of the Third World that were represented by the United Nations agency UNCTAD. In 1972 the international meeting of the UNCTAD took place in Santiago, at a purposely built conference centre in Alameda Avenue, a meeting that was hosted by the socialist government of Salvador Allende.[32]

However, Míguez Bonino was not part of the trade delegation sent by the Argentinean government but he was attending an international meeting of the movement Christians for Socialism that was taking part on the same days in Santiago, and without the blessings of the then Archbishop of Santiago, Cardinal Raúl Silva Henríquez.[33] Míguez Bonino saw hope in those priests, nuns and pastoral agents who were challenging the traditional view given to the Gospel and who were asking questions about social realities of poverty, violence and oppression, without knowing that a year later Chile was going to be dominated by the military while another Argentinean military coup was going to follow a couple of years later.

Míguez Bonino could have been accused of leaning towards Marxism but he was not. He lived the actions by Christians and Marxists at that particular time and thought that it had made a difference to the ongoing dialogue and understanding of Christians and Marxists within European circles. If within Europe Christianity and Marxism were understood as two different systems of thought, what united them within the Latin American experience was their common action for the poor and the marginalized that took precedence over systems of thought and intellectual debates about ontology or even theodicy. Despite further questioning of those contextual alliances Míguez stated clearly in the context of the 1974 London lectures in contemporary Christianity: 'The God of the covenant has himself designed a pattern of action which such words as justice, righteousness, the protection of the poor, active love, help us to discern'.[34]

Nevertheless, within the Latin American context in which Míguez Bonino was operating many Christians considered themselves Marxists and vice versa. For Míguez Bonino there was a 'strategic alliance' that responded to a common concern and a common project: the social and political challenges that arose out of a situation of poverty, oppression and marginalization of a larger part of the Latin American population and that in the case of Argentina and Chile had given way to socialist utopias led by Salvador Allende and by Juan Domingo and Evita Perón within their base among the Argentinean workers. In the Argentinean case Míguez Bonino allied himself with the Christian position of the minority as the Argentinean Bishops were much more conservative and traditional than those in Chile.[35]

For Míguez Bonino there could not be a person who could embrace a hybrid identity as a 'Christian-Marxist' or a 'Marxist-Christian'; however, there could be a contextual position in which a Christian could follow the Marxism paradigm in order to extend his own analysis of a social situation of injustice or oppression. On the other hand, there could be a Marxist who having been brought up as a Christian or realizing the challenging demands of 'love of neighbour' could also find useful and appropriate to follow those narrow parameters of Christian interpretation in order to achieve the same goal: the defence of the poor and the marginalized and the advent of a more just society. Four areas of common understanding did exist and were outlined by Míguez Bonino as follows:

(1) Knowledge is not abstract but an engagement with concrete social realities;
(2) There is a common shared ethos of human solidarity;
(3) There is a need for a historical mediation of any humanist intention; and
(4) The ultimate horizons of life as understood by Christians and Marxists are radically different.[36]

The 'strategic alliance' provided a contextual unity in action and within some limited theoretical understanding but separated Christians and Marxists when the aims of such alliance were achieved. At the end of the road Marxists wanted to achieve a socialist society through revolution with a base on the workers while Christians wanted to achieve the realization of the Kingdom of God with a base on the Christian communities. Both, Marxists and Christians sustained a utopian dream by the fact that neither the revolution [in Marx's understanding] nor the Kingdom was to be solely achieved within a particular moment in human history.[37] If a Marxist had a structural way of perceiving the world and of reading history, a Christian had a critical way of reading God's intervention in the world, called faith, which following Gutiérrez had to be critical and engaged with the realities of underdevelopment, oppression and sin.[38]

For Míguez Bonino this 'strategic alliance' serves the Church well because at the centre of his personal option is the moulding of a Church that has the poor at the centre and that is less involved in disappointing academic (and European) theological debates but comes out of a given individualism in order to be closer to the poor and thus to Jesus Christ and through other groups and communities that are also looking after and learning from the poor, including practitioners of the world religions.

His critical approach to Marxism and Marxists activists did not arise out of a critique or distrust of a 'strategic alliance' but from the fact that Míguez Bonino criticized the lack of power control within Marxist oriented groups, usually manifested in a personality cult or the uncritical behaviour in politics due to a total allegiance to a person, a party or a system.[39] However, Míguez Bonino also recognized that the Marxist is a person fully given to a way of life, a 'militant', who gives it all and puts the selfish individual comforts and aspirations of life as secondary. Christians and Marxists do not share a common spirituality but both have one common call, understood by Marxists as 'militancy'.

For the Christian that militancy is expressed as the revolutionary following of Jesus, symbolized by the actualization of faith, love and hope within a person's life and within the daily work in order to construct a more just society for all. For many that realization becomes an act of self-immolation in joy, as a person gives his life and comforts so that others may have life too.[40] For the Marxist the call to join the struggle and a militant struggle leads to the same state of self-immolation that one can see in Antonio Gramsci, dying slowly but with a purpose in one of Mussolini's jails or the life of Ernesto 'Ché' Guevara who left his sheltered existence and the possibility of a brilliant medical career in order to join others throughout Latin America and Africa who were struggling for a more just society.[41] Míguez Bonino prefers to call such 'militancy' a Christian spirituality because of the joy attached to a Christian life, so that

'Christian faith becomes an invitation under the conditions of responsible, joyful solidary militancy'.[42]

Christians and Atheists

Míguez Bonino engaged himself not only with groups of Marxists but also with others who did not believe in the existence of God (atheists). In the context of a church hall attached to a Protestant congregation in Buenos Aires he gathered a group of Christians and atheists in order to open an ongoing human dialogue about the Christian faith within the context of Argentina. The format of the meeting followed Míguez Bonino's preferred style of teaching: he gave a short presentation, immediately after this the participants formed small discussion groups and after the meeting he put together the initial presentation and the common thoughts shared during the meeting in a small publication available for further discussion.[43]

Míguez Bonino's exposition starts not from the point of view of asking if there is a God but from the fact that in order to show belief in a God there is the need to reject belief in others. Therefore, the Christian and the atheist have a common starting point of view in their rejection of some gods, rather than in their acceptance of a particular one. Once that initial foundation is laid Míguez Bonino accepts that faith is a gift and therefore the possibility of believing in God requires more than a human effort. In his words the free action of God provides the possibility of believing so that 'the Christian is like a beggar who says to another beggar "Let's go together. I know where they will give us bread"'.[44] However, he asserts that most of the further contextual disagreements between Christians and atheists come from a misunderstanding of Christianity, either by the atheists or by Christians themselves.

Those disagreements between Christians and atheists include issues of religion and science, suffering in the world, the wrong doings of the Christian communities, the separation of religion and politics and the spiritualization of religion with a distorted concept of the goodness of humanity. Míguez Bonino's conception of religion as an expression of belief in community is very clear: human beings become Christians in community so that without an incarnated principle of humanness and human goodness expressed in solidarity with the world and in community there is no belief in God, who after all is an incarnate God.

The issue of suffering in the world is not a metaphysical discussion but an expression of humanness, with its frailty and its need for care and compassion. The image of God's Son dying on a cross and its incarnation as a ministry of healing and solidarity with the people of His time brings not further metaphysical or ontological questions but the belief that God exists because His Son became one with us in suffering and death.

The spiritualization of religion provides a further bridge between Christians and atheists but the ministry of Jesus of Nazareth is not only an example of human [and divine] solidarity with others but also a lead in matters of religion and politics. Therefore, Míguez Bonino rejects the notion that they are separated only because some clerics tend to speak too soon about matters where they don't have proper technical expertise. Despite those bad examples, the immersion of Christ in the world and within the society of His time shows not only the possibility but also the mandate for Christians to get involved in the running of society and in the challenges that the creation of a more just society demands. For Míguez Bonino,

> Politics is the attempt at retrieving the world for people, at seizing power from the irrational, from the high-handedness of an inhuman system, and of then restoring it to its original proposition – to serve the enrichment and fullness of the human community. And this is a fundamental Christian obligation. You can't be a Christian without accepting it, because you can't be a human being without doing it.[45]

Within those discussions it is possible to see the liberating and social strand that Míguez Bonino brings to discussions that could be totally philosophical and ontological. For him, there is no contradiction between religion and science because Christians as human beings, first and foremost, take part in science research and are, as many others, interested in knowing more about the world which after all is the world that God created. God loved the world and so we do as well. However, he is very weary of a Christianity that dwells on too many intellectual arguments or that provides a middle-class isolation where people cannot share their faith and do not have any relation with a material and social world. Míguez Bonino provides a sharp critique of middle-class Argentinean society by asking if they actually live the Christian faith or is it that they believe in God rather than in practising their faith. His sociological analysis is both devastating and realistic when he writes: 'They live for themselves, introvertedly, dreaming of their houses, their own vacations, their own privacy. And their religion has the same characteristics. Since they do not share their lives, they do not share their faith'.[46]

Returning to an ongoing dialogue with atheists, issues of human fulfilment come to the core of his engagement with other human beings. The grace of believing in a God or in Jesus Christ presupposes the development of any human potential and the possibility of being human at all times. Thus, there are very good people who do not believe and others who come to believe through two different processes: challenge and consolation. Within the first process, those involved in changing society and making it better come to like and feel part of the process of liberation, individual and social, that Jesus offers in the New Testament, either by His own ministry or by those who became His followers in the early Christian communities. His project of liberation is the final triumph of life over evil and life over death, a theme that is common to all humans, believers of different faiths and non-believers as well. However, other people come to believe through a process of consolation, by realizing that the message, life and actions of Jesus of Nazareth are very clear: evil and wrong do not prevail but they are always embraced and conquered by a divine goodness manifested in the Son of God.

These two processes, these two sides of faith are interrelated so that if an individual comes to believe either because of challenge or consolation that same person quickly discovers and becomes part of the other side of faith. Many good and honest responses to the challenges of life are found outside Christian responses and for Míguez Bonino they all come from Jesus Christ who is at the centre of good human responses and remains the source of all goodness, even locating them outside the realm of Christianity.

Míguez Bonino's involvement with society and particularly non-Christians has made a different contribution to the history and development of Latin American theology in that most other Latin American theologians assumed that they were challenging and reflecting on the action of Christians within an unjust contemporary society. In doing so they did not see the possibilities of embracing the challenges of nations that for the most part had a majority of professing Christians but actually minorities of people involved directly in processes of human and societal liberation.

The movements towards dialogue and diversity in religious practice within Latin America affected whole societies that by the late twentieth century had realized that Christianity existed in dialogue with many other religious traditions/choices within Latin America. Tibetan Buddhist temples started to appear in Latin America and a sense of liberation from ignorance seemed to have replaced fear at the end of the era of military regimes.

For some this process of openness and diversity was perceived as a negative influence; for those opposed to any religious diversity this change only shaped societies in which commitment to God (the Christian God) was absent. Against this proposition I would argue that the fruits of Vatican II in Latin America stressed the fact that belief in God provided a vivacious model centred in God and love of neighbour, a model of open dialogue rather than a model of exclusive ecclesiological centrality and apocalyptic encounter. As a result, faith maturity led to maturity in dialogue rather than vice versa.

Notes

1 Robert McAfee Brown, 'Preface: After Ten Years', in Gustavo Gutiérrez, *The Power of the Poor in History: Selected Writings*. London: SCM Press, 1983, pp. vi–xvi at p. vii.
2 See for example the insightful analysis of the Gospels vis-à-vis Latin American society by J. Severino Croatto, 'The Political Dimension of Christ the Liberator', in José Miguez Bonino, ed. *Faces of Jesus: Latin American Christologies*, Eugene, OR: Wipf and Stock Publishers, 1998, pp. 102–22.
3 Jon Sobrino SJ, 'Central Position of the Reign of God in Liberation Theology', in Ignacio Ellacuría SJ and Jon Sobrino SJ, eds. *Mysterium Liberationis: Fundamental Concepts of Liberation Theology*, 1993, pp. 350–88 at pp. 378–9.
4 For the development of a global ethics within centre-theologies see Hans Küng, 'Global Business and the Global Ethic', in Karl-Josef Kuschel and Dietmar Mieth, eds. 'In Search of Universal Values' (*Concilium*, 2001/4), London: SCM Press, pp. 87–105.
5 Some of these arguments have been developed at length in Mario I. Aguilar, *The History and Politics of Latin American Theology*, 3 volumes, London: SCM Press, 2007–8.
6 For a detailed analysis of the relation between church and state at the period and within different Latin American countries see Jeffrey Klaiber SJ, *The Church, Dictatorships, and Democracy in Latin America*, Maryknoll, NY: Orbis, 1998.
7 At the theological level African and Latin American theologians encountered each other through the Ecumenical Association of Third World Theologians (EATWOT) and the first period of their work was coordinated by Enrique Dussel and François Houtart, see a useful historical overview in Enrique Dussel, 'Theologies of the "Periphery" and the "Centre": Encounter or Confrontation?', in Claude Geffré, Gustavo Gutiérrez and Virgil Elizondo, eds. *Different Theologies, Common Responsibility, Babel or Pentecost?* (*Concilium* 1984/1, 171), Edinburgh: T&T Clark, 87–97, see also EATWOT, *The Emergent Gospel*, Maryknoll, NY: Orbis Books, 1976. For a theological overview see Theo Witvliet, *A Place in the Sun: An Introduction to Liberation Theology in the Third World*, London: SCM Press, 1985. An Asian Christianity as a Christian project was more problematic; numbers of Christians in Asia, with the exception of the Philippines, remain small and the post-Vatican II discussions on salvation within the world religions created more than an impasse between those who adhered to a Christ centric option (exclusivists) and those who understood the world religions as places where God could save (inclusivists), see Paul F. Knitter, *No Other Name? A Critical Survey of Christian Attitudes towards the World Religions*, London: SCM Press, 1985.
8 For historical data on his life see Sergio Torres, 'Gustavo Gutiérrez: A historical sketch', in Marc H. Ellis and Otto Maduro, eds. *The Future of Liberation Theology: Essays in Honor of Gustavo Gutiérrez*, Maryknoll, NY: Orbis, 1989, 95–101.
9 Gustavo Gutiérrez, *Teología de la liberación: Perspectivas* (16th edn), Salamanca: Ediciones Sígueme, 1999 and Lima: Centro de Estudios y Publicaciones 1971; for a full review of the theological works of 18 Latin American theologians see Mario I. Aguilar, *The History and Politics of Latin American Theology*, 2007.
10 See Second General Conference of Latin American Bishops 1968, *The Church in the Present-Day Transformation of Latin America in the Light of the Council II Conclusions*, Washington, DC: United States Catholic Conference USCC, 1970.

11 For a comprehensive history of liberation theology and of some of the most prominent theologians of liberation see Mario I. Aguilar, *The History and Politics of Latin American Theology*, 2007–8.
12 Juan Luis Segundo SJ, 'Two Theologies of Liberation', Toronto, 22 March 1983 in Alfred T. Hennelly, ed. *Liberation Theology: A Documentary History*, Maryknoll, NY: Orbis, 1990, pp. 353–66.
13 Gustavo Gutiérrez, 'Option for the Poor', in Ignacio Ellacuría SJ and Jon Sobrino SJ, eds. *Mysterium Liberationis: Fundamental Concepts of Liberation Theology*, Maryknoll, NY: Orbis and North Blackburn, Victoria: Collins Dove, 1993, pp. 235–50 at p. 250.
14 Silva Henríquez gave the following thoughts in an interview with US News & World Report: 'Este proceso, válido para toda la Iglesia, se singulariza y reviste de connotación particular en América Latina. Continente en vías de desarrollo, el servicio eclesial a América Latina se concreta en un servicio al desarrollo, entendido en la acepción de Populorum Progressio: de condiciones menos humanas, hacia un humanismo integral, que incluye el don de la fe' (This process, valid for the whole Church, singles out and is of particular connotation in Latin America. A continent in the process of development, the ecclesial service to Latin America is in a specific service to development, understood in the meaning of Populorum Progressio: conditions less than human, towards an integral humanism, which includes the gift of faith), *Memorias* II, 137.
15 Josep-Ignasi Saranyana, director and Carmen-José Alejos Grau, coordinator, *Teología en América Latina*, vol. III: *El siglo de las teologías latinoamericanistas 1899–2001*, Madrid: Iberoamericana and Frankfurt am Main: Vervuert, 2002, p. 124.
16 Ibid.
17 Ibid., p. 125.
18 Ibid., p. 126.
19 Ibid.
20 Ibid.
21 Virgilio Elizondo, 'Emergence of a World Church and the irruption of the poor', in Gregory Baum, ed. *The Twentieth Century: A Theological Overview*, Maryknoll, NY: Orbis, 1999, p. 108.
22 See Mario I. Aguilar, *A Social History of the Catholic Church in Chile*, vol. I *The First Period of the Pinochet Government 1973–1980*, Lewiston, NY, Queenston, Ontario, and Lampeter, Wales: Edwin Mellen Press, 2004, 2006, 2007.
23 Provincials of the Society of Jesus, 'The Jesuits in Latin America', May 1968, in Alfred T. Hennelly, ed. *Liberation Theology: A Documentary History*, Maryknoll, NY: Orbis, 1990, pp. 77–83.
24 Provincials of the Society of Jesus, 'The Jesuits in Latin America', § 3.
25 Ibid., § 7.
26 Ibid., § 10.
27 Ignacio Ellacuría SJ, 'The Task of a Christian University', in Jon Sobrino, Ignacio Ellacuría and Others, *Companions of Jesus*, p. 150.
28 Jon Sobrino SJ, 'The University's Christian Inspiration', in Jon Sobrino, Ignacio Ellacuría and Others, *Companions of Jesus*, pp. 170–1.
29 Mario I. Aguilar, 'Dialogue without God: Reflections on Christian-Buddhist Dialogue', Paper presented at the meeting Where We Dwell in Common: Pathways for Dialogue in the 21st Century, Assisi, Italy, 17–20 April 2012.

30 José Míguez Bonino, *Revolutionary Theology Comes of Age*, London: SPCK, 1975, published in the United States as *Doing Theology in a Revolutionary Situation*, Philadelphia: Fortress Press, 1975.
31 José Míguez Bonino, *Revolutionary Theology*, pp. 78–9.
32 After the 1973 military coup and due to the destruction of the presidential palace (La Moneda) the military junta used it as their headquarters and it legally was owned by the Ministry of Defence. With the return to democracy in the 1990s the building became a conference centre until it was completely destroyed by a fire in March 2006 and the government of President Bachellet decided to sell it; see David Maulen, 'Chile: Se vende edificio de la Unctad III (1972)', *Política en el Cono Sur Latinoamericano*, 1715, 24 November 2006.
33 Fernando Castillo, 'Christians for Socialism in Chile', *Concilium*, 1977, pp. 105, 106–12 and John Eagleson, ed. *Christians and Socialism: Documentation of the Christians for Socialism Movement in Latin America*, Maryknoll, NY: Orbis, 1975. For a right-wing critique of Christians for Socialism, see Teresa Donoso Loero, *Los cristianos por el socialismo en Chile*, Santiago: Editorial Vaitea, 1975.
34 José Míguez Bonino, *Christians and Marxists: The Mutual Challenge to Revolution*, London: Hodder and Stoughton, 1976, p. 41.
35 The response of the Chilean and Argentinean Bishops to human rights abuses by the military was very different: the Chilean bishops led by Cardinal Silva Henríquez challenged the military regime for the most part, while the Argentinean bishops for the most part remained passive and kept silent within a political situation in which 25 times more Argentinean than Chilean citizens were arrested and forcefully made to disappear. For the Chilean Bishops' actions that questioned the Chilean military see Mario I. Aguilar, *A Social History of the Catholic Church in Chile* volumes I–IV.
36 José Míguez Bonino, *Christians and Marxists*, pp. 118–19.
37 With the collapse of the Soviet Union it was impossible to see how Christians and Marxists would have interacted in a democratic system as Marxism lost its momentum and Christians who allied themselves with them joined new political coalitions that departed from a contextual Marxist–Christian dialogue.
38 Gustavo Gutiérrez, *A Theology of Liberation*, Maryknoll, NY: Orbis, 1973, II.3 'Faith, utopia and political action'.
39 A contemporary example of this criticism can be found in the life of the Chilean poet Pablo Neruda, who as a member of the Chilean Communist Party always refused to condemn the persecution of intellectuals, writers and poets exercised by the Soviet regime and seemed to be enchanted by those who were in control of the Soviet Union during the period of the Cold War, see Adam Feinstein, *Pablo Neruda: A Passion for Life*, London: Bloomsbury, 2005, pp. 318–19.
40 José Miguez Bonino, *Christians and Marxists*, pp. 136–42.
41 Ibid., p. 135.
42 Ibid., p. 141.
43 José Míguez Bonino, *Espacio para ser hombres*, Buenos Aires: Tierra Nueva, 1975, English translation published as *Room To Be People: An Interpretation of the Message of the Bible for Today's World*, Philadelphia: Fortress Press, 1979.
44 José Míguez Bonino, *Room To Be People*, p. 8.
45 Ibid., p. 42.
46 Ibid., p. 78.

Chapter 7

BASIC TENETS

It is with the passing of age that one seems to believe in less but what one believes one believes more. Thus, with the passing of time the church returns to the central tenets of Christianity in order to mortify memories of a history of division and violence. Basic tenets such as Mt. 25.31–46 and Lk. 4.16–22 become entangled with a church that serves and that returns to the central commandments: to love God and to love neighbours. Dialogue has the same path: a return to the basic tenets in which God is loved and is loved in others. Those who are more loved by God between the love that encompasses all are the humble, the meek, the poor and the marginalized. Thus, if the church returns to basic tenets the dialogue with other faiths in general and with Buddhists in particular takes shape following the service to others and the love of the poor in the name of God. For the simplicity of compassion and service in Buddhism becomes a linking episteme for the church. In this chapter I explore some of those basic tenets that bring us towards dialogue with others in this world and not in the next.

Theologizing Dialogue

In between challenges of activism and theologizing at the periphery there are central statements that are forgotten or are taken for granted and as a result they remain unspoken. One of them was highlighted by the Dalai Lama in his Nobel Prize Lecture in 1989 when he opened the solemn occasion with the following remark:

> I am always reminded that we are all basically alike: we are all human beings. Maybe we have different clothes, our skin is of a different colour, or we speak different languages. This is on the surface. But basically, we are the same human beings. That is what binds us to each other.[1]

Latin American theology has followed that pattern of commonality by centring action and reflection within history, rather than centring the process of theologizing within the individual.² The comparison with other faiths and with other modes of being is striking because in an individualistic mode the person as individual makes history without depending on others. However, for the theologizing at the periphery where lesser materials means are available there is a need of cooperation and a certain dependency on others. With that cooperation in mind and that life of community at the centre it is possible to respond to the central calling: that of the Spirit. Jon Sobrino has summarized that calling and that questioning in a very dramatic way, as dramatic as Sobrino's life in Central America, in the following words:

> What are you, and what ought you to be? What do you hope for, and what might you hope for? What are you doing, and what should you be doing? What are you celebrating, and what could you be celebrating? From out of the midst of history itself, the call has sounded: Answer for the truth of history truthfully. Shape that history, do not be dominated by it or merely slip and slide passively through it.³

Market versus Person

One of the most challenging experiences of my visits to North America has been the visits to shopping malls. Shopping has become a way of life for some and at the same time a way of relating for others. Shopping in general and shopping malls in particular are not bad; however, they are the reflection of a human experience dictated by the market in which personal satisfactions arise out of a relation through things rather than through human attitudes. 'Are you coming?' 'We are going shopping?' becomes not a question about a human need for food, clothing or human pleasure in which because an item is needed there is the need to go to a place where one can get it but a reflection on the self, the human and the divine all together. Without realizing, some, if not many human beings, start relating to each other through what they have and how they look. Here, I express my deep ongoing satisfaction with a well-dressed person at any time; I am speaking of a phenomenon where human time and human self are defined by the market rather than by human relations. I am speaking about the need to spend; at its worst a human being goes to the mall in case there is anything interesting and returns with items that are not needed, not wanted or indeed above any financial consideration for the common good of others. Therefore, my theologizing about the shopping mall does not exclude the usefulness and even possible architectural beauty of a mall but the fact that human beings can substitute relatedness and human creativity for shopping and having. Two examples illustrate the substitution of a creative human activity for a material inclusion in a world fabricated by the market and by those who control the market through the media.

In the first example I refer to the creative theologizing of Ola Sigurdson who in her insightful analysis of pop music and God has argued that 'with regard to the question of God in pop-music I suggest that the common denominator is the quest for what it means to be an authentic human being' and that 'this quest often – not always – calls upon God or some higher spiritual being for help'.[4] Indeed, human creativity and the presence of God as beauty or companion of beauty are themes that have inspired the great cathedrals of Europe and the great musicians of church music and some of the pop music composers. It is a pleasure and a divine extension of eternal beauty when one listens to music that one enjoys. However, shopping as a human activity can relate to the possibility of listening to music, to the actual shopping at the mall or to any shopping via the Internet. As far as the shopping is controlled and creates beauty it is part of a human creative activity in which the restful human spirit can dwell on the refreshing notes of an activity that enhances the senses, the spirit and the communal sense of beauty. If that shopping of pop music becomes the central activity rather than the music then one is referring to a process of consumerism in which buying, having and consuming becomes the centre rather than the human activity of enjoying music.

In the second example I refer to the idea sold by the market that a common humanity, globalization and economic development relates to the possibility that all peoples in the world can drink Coca-Cola, can wear blue jeans and can use the Internet in order to feel part of one world. The market has pushed hard through the media for that idea of inclusion, an idea that collapses by the time that members of the Empire are drinking Coca-Cola at your doorsteps or when the poor and marginalized are turned away from a national frontier because they have the wrong nationality, the wrong papers or the wrong intentions. Those rejected at a border can still go away and drink Coca-Cola but they are not able to convince the officials that guard the wall that separates the United States and Mexico that they are both equal. They live in a world of a common humanity and common universal rights in which humanity is divided between those who create and open the markets and the rest, recipients of those ideas and market practices.

The market exists and a process of theologizing asks questions about God and about human beings in relation rather than sanctioning the possibility of existence of financial institutions and their policies. It is through that theologizing that a third part of the hermeneutical circle, the excluded, join the shopper and the seller at the market of the shopping mall. If there are significant numbers of human beings that cannot have enough to eat or that fail to acquire their basics needs is it possible for an honest Christianity to continue consuming rather than being? My answer is a categorical 'no' and the close reading of the Gospels point to the same message. There is a direct relation between the following of God and the compassion for the poor and there is a direct connection between centring the periphery and the demands for a simpler life, for poverty of the spirit and for a constant preoccupation for other human beings. It is here that the scandal of the consumerist world appears, because the values of the Kingdom of God through equality for all human beings disappear.

If the worth of a human being is what the person can acquire through shopping then there are more important human beings: those who shop better and acquire goods that attract attention and have a large home as to be able to store those hundreds of items. Instead, if one follows the values of the Kingdom all human beings have the same worth and within those human beings God takes immediate and more intensive care of the poor and the marginalized; God loves a human being and all human beings regardless of their possibilities at shopping and their prosperity and within those human beings God is closer to those who take care of other human beings and those who have put their heart in God rather than in material possessions. Further, as pointed out by William Cavanaugh, the celebration of God's Kingdom by the community, that is the Eucharist, 'places judgement in the eschatological context of God's inbreaking Kingdom' so that 'the Kingdom is not driven by our desires but by God's desire which we receive as gift in the Eucharist'.[5]

One of the difficulties in any foundational dialogue is the ever-growing division between the poor and the rich, between those under or just above the poverty line and those who have more and more and are able to become successful consumers.[6] The difficulty is not only financial but spiritual. It is financial because there are millions of human beings who cannot feed their families, have access to primary education or clean water but it is spiritual because it is very clear that the message of the Gospel does not make any difference in most of the policies and social approaches to basic human rights. In Latin America and within the period of the military regimes it was possible to blame the armies for spending most of the financial assets on defence and the fighting of insurgents; in democracy there is nobody to blame but the elected politicians who in their majority profess allegiance to the Christian faith and have been in the past victims of human rights abuses.

Within the contemporary world a dialogue between Christianity and Buddhism reminds society that there are higher spiritual values, common human values and that the market does not connect to one or the other.

Poverty and Beatitude

It is here that one looks for the possibility of spiritual centres of change, of Christian commitment and Buddhist practices. Throughout the history of the

Church and throughout the development of Christianity in Latin America the monasteries of contemplatives, men and women, have reminded us of the values of the Kingdom in a way that sometimes the structures of the churches have not.[7] Monasteries are located at the periphery because of monks' search for solitude, silence and God outside the urban places of noise where the shopping malls are located.

The centre of the monastic life relates to activities that are constant, daily routines of prayer, work and communal meals together with a constant reading of the Gospels in community, the search for a communal poverty, and a daily search for the voice of God within the walls of the monastery.[8] The monasteries are places of subversion and transgression because they refuse the possible acceptance of values outside the Kingdom and they do not comply with secular life or even with diocesan ecclesiastical structures. The head of an abbey, the Abbot, acts as a bishop towards the community without having to comply with the pastoral plans of the diocese in which they are located. Monasteries are signs of non-compliance and of the possibility of liberation from consumerism and from the slavery of the market. Monasteries are places where the Kingdom of God is proclaimed as master of all other political systems, the master of consumerism and the master of other processes associated with the centre.[9] The care of the poor and sometimes the defence of the poor are associated with walls in which men and women of courage proclaim that the King is still to come and that not everything is well in the contemporary world.

It is not by chance that there is a close connection between prayer, contemplation, mysticism, actions for peace and actions for non-violence.[10] There is, for example, a historical connection between the Trappist influence by Thomas Merton the Trappist monk, writer and political activist who lived at the Abbey of Our Lady of Gethsemani in Kentucky, USA on Ernesto Cardenal and the later foundation of the Trappists from the abbey of Gethsemani in Santiago, Chile.[11] If Merton supported the peace movement of the 1960s from his enclosure, he also encouraged Cardenal to go ahead with the monastic foundation at Solentiname, Nicaragua. To make matters ever more transgressive the Trappist monks of Santiago aided some politicians that had served under Salvador Allende's government by hiding them from Pinochet's security forces in the hermitage of the Trappist monastery.[12]

I am not advocating here that every Christian should become a monk but I am pointing to the fact that the increase in consumerism has a counter-discourse in the spiritual lives of those who guided by a somehow simple life and challenges the values of the market and consumerism. By their actions they make political statements that follow the values of the Kingdom rather than the values of a secular or an unjust state that oppresses the poor. I am certainly pointing to a certain style of life that has been the mark and trade of theologians, revolutionaries and utopian people who have realized that there is a close connection between one's style of life and the attitudes that one develops in daily life.

Theologizing against consumerism and with the poor and the marginalized takes a particular choice of lifestyle and location. Without that theological consciousness there is no hope of being there with the poor for without a lifestyle that challenges the values of the market there is no chance of acquiring the values of the Kingdom. The soft approach to spirituality is certainly not part of the life of the poor who struggle with inner strength through daily life and difficulties. Thus, since the fourth century monks have struggled with the institutional powers and already the Donatists, condemned as heretics, could be considered the first Marxists within the history of the Church because they challenged the lifestyle and centrality of Rome and the new Christian emperor and quarrelled with Augustine about an established Christianity that for them had too many traits and too many functionaries who had evolved into functionaries of the Church from the former Roman Empire.

The monk is a revolutionary, able to challenge the easy life of the market and who becomes active in a constant bridge between the human and the divine, the social and the monastic.[13] In 1978 I had the chance to spend a few days on retreat at the Trappist monastery in Santiago and I was struck by the fact that their work in the farm was very hard, that their habits were not as elegant as the Benedictines [later I learned that the Trappists have a more strict way of life than the Benedictines] and the most important one – that the community was well-aware of what was happening outside the walls as their bidding prayers throughout the daily offices and at the daily Eucharist requested protection for the persecuted, courage for the church and solidarity with those who had asked for their prayers and their protection. The liturgical act of praise towards God was also a political act of theologizing action and society's needs. Their early prayer at 3:15 am in the morning reminded me of a larger reality in which they were not escaping from the world of the poor and the marginalized; on the contrary they had become a sign and challenge against injustice by just being there – a physical thorn in the urban centre reminding the world that utopia could exist and that the tentacles of power and greed could not have the last say. It is of no surprise to me that they always had a flow of Chilean vocations particularly among those who had been socially and politically very active.

A lifestyle that relates to the Beatitudes provides a sign of the Kingdom that challenges the market; it prepares those who are going through actions of theologizing, be they helping or living among the poor, or taking part in political protests of non-violence against the state. A lifestyle that asks how much is too much and how God comes into every social and financial action creates solidarity with the poor that comes from the deeply rooted Gospel action of uttering the Beatitudes. 'Blessed are the poor!' expresses exclusion for those who oppress the poor and who use the message of the Gospel to pacify protests in order to sustain their power and their greed. 'Blessed' are those who chose to challenge the riches of this world because they preferred to ally with the poor, with God and with his Kingdom. 'Blessed' are the monks who challenge the possibility that the market controls time because through their ongoing marking of the hours through prayer and work they sanctify the hours with values of solidarity, community and divine violence. 'Blessed' are those who reject the possibility that human beings could become better by what they have; instead they are ready to embrace all human beings, particularly those who cry because they have been evicted from their lands or those who have been bombed because they were on the way to oil, resources and stability for the killing machines of the Empire.

A Spirituality of Transgression

The style of life of the periphery is marked by a spirituality of liberation, the liberation of oneself from the slavery of consumerism and the recognition that God works through the poor in the liberation of those oppressed within contemporary society. In the words of Pedro Casaldáliga and José María Vigil,

> We believe that today, in creative fidelity to this living tradition, we are called to live contemplation in liberative activity (*contemplativus in liberatione*), decoding surroundings made up of grace and sin, light and shade, justice and injustice, peace and violence, discovering in this historical process of liberation the presence of the Wind that blows where it will, uncovering and trying to build salvation history in the one history, finding salvation in liberation.[14]

Thus, within a contemplative tradition spirituality, previously associated with pious practices and little action, becomes the action of the Spirit through a person who within the periphery acts on behalf of the poor and continues building up a liberating consciousness by a daily following of a lifestyle that connects with the values of the Kingdom of God and by a daily conversation with the God of Life following the example of Jesus of Nazareth. Spirituality becomes in this way of life a life of transgression because the freedom of the Spirit means that such a person is not always complying with the rules of the market, the rule of the state, the rules of the Church or the rules of the monastery. Indeed, Thomas Merton had enormous problems with his Abbot because the Abbot did not understand the fact that a monk was being a writer, a political activist, a personal confidant and an inter-faith activist at the same time. There is no doubt that within the deepest disagreements between Merton and his abbot Merton spent longer periods in contemplation and for years became a solitary hermit in order to continue searching for the will of God as he continued corresponding with hundreds of people, including activists against the Vietnam War and even Buddhist philosophers.

The style of life that challenges the values of the unjust is a style of life that bears witness to the poverty of Jesus of Nazareth and declares openly the foolishness and injustice that creates multinational companies and financial wealth for the so-called billionaires of this world at the expense of the Third World and the poor of this world. A lifestyle becomes a continuation of a line of Gospel adherence through the centuries to the poor, starting with the Peruvian Saint Martin de Porres in colonial times and development of the convents into monasteries of the twentieth century.

Transgression and theological transgressions at the periphery are a way of theologizing because as in the case of the monk they are signs of a world to come 'not yet' but 'here now'. Theological transgressions challenge any impossibility of dialogue and foster the presence of God in all structures, all human beings and all religions. Theological transgressions remain prophetic when they are able to recognize the centrality of the poor and of the Kingdom even if there are contradictions in such theologizing with the contemporary realities of a particular tradition or a particular church. The unity of transgressing is the unity of hunger and poverty at the periphery not only in spirit and desire but also in form, matter and lifestyle. Theological transgressions such as those explored by Marcella Althaus-Reid within theology and sexuality are also explorations that conduce to ethical responsibilities that arise not out of unchangeable norms but of social relations and the realities of a common humanity. Therefore, 'the perceived excessive consumerism and carelessness of some sections of the population is seen as sinful by destitute people who do not understand why things (in this case, discarded goods) are not shared with the community'.[15]

A simpler style of life for those who have more and a richer style of life for the poor is the way forward. However, we become aware that the media and the market play with our desires for consumption. We are told that the more growth in the economy through our consumption we have the more jobs that could be created, the more prosperity we could enjoy and the happier we would be. This is a false strategy because an increased consumption by us does not solve the breach between the rich and the poor or in other words 'self-interested consumption does not bring justice to the hungry' but 'consumerism is the death of Christian eschatology'.[16] Instead, the search for the other is what drives our lives in the periphery for if consumption allows a non-human exchange of desire and eventually kills it the search for the other as co-human and as my own responsibility becomes a sign of the Kingdom. The prophets of the Kingdom are certainly those that drive others to desire the values of the Kingdom; in the words of Hadwig Ana Maria Müller 'they approach others not as rich people who have something to give but as those who are poor and want to receive from others. They do not suppress their search for relationships; they keep alive their desire, the hunger, within them'.[17]

It is here that the common humanity and the Christian eschatology meet because if Latin American theology, a theology of liberation, has become a well-known global phenomenon within Christian theological circles it has been because of the challenges it posed to the Empire in the times of the Reagan administration and later through the cooperation between Latin American theologians and other Third World theologians. In matters of lifestyle and spirituality I am tempted to argue that the future would need a further globalization of a Latin American spirituality because in matters of poverty, hunger, emptiness, longing, enlightenment, submission, Kingdom values, anti-poverty, relatedness, otherness, contemplation and non-violence a further cooperation is needed between Latin American theologians and the theologizing at the periphery with the theologizing of the Eastern peripheries of a globalized world. Ernesto Cardenal had the challenge of Thomas Merton's experience of the East in the 1960s and 1970s; is it not the time for a new and fresh encounter between Latin American theologians, theologizing at the periphery and Buddhism, particularly Tibetan Buddhism, and its sense of exile, refugee and periphery? Is it not the time to explore the sense of creation and ecological issues with Hinduism particularly through the Hindu masters' understanding of their 'sacred scriptures'? Is it not the time to theologize with other peripheries of the world in order to hear God's Kingdom at work? My answer is an unequivocal 'yes' to those dialogues and the search for a preferential option for the poor that becomes inclusive rather than exclusive and that relates the injustice and oppression of human beings in Latin America, Africa and Asia. This kind of opening to a cosmic theologizing was already stated by the Association of Third World Theologians meeting in Mexico in 1986 but has not been properly followed up from the point of view of dialogue between Latin American theologians and the world religions. It is understandable that matters of hunger, injustice and poverty come first, however the de-colonizing of other beliefs and other cultures by Christianity needs to be addressed as a matter of urgency following the rich theological statement given by the final document of that conference in number 65:

> Jesus reveals God, but does not limit or exhaust the divine. In the light of the risen Jesus and the cosmic Christ, nothing prevents God's self-revelation

to all God's people. It is liberating to confess that God is not confined to Christian traditions, churches, and scriptures. Wherever God makes self-disclosure and self-gift, the word enters the earth, becomes embodied in history, participates in people's struggles for justice and freedom, and helps propel them toward their (up)rising and liberation.[18]

I must admit that I have found enormous inspiration by connecting the values of the Kingdom of God as a globalized reality, by theologizing with those who follow other faiths, in the Gospels as well as in the sayings of the Buddha, in the poetry of Ernesto Cardenal as well as in the writings of the Dalai Lama, in the compassion exalted in the *Bhagavat Gita* or the Koran, values that in the search of a spirituality of justice and compassion for the world challenge consumerism and the possibility of a world and a Latin American society that does not care for justice and peace. The signs of the Kingdom through the contemporary experiences of monasticism, mysticism and contemplation challenge the media's assumption that we are all consumers and that we are happy to consume. I am not a happy shopper; I enjoy the fruits of the earth, a good glass of wine with fellow travellers and an oily chicken stew in the periphery. At the end of the day I would always argue that the future of humanity and the presence of the God of Life lies at that globalized periphery where not only enemies would cease to fight each other, where the machines of war would be dismantled, where the Empire would cease to understand the world of God in terms of power and where Christians, Buddhists, Hindu and Muslims would live together under the umbrella of the values of the Kingdom within a globalized world which is just and in peace because every single human being has decided to do so.

It is possible to argue that history repeats itself and that the challenges of the 1960s are still with us, or they have returned unsolved. There is a 'war on terror', poverty is still an issue that divides protestors, Christian activists and the leaders of the G-8 nations, secularism and freedom of conscience are at our doorsteps and millions still follow religious and ritual lives within the world religions. Gustavo Gutiérrez' assessment of Latin America still stands within a continent in which the realities of injustice and poverty are central to understand the possibilities and impossibilities of a theologizing in which the Kingdom of God is here but not yet, but a continent in which God is present. Gutiérrez wrote in the late 1980s,

> On this continent hope is born in the midst of suffering; it takes the form of life that comes through death. Its ultimate motivation is found in the living God, the God of tender love, who stoops to us in our suffering, our faith, and our efforts to be in solidarity with the Latin American poor and to win their liberation.[19]

Towards Common Tenets

It is the realization of suffering that assigns a central tenet of love and compassion to both Christianity and Buddhism. The service of neighbours, central to the golden periods of Christianity, finds a common thread in the Buddhist realization that all is suffering. Liberation comes from detachment from riches in Christianity, from detachment from a material world that is an illusion in Buddhism. The mediation of the two realms of experience and knowledge seem to be realized in the challenges to exclusion that in the context of Europe has been idealized and implemented by legislation. Legislation has not only proclaimed the total equality in rights and obligations of all citizens but has challenged any other mode of existence as selfishness without love for others, even in the secular realm. The end of the absoluteness of Christianity in Europe has not only opened the growth of a more inclusive Christianity but has also helped the conditions and additions to a contemporary inter-religious dialogue.

After Christianity in the Church

If after the collapse of the Berlin Wall the postmodern condition had suggested the possibility of the end of meta-narratives, the advent of a unified effort to develop Eastern Europe and other parts of the world brought a new meta-narrative into play: the neo-colonial paradigm of globalization. It is at this moment that the 'age of faith' and the 'age of reason' became obsolete because neither secularization nor the challenges to science made any difference to a world dominated by the United States and the meta-narratives of economic prosperity and the ontology of a divine being that became closely link with economic progress. Thus, economic blessings became associated with divine intervention and economic success was located within a divine understanding of the exclusion of others who did not agree with either 'the clash of civilizations' or the possibility of the end of a separation between the public role of religion and politics in the United States. President George W. Bush and Prime Minister Tony Blair used their own faith understanding to suggest that a new 'liberation' of Iraq from the dictatorship of Saddam Hussein in 2003 was not only necessary but willed by God and the values of Western civilization.

It is within this context that the lifelong philosophical work of Gianni Vattimo became a challenge to the dying humanism of a 'war in terror' by suggesting that a new 'age of interpretation' became the language of all, the language of those who had challenged the actual possibilities of theism and atheism such as Richard Rorty. For Vattimo argues, following Heidegger [section 1 of *Being and Time*], 'knowledge is always interpretation and nothing but this', and 'interpretation is the only *fact* of which we can speak'.[20] If Nietzsche introduced the possibility of nihilism and Heidegger the end of metaphysics by the possibility of letting events speak, Lyotard and his end of meta-narratives overlooked the possibility that the narratives still existed after being negated. Those narratives needed to be looked at once again because the condition of postmodernity did not provide a state of truth after the negation of the meta-truths. It is here that Vattimo argues strongly for a more mainstream understanding of Heidegger's sense of the end of metaphysics in the following words: 'we are called upon to grasp a guiding thread that we can use in order to project its further development; that is, to remain inside it as interpreters rather than as objective recorders of facts'.[21]

Vattimo's act of remaining within 'a guiding threat' explores the possibility of human creativity *vis-à-vis* the human experience of God because it provides limits to any ontological exploration that in the past was deemed as normative. The realization that an event has something to say to an ongoing humanity in search of meaning, in Vattimo's words 'to let the event speak', has a clear repercussion: 'this event comprises the end of Eurocentrism, the critique of ideology, the dissolution of the evidentness of consciousness through psychoanalysis, the explicit pluralisation of the agencies of information, the mass media'.[22] Thus, in my own reading of Vattimo, any event is meaningful by itself regardless of the possibility that for the witness the event could be nihilistic and somehow devoid of a possible interpretation. For it is possible to argue with Vattimo that the role of Christianity has been changed within contemporary society and Christianity cannot only be perceived as meaningful through the utopian connection between the practices of Christianity and public society. Truth lies not within the ontological definitions or the philosophical negations of particular truths but within the historical event and subject, within what in liberation theology was known as 'the first moment' or in the definition provided by Jung Mo Sung as 'the experience of ethical indignation'.[23]

This is where Vattimo's arguments connect with liberation theology and Tibetan Buddhism. If Christianity seems to be nihilistic and empty it is only because it has responded as an anti-metaphysical response to the dreams of an ontological way of appreciating the world that has made human beings prisoners of platonic worlds in which human beings do not find their identity any longer. Vattimo's response to this absence of a humane and democratic society relates to his own search and to his own experience of serving within the contemporary world of European politics. However, within Vattimo's theoretical development of a possibility of a Christian existence after the end of theism and atheism, he develops a third possibility that does not engage with the previous ontological realities but moves into a new understanding of the possibilities of a Christianity freed from an ontological and rational explanation for all. He writes:

> There is a third possibility between, on the one hand, the metaphysical demonstration of the truth of Christianity (the *preambula fidei* and the historical veracity of the resurrection) and, on the other, its falseness with respect to scientific reason (entailing the quasi-naturalistic acceptance of the differences among individuals, cultures, and societies): Christianity as a historical message of salvation.[24]

It is interesting that Vattimo argued, after a life full of doubt about the Church and Christianity, for the possibility of a historicity within a life as a Christian, while he asserted that 'if I were not a Christian I would probably be a metaphysician'.[25] For in Vattimo's understanding, and practice, belief is always on the making and it is not a given; for belief and the assertion of belief in God is no more than a personal assertion of a plausibility. He writes: 'well, I believe that I believe'.[26] In dialogue with a non-believer such as Richard Rorty, Vattimo expressed their absolute similarity in philosophy but the fact that Vattimo's sense of event and being was framed daily by the reading of the biblical text and by the fact that the text did not support ontology but the history of a living God. For Rorty, 1 Corinthians 13 and the centrality of love as kind, patient and enduring all have the capability of uniting believers and unbelievers. However, in his words: 'the difference between these two sorts of people is that between unjustifiable gratitude and unjustifiable hope'.[27]

It is within that 'age of hermeneutics' that Vattimo returns to the most traditional of meanings for hermeneutics, that reading and interpretation of a message, an event for a particular human being in search of identity and being. It is also within that ongoing hermeneutics that Vattimo took part in the world of active politics and questioned, as the Argentinean philosopher Enrique Dussel once did, the possibility of understanding wisdom or philosophy without understanding the actions of human beings within the real world and particularly within the world of contemporary politics. Thus, Dussel referring to how liberation theologians used Marxism argued that 'liberation theology uses a *certain* Marxism in a *certain way* – never in such a way as to be incompatible with the foundations of the faith'.[28]

In the case of Vattimo the possible comparison of praxis and action for the socially marginalized and liberation theology's preferential option for the poor and the marginalized connect through Vattimo's own historical journey. As in the case of Latin American liberationists Vattimo's journey started as a committed Christian, a Roman Catholic, who developed his interests in the world, and his social, religious and political interests through the church. He studied philosophy in order to continue taking part in that blend of human interests and in his own words 'I wanted to contribute to the formation of a new Christian humanism, which would be free from liberal individualism and from collective and deterministic Marxism'.[29] After reading Jacques Maritain on his intellectual youth he became engrossed with the critique of modernity by Nietzsche and Heidegger who were not only anti-modern but anti-Christian.[30]

It was through a hermeneutics of the actual human being in a historical perspective and the impossibility of negating the essence of God that Vattimo returned to the Christian faith. If atheists had understood Nietzsche's work as denying the existence of God, Vittamo's work with those original philosophical sources argued that in the interpretation of both, Nietzsche and Heidegger, commentators had not understood the fact that the philosophers' assertions were only interpretations and that the negation of God had not been logically proven. Thus, 'the decline of metaphysics as a systematic philosophy, which conferred a consistent, unified, and rigorously grounded representation of the stable structures of Being, has made the philosophical denial of God's existence impossible'.[31]

For Vattimo, the biblical text becomes credible after modernity because it can be studied, critically assessed as historically constructed and because at the end supports the idea of God as Verbum, as the Word who becomes incarnate, thus weakening any rational and ontological understanding of an essence with no connection with his history, event or being. With modernity and postmodernity a Western God linked to a European conception of society and the state has been weakened to the point that the Verbum cannot be tied and become a prisoner of reason or of a mediaeval faith. Instead, the notion of Verbum continues a process of historical connection with events and beings who provide diversity. Those events and beings engaged with a Verbum who is as much part of the history and event of the Cross and does not exist on an essence of wisdom that cannot be linked to human events.

However, the reclaiming of Christianity without colonialism and eurocentrism, that is with a sense that all societies and human beings are in a linear progression and evolution towards European societies, can only take place if Christianity 'recovers its profound solidarity with the destiny of modernization'.[32] Vattimo's engagement with this modernization occurs within his active participation in European politics where after joining the Italian Communists he served as a member of the European Parliament from 1999 to 2004 under the umbrella of the Party of European Socialists. It is this particular action that makes him connect once again with a God who as far as political and social action – as far as active charity is dispersed – cannot be dead. For this is the intellectual and philosopher who leaves the ivory tower of Turin where he had been full professor since 1969 in order to immerse himself in the complex and difficulties politics of the European Union. Vattimo does so at a time in which the political tendencies of the Italian electorate aim towards the far-right and Italy supports the 'war on terror' while Prime Minister Silvio Berlusconi becomes a close ally and even friend of the US President George W. Bush.

Vattimo had been fully involved in the 1992 Italian political crisis in which a police investigation into political parties managed to finish the party of his youth, the Christian Democrats. After the political revolution against bribes that took place in Italy Vattimo took part in the national debate through newspaper columns in *La Stampa* and *L'Unità*, criticizing not only the dissolution of this new political revolution but also challenging the Italian electorate's support for Berlusconi and his House of Liberty Coalition that included the neo-fascist National Alliance of Gianfranco Fini and the xenophobic Northern League of Umberto Bossi.[33] Within the European Parliament Vattimo was a member of the Commission for Freedom and Citizens' Rights, Justice and Internal Affairs, the Commission for Culture, Youth, Education, Communication and Sport and the inter-parliamentary delegation from the European Union to China. Vattimo helped to shape the European Union Constitution and contributed to the challenges to Berlusconi by journalists who wanted to highlight accusations against the Italian Prime Minister when he took over the European Union presidency in July 2003.

During those years Vattimo served European politics as a philosopher, a moral and ethical philosopher, who despite the possibility of all-embracing structures in politics managed to remind others of the centrality of the individual and his rights and the centrality of a political and philosophical project that could emancipate humanity. In the critical summary by Paolo Flores D'Arcais 'the task that Vattimo assigns to philosophy is, in fact, radically political' so that 'philosophy *as* philosophy must be the instrument of *liberation*. Such a liberating and emancipator vocation constitutes – also and above all – the *responsibility* of the philosopher'.[34] This kind of ethical responsibility unites once again Vattimo with Enrique Dussel and through Dussel with the first generation of theologians of liberation. But if Dussel made his enterprise to challenge any philosophical ethics devoid of history Vattimo managed to make history a divine ethics. This kind of divine ethics remains a challenging dissolution of a centralized essence by the fact that the God of the Bible becomes complex and historical and Christianity remains a European sectarian movement to be weakened not by discrimination but through the affirmation of the end of metaphysics.

It is this assertion that remains challenging to a non-dialogical position between Christianity and Buddhism; the 'end of Christianity' remains a dialogical position between God, Christianity and Buddhism.

Notes

1. The fourteenth Dalai Lama, 'The Nobel Peace Prize Lecture, Oslo, Norway', in Sidney Piburn, ed. *The Dalai Lama: A Policy of Kindness – An Anthology of Writings by and about the Dalai Lama*, Ithaca, NY: Snow Lion Publications, 1990, pp. 15–25 at p. 15. The connections between Thomas Merton and the Dalai Lama are important because Ernesto Cardenal and the new foundation of the Trappist monastery in Santiago were all connected through discourses that arose out of the influence of Merton on the American inter-faith dialogue and later on the Latin American challenges to violence, particularly at the time of the military regimes, see for example Joseph Quinn Raab, 'Comrades for Peace: Thomas Merton, the Dalai Lama and the Preferential Option for Nonviolence', in Victor A. Kramer and David Belcastro, eds. *The Merton Annual: Studies in Culture, Spirituality and Social Concerns* 19, Louisville, KY: Fons Vitae, 2006, pp. 255–66.
2. Ignacio Ellacuría, *Freedom Made Flesh: The Mission of Christ and His Church*, Maryknoll, NY: Orbis, 1976, pp. 1–19.
3. Jon Sobrino SJ, 'Spirituality and the Following of Jesus', in Ignacio Ellacuría SJ and Jon Sobrino SJ, eds. *Mysterium Liberationis: Fundamental Concepts of Liberation Theology*, Maryknoll, NY: and Northblackburn, Victoria: Orbis and Collins Dove, 1993, pp. 677–701 at p. 677.
4. Ola Sigurdson, 'Songs of Desire: On Pop-Music and the Question of God', in Werner Jeanrond and Christoph Theobald, eds. *God: Experience and Mystery* (*Concilium* 2001/1), London: SCM Press, pp. 34–42 at p. 41.
5. William T. Cavanaugh, 'Consumption, the Market, and the Eucharist', in Christophe Boureux, Janet Martin Soskice and Luiz Carlos Susin, eds. *Hunger, Bread and Eucharist* (*Concilium* 2005/2), London: SCM Press, pp. 88–95 at p. 94.
6. For a contemporary globalized view of global inequality see Iván Petrella, 'Liberation Theology: A Programmatic Statement', in Iván Petrella, ed. *Latin American Liberation Theology: The Next Generation*, Maryknoll, NY: Orbis, 2005, pp. 147–72.
7. Santo Domingo § 37.
8. *Perfectae Caritatis* § 15.
9. Santo Domingo § 86.
10. See for example Dorothee, Soelle, *The Silent Cry: Mysticism and Resistance*, Minneapolis, MN: Fortress Press, 2001.
11. Thomas Merton wanted to relocate to Latin America, either to the Chilean foundation or to Nicaragua to be in Solentiname with Ernesto Cardenal. On 3 July 1966 Merton wrote to Cardenal: 'You will interested in the important news that Gethsemani is taking over the Spencer foundation in Chile. This is important because it now means that Gethsemani is engaged in work in Latin America. Some monks are going down in August and others in October. I do not think I am likely to be sent there but anything may happen', in Christine M. Bochen, ed. *Thomas Merton: The Courage for Truth – Letters to Writers*, New York: Farrar, Straus and Giroux, 1993, p. 156.
12. A few years ago the Trappist moved to Rancagua, a city south of Santiago, searching for a quieter place as the expansion of urban Santiago had reached the vicinity of the Trappist monastery in Santiago.
13. For theological reflections on the active apostolate of the religious congregations in Latin America see Jon Sobrino SJ, 'Religious Life in the Third World', in *The True Church of the Poor*, London: SCM Press, 1985, pp. 302–37.

14 Pedro Casaldáliga and José María Vigil, *The Spirituality of Liberation* (*Liberation and Theology* 12), Tunbridge Wells: Burns & Oates, 1994, p. 103.
15 Marcella Althaus-Reid, *From Feminist Theology to Indecent Theology: Readings on Poverty, Sexual Identity and God*, London: SCM Press, 2004, p. 161.
16 William T. Cavanaugh, 'Consumption, the Market, and the Eucharist', p. 91.
17 Hadwig Ana Maria Müller, 'Hunger for Bread – the Desire of the Other', in Christophe Boureux, Janet Martin Soskice and Luiz Carlos Susin, eds. *Hunger, Bread and Eucharist* (*Concilium* 2005/2), London: SCM Press, pp. 73–9 at p. 76.
18 'Commonalities, Divergences, and Cross-fertilization among Third World Theologies: A Document based on the Seventh International Conference of the Ecumenical Association of Third World Theologians, Oaxtepec, Mexico, 7–14 December, 1986', § 65, in K. C. Abraham, ed. *Third World Theologies: Commonalities and Differences*, Maryknoll, NY: Orbis, 1990, pp. 207–8.
19 Gustavo Gutiérrez, *The God of Life*, London: SCM Press, 1991, 189.
20 Gianni Vattimo, 'The Age of Interpretation', in Rorty and Vattimo, *The Future of Religion*, pp. 43–54 at p. 44.
21 Ibid., pp. 43–54 at p. 46.
22 Ibid.
23 Jung Mo Sung, 'The Human Being as Subject: Defending the Victims', in Iván Petrella, ed. *Latin American Liberation Theology: The Next Generation*, Maryknoll, NY: Orbis, 2005, pp. 1–19 at p. 4.
24 Gianni Vattimo, 'The Age of Interpretation', pp. 43–54 at p. 52.
25 Richard Rorty, Gianni Vattimo and Santiago Zabala, 'Dialogue: What is Religion's Future after Metaphysics?', in Rorty and Vattimo, *The Future of Religion*, pp. 55–81 at p. 63.
26 Gianni Vattimo, *After Christianity*, New York: Columbia University Press, 2002, p. 2.
27 Richard Rorty, 'Anticlericalism and Atheism', in Rorty and Vattimo, *The Future of Religion*, pp. 29–41 at p. 40.
28 Enrique D. Dussel, 'Theology of Liberation and Marxism', in Ellacuría and Sobrino, eds. *Mysterium Liberationis*, pp. 85–102 at p. 92.
29 Gianni Vattimo, *After Christianity*, p. 2.
30 Maritain also became important for Latin American liberation theologians, particularly for the first generation of those who studied in France such as Juan Luis Segundo SJ and Gustavo Gutiérrez, see Enrique D. Dussel, 'Theology of Liberation and Marxism', pp. 85–102 at p. 87.
31 Vattimo, *After Christianity*, p. 15.
32 Ibid., p. 97.
33 I have relied for these biographical notes on Santiago Zabala, 'Introduction: Gianni Vattimo and Weak Philosophy', in Santiago Zabala, ed. *Weakening Philosophy: Essays in Honour of Gianni Vattimo*, Montreal and Kingston: McGill-Queen's University Press, 2007, pp. 3–34 at pp. 26–7.
34 Paolo Flores D'Arcais, 'Gianni Vattimo; or rather, Hermeneutics as the Primacy of Politics', in Santiago Zabala, ed. *Weakening Philosophy*, pp. 250–69 at p. 250.

Chapter 8

A Fresh Christian Ecclesiology and Buddhist Challenges

The previous chapters have outlined the experiences of dialogue between world religions that have taken place over the twentieth century, including reflections on the experience of Christians who became heavily involved in a personal quest for dialogue.[1] From the experiences of ashrams (a spiritual community gathered around a guru) in India to the dialogue between Jesuits and Buddhists it is clear that the advent of Vatican II was not only an auspicious event for dialogue but also the fruit of a dialogue that had taken place previously.[2] Those previous experiences influenced the spirit of the ecumenical council and later the council inspired others to seek dialogue for the sake of finding God and the divine in their lives.[3] It is very striking then that within more open and globalized societies present in the twentieth-first century there seems to be less tolerance and openness to other religions at the international level.[4] There is no doubt that the criminal actions of Islamic extremists in the Middle East, Europe, the United States and more recently in northern Nigeria (January 2012) has not helped the possibility of religion being perceived as a threat to democracy and diversity.[5]

Divisions by practitioners of different world religions are played up in the media and the teachings of Pope Benedict XVI stress the centrality of the Roman Church as the only holder of the real 'truths' of Christianity.[6] In the analysis by Leonardo Boff 'fifty years of ecumenical work, of inter-religious dialogue, have apparently vanished because the old medieval theses of the Church as the sole holder of the intentions of God and as the path to salvation have been resurrected'.[7] There are criticisms that not only have arisen from within the Catholic Church but in a recent book-length assessment of Benedict XVI's pontificate Marco Politi has argued that there is a paralysis in ecumenical relations and a worrying lack of agenda and international presence by the papacy.[8]

One is mindful that bases for dialogue are indeed always threatened by national and international conflicts in which, it seems, religions seem to clash and religious sectarianism seems to be rampant.[9] However, following Alan Mittleman's analysis of 9/11 one must recognize that 'the problem of religious violence, of terror in the name of God, is very old'.[10] It is this religious violence that creates a climate where inter-faith dialogue seems like a dying activity and as such an activity that is detached from the ordinary human experience be it at the level of the state or of the individual.[11] A clear example of this has been the distrust of Islam in the United States and Europe following the appalling events of 9/11 in the United States and the subsequent 'war on terror' as well as the military interventions in Iraq and Afghanistan.[12] Both religious distrust and religious contestation assume an essentialist view of Islam and of Christianity rather than the diversity of several Islamic traditions and Christian traditions when it comes to the role of religion within the state and the possible dialogue between Christianity and Islam.[13] Reza Pankhurst has outlined this diversity very clearly in the context of the 'Arab spring' of 2010 and the always uncertain model of political unity in the Middle East:

> While one train of thought posits Islamic governance as an authentic and correct form of polity for the region which would bring about accountable, elected government, the other claims that 'Islam' is fundamentally silent on the issue of the 'state', and that notions of an 'Islamic state' or caliphate are in fact dictatorial and antithetical to orthodox Islam, though Islamic values can inform the individual in their role as citizens within a democratic state.[14]

However, less publicized has been the ongoing attempt at dialogue and conversation that took place after 9/11 in the United States and elsewhere in what Jane Smith has labelled 'the dialogue of engagement'.[15] Such 'dialogue of engagement' arose out of an event of death, indeed many deaths, within the history of the United States. It sadly linked the history of parts of North America with South America in general and with Chile in particular because of the coincidence on day (11) and month (September) of the military coup in Chile and the events of the widely called 9/11 in the United States. Following from such correlative date and in a very insightful analysis of remembering and forgetting Asma Barlas inscribed and commented on the Chilean playwright Ariel Dorfman's writings in which he reminded his readers that,

> During the past 28 years, 11 September has been a date of mourning, for me and millions of others, ever since that Tuesday in 1973 when Chile lost its democracy in a military coup, that day when death irrevocably entered our lives and changed us forever. And now, almost three decades later, the malignant gods of random history have wanted to impose upon the same country that we blamed for the coup that dreadful date, again a Tuesday, again an 11 September filled with death.[16]

Fresh Christian Ecclesiology and Buddhist Challenges 145

Barlas questions why these two events of 11 September are not remembered together; the answer is clear for her: 'it would require the US not only to acknowledge its own 9/11 against Chile, but also to engage in this process of mutual recognition'; in Dorfman's words to 'look into the mirror of our common humanity'.[17] Of course, the idea of a common humanity springs out in every conference given by the fourteenth Dalai Lama and those involved in a dialogue of a common humanity.[18]

In examining Islam and its diversity I am not losing sight of the Christian–Buddhist line of opening and assertions, I am suggesting that if within tense and contested historical situations dialogue and the acceptance of diversity is possible, even when difficult, in the case of Christianity and Buddhism this is also possible and desirable. The answer lies on focusing in the diverse actions of practitioners rather than in epistemological truths that after all can change according to times, fashions and cultural forms.[19] In fact, cultural forms remain embodied in symbolic caskets in which hermeneutical understandings and reasons of existence are bounded. Two cultural caskets have been previously mentioned as modes of awareness of being in society: Buddhism in its cultural Tibetan form and liberation theology as a form of Christianity that emerged in the bounded ecclesial experience of Latin America. A common characteristic for these two contextual forms of different world religions is the desire for 'liberation' expressed through a concern for other human beings: the poor and the marginalized in the case of liberation theology and sentient beings in the case of Tibetan Buddhism. Within the two religious traditions actual realization of this liberation is linked to actions based on meditation, contemplation and prayer. This is a tradition and a practice common, for example to the Bishop of Amazonia Pedro Casaldáliga in Latin America and to the Geluk order of Tibetan Buddhists (the order of the Dalai Lama) in India. Thus, the founder of the Geluk Rje Tsong Khapa (Lobsang Dakpa/bLo bZang Grags pa) argued that 'the development of a correct view of the ultimate nature of things requires rigorous analytical argument as well as meditative practice; that the deliverances of proper analysis and of proper meditation are completely congruent; and that the practices of study, contemplation and meditation should be inseparable in a practitioner's life'.[20] Tsong Khapa's argument and way of life was also the way of life of Pedro Casaldáliga and Ernesto Cardenal in Latin America.[21]

The three practices of study, contemplation and meditation are truly foundational for a Christian–Buddhist dialogue because these activities are experiential. Moments of dialogue require the actual sensorial experience of a religious moment rather than the sole academic study of a subject. Those involved in dialogue share something they have experienced and their conversation proposes the possibilities of further understanding and further experiential common experiences. Previous chapters have dwelt upon the experience of Thomas

Merton and the fourteenth Dalai Lama, of Daniel Berrigan SJ and Thich Nhat Hanh, as well as the ongoing conversations between Trappists and Buddhist monks. It is the shared experience rather than the documents that create the inter-religious experience, the common pilgrimage, the moment of prayer, the moment of silence and contemplation together, the appreciation of the Gita and the sayings of the Buddha read together with the Gospels, moments that open one's heart to the presence of the divine in different forms in somebody else's life and journey.

Dialogue as Love

Twenty five years after Bede Griffiths wrote his autobiography he returned to write a prologue to a new edition after having spent many years in an Indian ashram; he argued that 'there is only one absolute religion and that is the religion of the Holy Spirit which is the Spirit of Love, present in some measure in every religion and in every man, and drawing all men into the unity for which man was created'.[22] Following from this thought one must connect dialogue with the action of love because dialogue, from a Christian point of view, thrives on the foundational commandments of loving God and loving neighbours. Love is at the essence of life and love is what creates the ontological and practical capabilities for dialogue. When Christian communities in Latin America took an interest in dialoguing with Marxists in the 1960s and 1970s it was not only an 'unholy' alliance because of the historical oppression created by the military governments of the time but it was also an extension of the love of God for all. When Mother Theresa of Calcutta created the conditions of dialogue with Hindus and Muslims in Calcutta it was because she went determined, together with a group of nuns, to serve and love the destitute and the dying. God is love and human beings have the capacity to love and it is that love in action that creates dialogue.

I find it difficult to isolate the experience and theory of Christian dialogue with Buddhism from a larger dialogue with the world religions. There are comparative similarities in the human love required by each follower of a world religion towards the 'Lord'. For examples of dialogue and its necessity arises, as already stated, from the love of God and neighbour in Christianity, from the five pillars of Islam and the submission to the One God, from the Jewish covenant with Adonai as the only Lord, from the non-duality of the soul (*atman*) and the Lord Bhrama in Hinduism and from the compassion and sense of a common humanity in Buddhism.

The love of the divine and His presence within Christianity has an effect on the contemplative, the devotee who takes seriously the love and contemplation of God; God disappears in a common silence and the desolation of the mystic and the contemplative resembles the dryness of Mother Theresa's soul, a soul that in her own letters longed for God 50 years but God never spoke to her during that period. For the Benedictine Henri Le Saux, known as Swami Abhishiktananda, the challenges of dialogue and love meant that he agonized between a clear path to Christian salvation with a God in silence and the need to reject the duality of soul and body, of self and God and to immerse himself in the *advaita*, the non-duality of Hinduism. Within that self-emptying even a dialogue with God disappears, not being there, as outlined by Abhishiktananda in his own words: 'No longer a You to embrace, no longer a You to kneel before, no longer a You at whose feet to sit.'[23]

For the Church, always in need of reform, the path forward is a path of dialogue as a path of love. It is not, I would argue, a path of restoration or re-assertion of given truths, assumed cultural tenets or extraordinarily complex treatments of high theologies of essences and unlocated paradigms. If Vatican II made a clear contribution to a fresh ecclesiology it was in locating the church within society, within the experiences of human beings and to consider herself as servant and prophetic, returning to the figure of Jesus as friend of sinners, a friend of the poor and the marginalized and a friend of those ritually unclean within a cultural model of first century Judaism. The companions of Jesus gave their lives for others and in poverty and detachment they served the sick, the lonely, the prisoners and those without support from others. The call of Pope John XXIII for a council that would help shape a church of the poor in January 1959 coincided with a period of final suppression of Tibetan religious rights in Lhasa by the Chinese Army and the fleeing of the fourteenth Dalai Lama into exile in India in March 1959. This historical coincidence remains in my opinion an ecclesiological opportunity to discern the signs of the times in what Gutiérrez has called 'historical facts'. However, Gutiérrez has also suggested that 'these are not only a starting point for reflection; they are also a point of arrival, a way to verify all theoretical formulation'.[24]

What follows are a few general reflections on a fresh ecclesiology of a Church in dialogue with the world and with the world religions, particularly Buddhism, following from the historical and theological explorations of dialogue within the twentieth century outlined in the previous chapters of this work. It is my final argument that the centrality of the Christ understood as religious superiority has managed not only to bring a certain sectarian connotation to the commandments of love of God and neighbour but also has limited the possible theological reflection of a cosmic Christ present in all spheres of life and of a God that actually knows what He is doing with history, creation and humanity.

Signs of Hope

The previous chapters have highlighted the joys and wonders of inter-religious dialogue within the context of a spiritual search and a spiritual life based on a search for the common good, for a common humanity and for a spiritual experience of wholeness in which abandonment, prayer, contemplation and love are at the centre. Distrust of Islam, evangelical movements advocating the superiority of Christianity and an affluent Christianity associated with prosperity have not managed to water down experiences of dialogue based on common trust, genuine affection and the centrality of God rather than 'my religion'. Contemporary examples of these positive developments in dialogue have been the common encounters of study, prayer and common conversations between Christian monastic orders and Buddhist monks, an expression of an ongoing search by Christian monks since the 1960s for an experience of contemplation across world religions. If Thomas Merton was one of the leading figures of this possible encounter in faith, full communities have followed such as the Trappists of the Abbey of Gethsemani in Kentucky, the Camaldolese Benedictines of California and the Benedictine Federation throughout the world. These are signs of hope for dialogue and instances of religious dialogue that will make an impact on a larger and globalized society.

The presence of Buddhism seems to be non-threatening within the northern hemisphere where Buddhist temples are seen as places of peace and prayer while the fourteenth Dalai Lama, as spiritual leader of Tibetan Buddhists, is definitely seen as a good influence for nations and societies in Europe and the United States. The basis for this non-threatening perception stems from the fact that Buddhism is not a missionary religion. In fact, over the past 40 years the Dalai Lama has discouraged Westerners from becoming Buddhists stating that they should be good and honest Christians wherever they are and work together with all religious practitioners for the happiness of all sentient beings. It should be noted here that other great religious and political figures such as Mother Theresa of Calcutta and Mahatma Gandhi advocated the same option encouraging others to seek the truth in their own traditions, studying each other's traditions and assuming the goodness of God in all of them. The non-violence proclaimed by Gandhi was an expression of political commitment arising out of his own sense of respect and peace for other traditions, political systems and beliefs.[25] Thus while in jail Gandhi wrote a candid and honest letter to his friends thanking them for their support but exhorting them not to ask him to either practice other religions or say anything against other religions. He wrote: 'I regard both the religions as equally true.[26] But my own gives me full satisfaction. It contains all that I need for my growth. It teaches me to pray not that others may believe as I believe but that they may grow to their full height in their own religion. My constant prayer therefore is for a Christian or a Mussulman to be a better Christian and a better Mahomedan'.[27]

The Way Forward

It must be recognized that any dialogue starts with the admission of both differences and similarities between practitioners of Christianity and Buddhism. The main one, not usually expressed clearly, is that Christianity believes in a Creator God who will judge people on their actions at the end of their lives while Buddhism does not propose the existence of a God involved in creation and eschatology. Christians have become aware of the goodness and immense spiritual possibilities of Buddhism in service, prayer and contemplation, engagement with animals and the planet in general and have admired the Buddhist sense of integration between the material and the spiritual. Buddhists have had less experience of Christians as Christians but have explored the positive attitudes towards creation and science, and the monastic tradition within Western Christianity.

Within this realization of religious differential awareness rests a very foundational principle – the principle of commonality, of a common humanity. Thus, many of those involved in dialogue do not seem to see the need for a theoretical or intellectual dialogue but they are willing to cooperate with other religious practitioners within the context of their local, national and global experiences. It is within this realm that Tibetan Buddhism has made a public impact through the involvement of the fourteenth Dalai Lama in a call for spiritual renewal, openness to others and dialogue between religion and the hard sciences. In the case of Christianity, the figure of John Paul II created openness to the possibilities of religion due to his personal charisma, political outreach and his status of 'pop-star' among the young.

In these final reflections I would like to outline some of the major challenges and themes that can make a Christian and Buddhist dialogue meaningful. I avoid the possibility of using the expression 'fruitful' simply because there is a dangerous undertone of achievement in this word associated with a contemporary search for the usefulness of things and of personal achievements for personal gain. It is crucial to understand that dialogue is not an activity to be planned, evaluated and re-assessed but a way of life by human beings who encounter each other searching for human and divine dimensions, spiritual and material, because they find goodness and creativity in all human beings thus reiterating the dignity of the human as God's creation.

These themes or actions or thoughts remain characteristically ongoing and changeable as it is all dialogue. Dialogue takes time and it could be described as a constant conversation in search for meaning. For it is in a divine conversation that we find human meaning so that the initial basic questions associated with religion, creation, birth, death and eschatology disappear. These reflections on the beginning and the end reflect a human search for certainty, and certainty when it is religious makes dialogue impossible and creates a situation where 'religious superiority' appears. The possibility and the reality of any dialogue points to a possible means to an end and ends for the sake of means in order to return to a dialogue that is in the making, and rooted in history and a common humanity, Christian and Buddhist.

Dialogue as Liberation

The experience of Latin American Christian communities and of Tibetan Buddhists in the past 50 years has been a common experience of human beings who are oppressed, who live in poverty, who are sent into exile from their land and who are tortured and killed because they want to live their religious experience in a particular manner in a particular land. Testimonies are abundant of imprisonment and discrimination by the military of China, El Salvador, Chile or Brazil because of the belief that all human beings are equal in the eyes of the Christian God and that all human beings share a common humanity and the freedom of religious practice in the case of Tibetan Buddhism.[28] It is very striking that after Mao's successful taking over of the Chinese government he spoke about the oncoming 'liberation' of Tibet.[29] Thus, and regardless of Chinese assurances to the Indian Ambassador to China that China would not use force to liberate Tibet the imminent happened and on 7 October 1950 Chinese troops launched an attack on Eastern Tibet and the Chinese army entered Tibet reaching Lhasa on 9 September 1951 and keeping a military force of 250,000 across the whole of Tibet.[30] The Chinese 'liberation' of Tibet started and what was to follow was a very delicate period for the Tibetan government and the Dalai Lama that was to last until the full occupation of Tibet by the Chinese army in March 1959 and the flight of the Dalai Lama into exile in India.[31]

Out of these common experiences of suffering and oppression emerged a fresh theological reflection through theologies of liberation and the centrality of the poor in Latin America. In the case of Tibetan Buddhism theologies of emptiness and compassion arose that involved practices of compassion not only towards Tibetan Buddhists in Tibet but also towards Tibetans in India, Nepal, Europe and the United States. The opening of Tibet to the world provided a sense of a real common humanity in need of enlightenment, liberation and a sense of human commonality.[32]

Fresh Christian Ecclesiology and Buddhist Challenges

The theme of liberation arises as a central tenet within the Christian pioneers who have fostered and lived the dialogue with the world religions mentioned in the previous chapters. Liberation from personal and social sin remains a tenet for the Christian communities in Latin America while the liberation from the senses and material attachment remains a central tenet for all Tibetan Buddhists. Liberation from material oppression and poverty remains a Latin American Christian goal as much as Tibetan monks in Tibet desire liberation from the oppression of the Chinese army. So it is that common attitudes of protest and peaceful protest mark the desire for land by peasants in Brazil or by Tibetan monks who desire to be able to show publicly their common humanity through their reverence for the fourteenth Dalai Lama, for them the incarnation of the Lord Buddha, within the Tibetan autonomous region of China.

It is clear that a common dialogue starts by feeling a common experience of humanity, suffering and liberation, an experience common to the church and to the monasteries in Tibet, an experience common to the victims of globalization and capitalism as well as to the victims of progress and the economic boom of the elites in China. Thus, I would argue that dialogue begins with the practice of one's own religion and the conviction that attitudes and sacred texts of other religions can also help one to attain liberation, and thus freedom, from what creates violence, division, discrimination, anger, hate, envy and ultimately does not allow a Christian to love. It becomes clearer that in my opinion dialogue does not take place without a change of heart and an attitude of humility towards God, towards others and in the context of a believing community.

Dialogue as liberation presupposes love for others so that a Christian in dialogue is a Christian who serves others within society and who risks acceptance and security for the liberation and salvation of all. These attitudes create the unity of dialogue with Tibetan Buddhists because Tibetan Buddhists who hold dear the liberation from this life and the exiting of the cycle of life have chosen not to do so until all sentient beings can exit a cycle of suffering. To begin with, these altruistic attitudes create the necessary conditions for dialogue so that the affirmation of altruistic religious values, common to all humanity, provides not the end of a journey but the start of a journey for Christians and Buddhists.

The ecclesiology that arises out of this movement returns to an early Jesus' movement that preaches good news to all, even sinners and prostitutes, and proclaims the personal repentance from sin and the search for the values of the Kingdom of God. The Christian emptying and the Buddhist emptying require an ongoing ecclesial and personal process of material trimming and spiritual generosity that can only come from God and His presence rather than from the assurances of material comfort, prosperity and ultimately human greed. Emptying does not relate to nihilism but to renunciation. A Christian is called to a deeper search for love of neighbour in concrete deeds; the Buddhist is called to examine the teachings of the Buddha (Buddha-darma) and also to help other human beings with actions. The Buddha-darma, in the words of Steve Hagen who is commenting on the possibility of emptying as nihilism, does not relate to the abstract, 'the task it presents us with is to attend to what we actually experience'.[33] Through that experience of contemplation the Buddhist helps others in their lives and makes a clear act of dialogue with others.

We return here to an ecclesial model of human experience, to a radical model of a lifestyle that brings us back to a group of Jesus' friends, associates and followers that journeyed from Galilee to Jerusalem learning along the way the values of their commitment and ultimate journey. I have, somewhere else, spoken of 'a theology of the periphery' whose main manifesto is 'God lives at the periphery' because he chooses to be found within the history of the periphery, the history and journey of the victims, outlined by Jon Sobrino as creating 'the civilization of poverty that brings humanization within it'.[34]

Liberation from riches as opposed to the values of the Kingdom of God outlines the possibility of encounter with Buddhists who, in their own understanding, assume emptying of senses and attachment as part of their finding of liberation. Here, the Kingdom of God manifests itself in the shared values present in all religious texts whereby matter conduces to the divine but it is not the ultimate goal of any human activity that after all tends to leave earthly possessions in order to find human beings and ultimately to find God. Liberation represents an emptying by the church and its leaders from the possibility of power and riches that created in the past the phenomenon of Christiandom rather than Christianity, of a supra-structure rather than an ecclesial community of love and service to others.

Thus, the signs that accompanied the disciples' return to Galilee in order to recreate their experience somewhere else were the cure of the sick, the inclusion of sinners and the unclean, the possibility that slaves were not part of the values of the Kingdom of God and the life of a community that looked after the widows and orphans and took part in the local life of social communities. In the words of Marcus Borg: 'Out of that experience flowed an awareness of a way other than the normative ways of the other renewal movements, one open to the outcasts and not dependent on holiness, but on self-emptying and dying to self and world.'[35]

It is clear that I am less concerned here with a dialogue between theological commissions or learned theologians, something that Buddhists have not attempted so far. I am concerned with dialogue as part of a Christian way of life, as part of a journey in which the attainment of holiness and the daily conversation with God takes precedence over any intellectual exercise. The commonality of any inter-faith dialogue arises then out of a common experience rather than out of a common understanding of particular truths regarding the world. It requires 'learned ignorance' instead of the citing of texts containing truths and the inclusive pronouns of constructive inter-religious dialogue contained for example in the Muslim document sent to Christian leaders in the West after 9/11 entitled 'A Common World Between Us'.[36]

Dialogue as Personal Re-Shaping

It is first of all a human being that dialogues with another human being. Dialogue with other human beings require empathy, so that in the words of the fourteenth Dalai Lama, 'one of the Buddhist techniques for enhancing compassion involves imagining a situation where there is a sentient being suffering'.[37] It is the first outline of a newness of knowledge that arises out of the mind of a child who asks questions and in asking those questions remembers to accept diversity and a new search. It was the message given by the Benedictine monk Henri Le Saux, later to become the Hindu Swami Abhishiktananda, who wrote: 'dialogue may begin simply with relations of mutual sympathy. It only becomes worthwhile when it is accompanied by full openness ... not merely at the intellectual level, but with regard to [the] inner life of the Spirit. Dialogue about doctrines will be more fruitful when it is rooted in a real spiritual experience at depth and when each one understands that diversity does not mean disunity, once the Center of all has been reached'.[38]

This spiritual experience is the experience of emptying in order to fill senses and knowledge with the experience of contemplation and the divine. It is an experience, sensorial and personal, by which questions of definitions and differences disappear not because they do not exist but they become non-threatening, not centralized and non-discriminatory. The filling in of a spiritual experience in Christianity remains after all the experience of emptying the self from all preoccupations in order to to fill the self with the centrality of the experience of the divine self.

By dialogue, prayer and contemplation every agent and participant of dialogue discovers the centrality of the experience of looking at the centre of all rather than explaining the centre through other means, symbols and metaphors. Those symbols create the sense that the spiritual realm and the values of the spiritual are areas in which humans have to engage through conceptual means of human value actions rather than the acceptance of the mystical presence of silence and presence, of God and godless. Those binary oppositions bring a Christian and a Buddhist together in a pilgrimage of the soul rather than a pilgrimage of common ideas or words that lose their meaning and create strife and division. The pilgrimage towards holiness, a much misunderstood notion, has been explored by Denise and John Carmody suggesting a Christian appreciation of Buddhist values of holiness as the right path of a journey where the holy stands within the secular in terms of spaces filled by different religious traditions.[39]

The first step of dialogue is to accept the challenge of diversity and the warmth of the dichotomies of dialogue: for some moments of spiritual silence and search, for others moments of intense activity helping people in a common purpose of alleviating poverty, suffering and injustice. The two processes constitute the second challenge of possible contradictions. These notions of the apophatic or negative theology have already been explored as to suggest that religious experiences can go beyond the doctrinal and the rational in the works of Dionysius the Areopagite and St Maximus the Confessor. However, these notions assume a fresh understanding for the self in dialogue when they are compared to Zen Master Dogen and the impact of Zen Buddhism in the possibilities of a dialogue of self-contradiction.[40]

Dialogue as Religious Contradiction

There is one single contradiction between Christianity and Buddhism: Christianity upholds creation and eschatology as works of God while Buddhism does not uphold or believe in a creator but in energies that can be used for good through a process of human emptying and human detachment. The principle of contradiction in dialogue suggests that dialogue conduces not to a mutual conviction of a common awareness or a common epistemology but the assertion of a contradictory self-explanation. This contradiction leads to the awareness of commonality in contemplation and liberation from earthly desires, a utopic state of commonality that finds its peak within those who practice meditation, silence and emptiness in their daily life. The contradiction of creation/non-creation relates to the possible adherence to a common challenge to material actions that negates the possibility of achieving liberation through utopia and detachment. However, the engagement with contradiction in truth points to experiential self-understandings and common-understandings that are marked by the experience of speaking rather than silence, of listening rather than teaching. Thus, a recent work on the Catholic Church and dialogue with other religions edited by James Heft has emphasized not only the construction of academic chapters on the Catholic Church and each religion chosen but also has provided the possibility of a written response to the writing by practitioners of the religious tradition in question.[41]

The Meaning of Suffering

Golden moments of the church have taken place when the love and service of those suffering was taken seriously. The ecclesiology that arose out of the option for the liberation of the poor and the marginalized by the Latin American church created an immediate impact on the experience of the church. Suffering equated to poverty and discrimination related not only to a Christian option but allows a clear dialogue with Buddhism, tradition that considers suffering as a common phenomenon of all humanity. Suffering as one of the Buddhist truths extends to sentient beings, human beings and animals in the classification of a creation united in God, a theme that has been neglected by theologians of the world religions but discussed extensively by philosophers. The concept of speciesism, coined in 1970 as an analogy to racism and discussed almost exclusively within philosophical circles becomes for Paul Waldau a common dialogical trope for dialogue that goes back to ancient understandings in Christianity and Buddhism and provides the possibility of deepening dialogues on suffering and non-suffering related to animal rights and human rights in the two traditions.[42]

Texts for the Journey

The study of one's rule and of other religions such as Buddhism creates the valuable feeling that behind the experience of a religious practitioner there is a vast body of writings that express teaching, life and common values. There is no doubt that the choice of texts for a journey of dialogue is completely personal; thus I would like to share some of the texts that as a contemplative, as a hermit, scholar, human being and Latin American I have found meaningful for a journey of dialogue.

When I grew up in my native Chile the texts on dialogue with Buddhism were limited and during my adolescence I moved from the reading of Marx to the writings of the Tibetan Lobsang Rampa.[43] Later, in my move to Europe I felt that the diaries of Thomas Merton gave me an insight into a different world triggered by encounters with the Trappists and the Benedictines. The main text for grounding in faith and discipleship is certainly the Gospel of Mark. As the first Gospel it is the shortest and the clearest in what to be a disciple of Jesus entails and among these qualities there is the dialogue with other human beings, including sinners and outcasts. I have commented extensively on the message of Mark in my theological writings on Latin America stating clearly that 'the hermeneutical model of Mark's Gospel as a tool to read history, past and present, becomes not the traditional Galilee > Jerusalem > ends of the world but Galilee > Jerusalem > mimetic Galilee of the Gentiles or periphery > centre > periphery'.[44]

A good complement for a journey of dialogue, somehow monastic, that links with the Tibetan meditation and monasticism is the rule left by St Benedict whose first sentences set the pace for that dialogic imagination of a journey in dialogue: 'Listen [. . .] to your master's precepts, and incline the ear of your heart'.[45] There is no doubt that the listening as part of the daily life of Christian monasticism and Buddhist monasticism plays a very central part in the daily encounter and in the fostering of attitudes towards dialogue. If I listen I hear the meaning of life offered by others and after reflection I can offer the ones that I hold dear. For an attitude of a listener creates the possibility of fostering the advent of a listening church. A listening church instead of a teaching church is not afraid of the world but perceives human activity as part of God's creation.

A good complement to the savouring of the Gospel of Mark is the continuous reading of the Bhagavad Gita and the Upanishads as well as the sayings of the Buddha and the writings of the Tibetan monk Tsong-Kha-Pa.

Dialogue as a Second Step

Dialogue then becomes a second step, as theology for a Latin American starting with Gutiérrez has been a second step. The first step has been experience and action: the action of listening, the action of critically engaging with signs of death and discrimination, the action of reading and studying other traditions, the action of taking part in community activities in which the different religious traditions are taking part, the action of meditating and contemplating as a path of preparation for a fuller dialogue.

It is possible to forget that within the empathy for other traditions we study and read other religious traditions' texts remembering their sacredness for others, their sense of explaining the journey and the mapping of life. In the case of the Buddhist text *The Dhammapada* as a selection of the sayings of the Buddha, Carter and Palihawadana have reminded us that 'it is a religious work, meant to inculcate a certain set of religious and ethical values and a certain manner of perception of life and its problems and their solutions'.[46]

Conclusions: The Church Servant Witness to Dialogue

At the start of this work I intended to survey the historical possibilities of dialogue and to set a theological agenda: the possibility of a servant church that reflected on dialogue as a central ecclesiological paradigm. The values outlined by Vatican II are central in this ecclesiology. However, this theological exploration has also outlined some of the connections and similarities, basic

Fresh Christian Ecclesiology and Buddhist Challenges 157

for dialogue, between the experience of Latin American Christians and Tibetan Buddhists.

In this freshly dialogical ecclesiology, the Church, servant of all in words and deeds, finds her joy in the liberation of all, be it from personal or social sin or from the selfish attachment to matter and flesh that do not express love and a common humanity. It is difficult not to feel joy in exploring the spiritual and contemplative treasures of Buddhism. It is not difficult to share the possibilities of knowledge and liberation in other religions as part of a Christian tradition rooted in a Church – universal, globalized and universalistic.

I am afraid that this work has opened more questions than given practical answers to dialogue; it has challenged the possibility of a non-dynamic ecclesiology that brings together many ways of living a Christian life in dialogue and dialogue with Buddhism, a world religion that does not expand on the theological virtues of a God, as it does not have one. Therefore, the ecclesiology that arises is of a church always learning ways of dialogue, always in conversation with other traditions, always seeking to connect with every human being, all of them created by God. The shared experience of religious practitioners can only bring goodness and peace to society and the journey of a pilgrim church can only be an assurance of newness, of divine surprises and divine silences. For a servant church in dialogue becomes a prophetic church in a contemporary world divided and in strife where all human beings deserve to be heard and all religious practitioners deserve the place and space for their mutual communication and dialogue.

In concluding this work in progress I would argue that dialogue is an ongoing daily activity. One can with refreshed emphasis return to the figure of a restless monk in dialogue, Thomas Merton, who at the start of his journey of spiritual discovery towards the East wrote: 'I am going home, to the home where I have never been in this body, where I have never been in this washable suit [. . .], where I have never been with these suitcases [. . .], where I have never been with these particular books [. . .].[47] Inshalah!'

Notes

1 The Benedictine monk Henri Le Saux remains one of the most remarkable pioneers of dialogue with the world religions in the twentieth century, see Harry Oldmeadow, *A Christian Pilgrim in India: The Spiritual Journey of Swami Abhishiktananda (Henri Le Saux)*, Bloomington, IN: World Wisdom, 2008.
2 The experience of Christian missionaries living in ashrams in India remain an important sign of dialogue and respect for Hinduism and an Indian way of communicating with the divine, see Henri Le Saux and Jules Monchanin, *A Benedictine Ashram*, Douglas: Times Press, 1964.

3 It is clear that Vatican II's emphasis on dialogue made the experience of monks such as Bede Griffiths established when previously they had been considered experimental, see Bede Griffiths, *The Golden String: An Autobiography*, London: Medio Media, 2003.
4 No doubt that this has been the case after the events of 9/11 in the United States and particularly in George W. Bush's self-understanding of the role of religion in the United States, namely a particular type of Christianity, see the helpful analysis by Helen Daley Schroepfer, 'Pursuing the Enemies of Freedom: Religion in the Persuasive Rhetoric of the Bush Administration', *Political Theology*, 2008, 9(1), pp. 27–45.
5 For the negative media portrayal of Islam in Sweden see Therese Rudebeck and Mario I. Aguilar, *Terrorist Reporting in the Swedish Media: Reinforcing an Oriental/Occidental Division?* Series Current Issues in Religion and Politics volume I – Working Papers of the Centre for the Study of Religion and Politics (CSRP), University of St. Andrews. St. Andrews: CSRP and Santiago, London and New York: Fundación Literaria Civilización, 2011.
6 *Dominus Jesus*, London: Catholic Truth Society, 2000.
7 Leonardo Boff, 'Roman Catholic Fundamentalism', in *Fundamentalism, Terrorism and the Future of Humanity*, London: SPCK, 2006, pp. 9–13 at p. 9.
8 Marco Politi, *Joseph Ratzinger: Crisi di un papato*, Rome: Laterza, 2011.
9 For the possibility of religiously inspired governments that could operate outside of 'the paradigm and vocabulary of universally claimed democratic ideals' as a kind of same-religion violence and lack of dialogue see Reza Pankhurst, 'Muslim Contestations over Religion and the State in the Middle East', *Political Theology*, 2010, 11(6), pp. 826–45 and for the bipolarity of institutionalized religion see R. Scott Appleby, *The Ambivalence of the Sacred: Religion, Violence and Reconciliation*, New York and Oxford: Rowan and Littlefield, 2000.
10 Alan Mittleman, 'The Problem of Religious Violence', *Political Theology*, 2011, 12(5), pp. 722–6 at p. 722.
11 A clear case of this total lack of the possibility of dialoguing along religious lines was the case of the violence in Northern Ireland, see Cillian McGrattan, *Northern Ireland 1968–2008: The Politics of Entrenchment*, Houndmills, Basingstoke, Hampshire and New York: Palgrave Macmillan, 2010.
12 For an overview of the problems concerning a post-9/11 world, see the different papers edited as 'Ten Years After 9/11', in *Political Theology*, 2011, 12(5).
13 Leonardo Boff has argued that 'the original Islam is neither warmongering nor fundamentalist (in fact, Islam means "total submission to God")', in Leonardo Boff, *Fundamentalism, Terrorism and the Future of Humanity*, London: SPCK, 2006, p. 18.
14 Reza Pankhurst, 'Muslim Contestations over Religion and the State in the Middle East', *Political Theology*, 2010, 11(6), pp. 826–45 at p. 826.
15 Jane I. Smith, *Muslims, Christians and the Challenge of Inter-Faith Dialogue*, New York: Oxford University Press, 2007.
16 Ariel Dorfman, 'America's No Longer Unique', *Counterpunch*, 3 October 2011 at www.counterpunch.org/dorfman.html, cited in Asma Barlas, 'September 11, 2011: Remember Forgetting', *Political Theology*, 2011, 12(5), pp. 727–36 at p. 729.
17 Asma Barlas, 'September 11, 2011: Remember Forgetting', *Political Theology*, 2011, 12(5), pp. 727–36 at p. 731.

18 See for example, the fourteenth Dalai Lama's address at Aurobindo Ashram at Auroville, 'On Humanity' 24 December 1993 in A. A. Shiromany, ed. *The Spirit of Tibet: Vision for Human Liberation – Selected Speeches and Writings of H.H. The XIV Dalai Lama*, New Delhi: Tibetan Parliamentary and Policy Research Centre and Vikas Publishing House, 1996, pp. 157–65 at p. 157.
19 For a larger discussion on a post-colonial theological diversity see Jenny Daggers, *Postcolonial Theology of Religions: Particularity and Pluralism in World Christianity*, London: Routledge, 2012.
20 Geshe Ngawang Samten and Jay L. Garfield, 'Introduction' to *Ocean of Reasoning: A Great Commentary on Nāgārjuna's Mūlamadhyamakakārikā*, New York: Oxford University Press, 2006, pp. ix–xxiv at pp. x–xi.
21 For an outline of these contemplative side of Latin American liberationists, see 'Ernesto Cardenal', in Mario I. Aguilar, *The History and Politics of Latin American Theology*, vol. I, London: SCM Press, 2007, pp. 91–104 and 'Pedro Casaldáliga', in Mario I. Aguilar, *The History and Politics of Latin American Theology*, vol. II: *Theology and Civil Society*, London: SCM Press, 2008, pp. 135–49.
22 Bede Griffiths, 'Preface' to The Golden String: An Autobiography, Tucson, AZ: Medio Media, 2003, pp. vii–xii at p. x.
23 Shirley Du Boulay, *The Cave of the Heart: The Life of Swami Abhishiktananda*, Marynoll, NY: Orbis, 2005, p. 140, see also the works by *Abhishiktananda*, *Intériorité et revelation: Essais théologiques*, Sisteron: Editions Présence, 1982 and *Saccidananda: A Christian Approach to Advaitic Experience*, Dehli: ISPCK, 1997.
24 Gustavo Gutiérrez, 'The Gospel of Work: Reflections on Laborem Exercens', in *The Density of the Present: Selected Writings*, Maryknoll, NY: Orbis, 1999, pp. 3–38 at p. 9.
25 This respect for the beliefs of others created an impact on the possibilities of a democratic post-colonial India and spread to other movements and other struggles, some of them unexpected such as the democratic movement of women who wanted the return to democracy in Chile during the dictatorship of General Pinochet (1973–90); see Patricia Verdugo, *Bucarest 187: mi historia*, Santiago: Catalonia, 2006, p. 169.
26 Gandhi is referring here to Christianity and Islam.
27 Mahatma Gandhi, 'My jail experiences – XI', *Young India* 4 September 1924 in Judith M. Brown, ed. *Mahatma Gandhi: The Essential Writings*, Oxford World's Classics, Oxford: Oxford University Press, 2008, pp. 52–3 at p. 53.
28 In the case of Latin America see for example Carlos Christo, *Letters from a Prisoner of Conscience*, London: The Catholic Book Club, 1978 and Sheila Cassidy, *Audacity To Believe: An Autobiography*, London: Fount, 1978. In the case of Tibet see Ama Adhe, *The Voice that Remembers*, Boston: Wisdom Publications, 1997 and Tubten Khétsun, *Memories of Life in Lhasa under Chinese Rule*, New York: Columbia University Press, 2008.
29 See 'Chairman Mao's Conversation with Dalai and Panchen 23 February 1955 (Tibetan calendar: First month, First day', in Melvyn C. Goldstein, *A History of Modern Tibet*, vol. II: *The Calm before the Storm 1951–1955*, Berkeley, Los Angeles and London: University of California Press, 2007, pp. 505–7.
30 Heinrich Harrer, *Return To Tibet*, London: Weidenfeld and Nicolson, 1984, p. 20.
31 Tsering Shakya, *The Dragon in the Land of Snows: A History of Modern Tibet since 1947*, London: Pimlico, 1999, pp. 196–211.

32 See for example Gustavo Gutiérrez, *A Theology of Liberation: History, Politics and Salvation*, London: SCM Press, 1974 and A. A. Shiromany, ed. *The Spirit of Tibet: Vision for Human Liberation – Selected Speeches and Writings of H.H. the XIV Dalai Lama*, New Delhi: Tibetan Parliamentary and Policy Research Centre and Vikas Publishing House, 1996.
33 Steve Hagen, *Buddhism, Plain and Simple*, London: Penguin, 1999, p. 23.
34 John Sobrino borrows this concept from Ignacio Ellacuría, see John Sobrino, 'Redeeming Globalization through Its Victims', in Jon Sobrino and Felix Wilfred, eds. *Globalization and Its Victims* (*Concilium* 2001/5), London: SCM Press, pp. 112–14; for an expansion of these ideas see Mario I. Aguilar, *The History and Politics of Latin American Theology III: A Theology of the Periphery*, London: SCM Press, 2008, p. 16.
35 Marcus J. Borg, *Conflict, Holiness & Politics in the Teachings of Jesus*, New York and Toronto: Edwin Mellen Press, 1984, p. 261.
36 See James L. Heft, Reuven Firestone and Omid Safi, eds. *Learned Ignorance: Intellectual Humility among Jews, Christians and Muslims*, New York: Oxford University Press, 2011.
37 HH the Dalai Lama and Howard C. Cutler, *The Art of Happiness: A Handbook for Living*, London: Hodder & Stoughton, 1999, p. 69.
38 Abhishiktananda, *Saccidananda: A Christian Approach to Advaitic Experience*. Dehli: ISPCK, 1984, p. xiii.
39 Denise Lardner Carmody and John Tully Carmody, *Serene Compassion: A Christian Appreciation of Buddhist Holiness*, New York: Oxford University Press, 1996.
40 See J. P. Williams, *Denying Divinity: Apophasis in the Patristic Christian and Soto Zen Buddhist Traditions*, Oxford: Oxford University Press, 2000.
41 See James L. Heft, ed. *Catholicism and Interreligious Dialogue*, New York: Oxford University Press, 2011.
42 See Paul Waldau, *The Specter of Speciesism: Buddhist and Christian Views of Animals*, New York: Oxford University Press, 2003.
43 Lobsang Rampa, *The Third Eye*, London: Ballantine Books, 1986 and *Wisdom of the Ancients*, Cutchogue, NY: Buccaneer Books, 1991.
44 Mario I. Aguilar, *The History and Politics of Latin American Theology III: A Theology at the Periphery*, London: SCM Press, 2008, p. 63.
45 'Preface', *The Rule of Saint Benedict*, Collegeville, MN: The Liturgical Press, 2001, p. 13.
46 John R. Carter and Mahinda Palihawadana, 'Introduction' to *The Dhammapada: The Sayings of the Buddha*, Oxford: Oxford University Press, 2000, pp. xi–xxvi at p. xxvi.
47 *The Asian Journal of Thomas Merton*, 15 October 1968, New York: New Directions, 1975, p. 5.

Index

Abraham 20
advaita (non-duality) 29, 147
  of the soul (*atman*) 146
Algerian civil war, the 12
Allende, Salvador 97, 100, 118, 130
Alonso, Esther Paniagua (Augustinian Missionary Sister) 59–60
Althaus-Reid, Marcella 133
Althusser, Louis 100
Arguedas, José María 39
  El zorro de arriba y el zorro de abajo 39
Armed Islamic Group (GIA) 58, 63, 68
Arns, Evaristo 43
Attiyah, Sayah 68

Bamberger, John 55
Barnes, Michael 31
Barth, Karl 11
Based Ecclesial Communities (CEB) 36
Beauvois, Xavier 70
Benedict XVI, Pope 4, 16, 143
Benedictines, the 31, 91, 92, 131, 155
Benjedid, Chadli 58, 63
Berlusconi, Silvio 140
Berrigan, Daniel 9, 12, 74, 77–84, 146
  and Thich Nhat Hanh 82–4, 146
  Trial of the Catonsville Nine, The 82
Berrigan, Freda 81
Berrigan, Philip 78, 80, 81, 82
Bible, the 40–1, 44, 60, 140
  New Testament, the 22, 122
  Old Testament, the 22, 38, 40
Blair, Tony 136
Boff, Clodovis 49
Boff, Leonardo 5, 6, 143
Bonhoeffer, Dietrich 48

Borgman, Erik 5
Bossi, Umberto 140
Bouteflika, Abdelaziz 58
Brown, Margrethe 1
Brown, Robert McAfee 107
Buddha, Gautama 7, 83, 84, 135, 146, 151, 156
Buddha-darma, the (teachings of the Buddha) 152, 156
Buddhism 3, 4, 12, 13, 17, 19, 27, 28, 30, 89, 106, 126, 134
  concept of God 4
  contemporary 84
  Hinduism, close relation to 4
  Tibetan 12, 92, 93, 145, 149, 150
    see also dzogchen
  Zen 83, 92, 94, 154
Bush, George W. 136, 140

Camaldolese Constitution, the 4
Camara, Helder 43
Camus, Albert 95
Carmody, Denise 154
Carmody, John 154
Carter, R. 156
Casaldáliga, Pedro 43, 132, 145
Cavanaugh, William 129
Chessel, Christian (White Father) 61
Chevillard, Jean (White Father) 60
Chinese Revolution, the 106
Christian humanism 139
Christianity *see also* dialogue, inter-religious
  and Buddhism 74–84
    colonial encounters 74–5
    common tenets 136
    concept of ignorance, the 98

Dan Berrigan and Thich Nhat
    Hanh 77–84
  Jesuits in Tibet, the 75–7
  and Hinduism 27–31
  and Islam 26–7
  and Judaism 25–6
  as the only path to God 11
church,
  at the centre of the world 6
Cistercian Order of the Strict
    Observance *see* trappists, the
Cold War, the 91, 100, 108
Columbus, Christopher 75
Concha, Luis 111
Cornell, Tom 78
Council of Trent, the (1545) 16
Cox, Harvey 81
creation 7
Cuban missile crisis, the 108
Cuban Revolution, the 108, 110
Cunnane, Robert 78

Dalai Lama, the 13th 1
Dalai Lama, the 14th 1, 2, 8, 12, 82, 87,
    92–5, 126, 145, 148–51, 153
  on Marxism 93
  Nobel lecture of 87, 126
Day, Dorothy 78
De Andrade, Fr Antonio 75, 76
de Chergé, Christian 56–7, 63, 65–9
  Quand un à-Dieu s'envisage 63
death of Christian missionaries 58–62
  see also trappists, the
    assassination of
Deckers, Charles (White Father) 60–1
Des homes et des dieux (film) 70
Desideri, Fr Ippolito 75–7
Dhammapada, The 156
dialogue,
  as absence 8–9
  basic tenets 126–40
    common tenets, towards 136
    market versus person 127–9
    poverty and beatitude 129–32
    spirituality of transgression 132–5
  and ecclesial experience 5–8
  inter-religious 2–3, 63–5
    see also Christianity

future of, the 149–50
innovations 67–9
issues related to 69–70
as liberation 150–3
as love 146–7
as personal re-shaping 153–4
possibilities of a Christian-Buddhist
    dialogue 4–5
as religious contradiction 154
as a second step 156
signs of hope for 148–9
texts for a journey of 155–6
theological markers of 65–7
as knowledge 9–10
as presence 8
theologizing 126–7
before Vatican II 24–5
in Vatican II 16–31
  Ecclesiam Suam 19, 21–4
  Nostra Aetate 18–20
Dialogue and Proclamation 67
Dieulangard, Alain (White Father) 60
Dignitatis Humanae 6
Dionysius the Areopagite 154
Dochier, Luc 56
doctrine of original sin, the 98
Dogen Zenji 154
Domingo, Juan 118
Dorfman, Ariel 144, 145
Douglass, Jim 78
Du Boulay, Shirley 30
Dussel, Enrique 138, 140
dzogchen 93 *see also* Buddhism, Tibetan

ecclesio-genesis 6
Ecumenical Association of Third World
    Theologians 55
Elizondo, Virgilio 112
Ellacuría, Ignacio 56, 57, 114, 115
Elsberg, Robert 9
Enlightenment, the 16
eschatology 7

family,
  as the unit of divine manifestation 5
Favre-Miville, Paul 56
Ferry, W. H. 78
Fini, Gianfranco 140

Fleury, Michel 56
Forest, Jim 78
Foucault, Charles de 27
Freyre, Fr Emanuel 76

Gaudium et Spes (7 December 1965) 3
Gelug school of Tibetan Buddhism,
    the 94 *see also* Tsong-Kha-Pa
Gilkey, Langdon 38
Gita, the 28, 99, 135, 146, 156
    see also Upanishads, the;
    Vedas, the
God,
    as Verbum 139
Gospel of Mark, the 155, 156
Gramsci, Antonio 119
Grande, Rutilio 114
Gregory the Great 46
Griffiths, Bede 28
Griffiths, Bede (Swami
    Dhayananda) 30, 146
    Christ in India 30
Guevara, Ernesto Ché 108, 119
Gutiérrez, Gustavo 37–48, 109, 112, 119,
    135, 147, 156
    on the dignity of the person 45
    and God 44
    and spirituality 43
    theology of, the 37–49
        during his first theological
            period 37–9
        during his second theological
            period 39–43
        during his third theological
            period 43–7
    Theology of Liberation, A 41–2, 109

Hagen, Steve 152
Heft, James 154
Heidegger, Martin 136–7, 139
    Being and Time 136–7
Henríquez, Silva 111, 117
Herz, Alice 79
Heschel, Abraham 25–6
Hick, John 3, 9, 10
Hinduism 4, 19, 27–31, 134,
    146, 147
Holy Spirit, the 43, 146

Humanae Personae Dignitatem
    (28 August 1968) 3
Hussein, Saddam 136

Inter-American Development Bank
    (Banco Interamericano del
    Desarrollo-BID) 114
International Eucharistic Congress,
    the 39th 111
Islam 4, 20, 26, 27, 144–6, 148
Islamic Armed Movement
    (MIA) 58, 63
Islamic Salvation Army (AIS) 58
Islamic Salvation Front (FIS) 58, 63

Jesuit Missions 80
Jesuit University of Central America
    (UCA) 114
Jesuits, the 25, 75, 113, 114, 143
    see also Society of Jesus, the
    in Tibet 75–7
Jesus Christ 3, 7, 83, 84, 90, 119, 122,
    133, 134, 147, 155
    body of, the 21
    death of, the 20
John Paul II 16, 45, 149
    Laborem Exercens 45
    Redemptoris Missio 67
John XXIII 6, 16, 18, 19, 22, 25, 26,
    88, 109, 147
    Pacem in Terris 109
Judaism 4, 18, 26, 84, 146, 147

King, Martin Luther 83
Knitter, Paul 9, 10
König, F. 21
Koran, the 135
Korean War, the 77
Küng, Hans 9

La Porte, Roger 79
Larraín, Manuel 43, 108
Las Casas, Bartolomé de 41
Lash, Nicholas 47
Le Saux, Henri (Swami
    Abhishiktananda) 28–9, 31,
    147, 153
Lebreton, Christophe 56

Index

Leclercq, Denise (Sister of Our Lady of The Apostles) 62
Lemarchand, Bruno 56
Leo XIII 21, 23
Lewis, C. S. 30
liberalism 16
Littlejohn, Jeanne (Sister of Our Lady of the Apostles) 61–2
López, Amando 56
Lyotard, Jean-François 137

McDade, John 7
McDole, Bob 78
Mahatma Gandhi 31, 148
Mahieu, Fr. Francis 28
Mao Zedong 150
Marcuse, Herbert 96, 97, 106
María Vigil, José 132
Maritain, Jacques 139
Marques, Brother Manuel 75
Martín, Caridad Álvarez (Augustinian Missionary Sister) 60
Martín-Baró, Ignacio 56, 57
Marx, Karl 96, 119, 155
Marxism 93, 96–100, 110, 116, 118–19, 138–9
  collective 139
  deterministic 139
  French 99–100
  orthodox 96, 98
Massignon, Arabist Louis 26
  conversion of 26–7
  works of 26
Medellin conference, the 106–22
  challenges 107–8
  Christianity and atheism (within the Latin American context) 120–2
  Christianity and Marxism (within the Latin American context) 117–20
  impact of, the 112–15
    on dialogue and religious cooperation 115–16
    on dialogues with the secular 116–17
  kairos of, the 108–12
  liberation and poverty 106–7

Merton, Thomas 1, 8, 12, 55, 78, 79, 82, 87–100, 106, 130, 134, 146, 148, 155, 157
  experiences of the Stranger 88–92
    ecclesial 88–91
    monastic 88
    Tibetan 91–2
  and the fourteenth Dalai Lama 92–3, 146
  last lecture of, the 95–9
  Literary Essays of Thomas Merton 95
  and Marxism 99–100
  Seven Storey Mountain, The 78
Metz, Johann Baptist 37–8
Míguez Bonino, José 116–22
  Marxism, affinity for 118
  Revolutionary Theology comes of Age 117
Mission and Dialogue 67
Missionaries of Africa, the 25
Mittleman, Alan 143
Molina, Arturo Armando 114
Monchanin, Jules (Swāmi Paramārūbyānanda) 28, 29, 31
Montes, Segundo 56
Morrison, Norman 79
Moses 20
Müller, Hadwig Ana Maria 134
Murray, John Courtney 17
  Dignitatis Humanae 17
Muste, A. J. 78

National Democratic Rally (RND) 58
National Liberation Front (NFL) 58
Nazi, the 25
Nhat Hanh, Thich 9, 12, 77, 82–4
Nicholl, Donald 5, 24
Nietzsche, Friedrich Wilhelm 137, 139
Nixon, Richard 82
Nostra Aetate (28 October 1965) 3

O'Brien, Patrick 81
Of Gods and Men (film) 69 *see also* Des homes et des dieux
O'Grady, Jim 81
O'Hare, Joseph 57
Oliver Nelson, John 78

Palihawadana, Mahinda 156
Pankhurst, Reza 144
Paul VI 7, 19, 21, 22, 23, 24, 25, 108, 111, 112
   Populorum Progressio 109
Paul-Hélène (Little sister of the Assumption) 59
Perón, Evita 118
Peter Grady, John 78
Pious IX 17
   Syllabus of Errors 17
Pious XI 23
Pious XII 7, 23, 25, 26, 27
Politi, Marco 143
Polner, Murray 81
Prévost, Odette (Little Sister of the Sacred Heart) 62
Propaganda Fide 75

Ramana Maharshi 29
Rampa, Lobsang 155
Ratzinger, Cardinal 5
   Dominus Jesus 5
Rault, Claude 67
Ribât-es-Salam (Link of Peace) 61, 67
Ringeard, Celestin 56
Roman Catholic Church, the 1, 5, 6
   extra ecclesiam nulla salus (dictum) 6
Romero, Oscar (Bishop) 2, 43, 114
Rorty, Richard 136, 138
Russian Revolution, the 100

St Augustine 39
   De Civitate Dei 39
St Benedict 88, 98, 156
   rule of, the 88
St Francis Xavier 75
St Martin de Porres 133
St Maximus 154
St Paul 6, 16, 22, 100
Salenson, Christian 66, 68, 69
samsara 30
Schmidt-Leukel, Perry 9
School of Youth for Social Services, the (SYSS) 83
Second Vatican Council, the
   see Vatican II
Segundo, Juan Luis 109, 110

Self,
   and nonself 84
Sigurdson, Ola 128
Sobrino, Jon 47, 114, 115, 127, 152
Society of Jesus, the 77 *see also* Jesuits, the
Society of the Divine Word, the 25
speciesism 155
Sullivan, William (US ambassador) 80
Suzuki, D. T. 93
Swidler, Leonard 9

Talbott, Harold 92
Theresa (Mother) 2, 146, 147, 148
theology,
   as history 39–43
   liberation theology 37, 47, 107, 110, 117, 137, 145
      first moment, the 137
      kinds of 109
      Latin American 109
      and Marxism 138
   and politics 47–9
   within a post-socialist world 43–7
   as a Second Act 37–9
   tasks of 7
Torres, Camilo 108
Torres Restrepo, Fr Camilo 110, 111
Trappists, the (of Algeria) 55–70, 130, 131, 146, 155
   and Algerian Civil War 57–8
   the assassination of 62–3
   see also death of Christian missionaries
Tsong-Kha-Pa 94, 145, 156
   see also Gelug school of Tibetan Buddhism
Tutu, Desmond (Archbishop) 2

Upanishads, the 156 *see also Gita*, the; Vedas, the

Vallejo, César 44
Vatican I (1869) 16
Vatican II (second Council) 1, 3, 4, 6, 38, 45, 74, 80, 87–90, 96, 108–11, 114, 116, 122, 143, 147, 156
Vattimo, Gianni 12, 136–40

Vedas, the 84 *see also Gita*, the; Upanishads, the
Vergès, Henri (Marist Brother) 58–9
Vietnam War, the 26, 70, 74, 77, 78, 79, 80, 83, 91, 133
   dialogue and 77–82

Waldau, Paul 155
Walsh, Anthony 78
Westmoreland, William 80
World Council of Churches (WCC), the 1
   'Dialogue with People of Living Faiths' 1
   'Seeking Community' (document) 2
   inter-faith dialogue (in Ajaltoun) 1
World War II 25, 77, 80

Yoder, John H. 78

Zéroual, Liamine 58
Zinn, Howard 80

www.ingramcontent.com/pod-product-compliance
Lightning Source LLC
Chambersburg PA
CBHW070642300426
44111CB00013B/2212